ASIAN CASE STUDIES

Lessons from Malaysian Industries

Firend Al Rasch, Ph.D

Copyright @ 2016 by Firend Al Rasch. All rights reserved. Published by IJBMR.

No part of this publication may be reproduced, stored in a retrieval system, or transmitted in any form or by any means, electronic, mechanical, photocopying, recording, scanning, or otherwise, except as permitted under Section 107 or 108 of the 1976 United States Copyright Act, without either the prior written permission of the publisher, or authorization through payment of the appropriate per-copy fee to the publisher.

Limit of Liability/Disclaimer of Warranty: While the publisher and author have used their best efforts in preparing this book, they make no representations or warranties with respect to the accuracy or completeness of the contents of this book and specifically disclaim any implied warranties of merchantability or fitness for a particular purpose. No warranty may be created or extended by sales representatives or written sales materials. The advice and strategies contained herein may not be suitable for your situation. You should consult with a professional where appropriate. Neither the publisher nor author shall be liable for any loss of profit or any other commercial damages, including but not limited to special, incidental, consequential, or other damages. For general information on our other products and services or for technical support, please contact: firendr@gmail.com

Table-of-Content

Introduction

AirAsia	7
Avialite	32
Encorp	50
Felda Global Ventures Holdings	64
Eco World	76
Southern Coated Peanut "A Better One"	93
Boustead Heavy Industries Corporation (BHIC)	109
BHIC Bofors Asia	124
APM Automotive Holdings	172
VADS	184
Asia Assistance Network	196
D'YANA	222
The Humble Chef	230
Jeonsa Centre	237
Materialise	251
Takaful	273

References   291

Introduction

With Asia as a collective and diverse region, it poses a significant importance to the world of trade and commerce. In terms of absolute sales and revenue, Asia is the largest global market player. Companies small and large are constantly looking for growing markets, as developed economies matures they becomes saturated and crowded. The significance of Asia lies is not only in the number of people (4.5 billion), 500 million live in South East Asia alone, additional 1.2 billion in India and about 1.5 billion in China, but, the significance of Asia rests in its collective growing economies. The South East Asian market, which comprises of (Indonesia, Singapore, Malaysia, Thailand, Myanmar, Cambodia, Vietnam and the Philippines) is a market greater of 500 million people. The growing middle-class in Asia is creating an unprecedented demand for products and services, and fueling global growth. A slowdown in the Chinese economy (the world's second largest) most definitely will impact global economic growth. Although Malaysia is a relatively small economy with population of 30 million, yet it provides an insight into the Asia-Pacific region with its strategic location in South-East Asia. This book will be followed by a series of other books that provides insight into more Asian companies.

In 2010, Malaysia sat a target to become a high-income nation by the year of 2020 with the initiation of Economic Transformation Program (ETP). ETP is a comprehensive blueprint to move Malaysia's economy into developed economy with a projected Gross National Income (GNI) of US$523 billion and per capita income at US$15,000 by 2020. The blueprint has included many sectors in its transformation plan such as palm oil, electrical & electronics, business services, oil & gas etc. Being a manufacturing and services center in a number of areas in the global outsourcing business, Malaysia needs to adapt to become more specialized, by identifying strong niches and subsectors to serve of the global market. Malaysia is urgent need to offer high-value services if they plan to remain relevant to international business and ultimately compete in the global marketplace. Malaysian companies are also encouraged to ready for changing nature of competitive landscape in the eve of the Transatlantic Trade and Investment Partnership (TTIP). TTIP will force many companies and industries in Malaysia to either become obsolete, or lack the competitive advantage needed to remain in business. The Malaysian consumer will also be forced to make adjustments in the post-TTIP agreement and with lower oil & gas prices. As we see in numerous cases presented in this book, many Malaysian firms are heavily subsidized by the government, and that's how they manage to support operational costs and remain in business. The biggest challenge to Malaysian industries today is to compete in a crowded and competitive region. Gaining new market share and finding new segments to serve is a serious challenge for Malaysian industries in their quest to remain relevant and competitive. Corporate Malaysia and individual consumers are risk avers by nature, and not willing to charter in and unfamiliar territories. This is reflective in the level of technological advancement and innovation Malaysian industries enjoy today. VADS for instance is a very representative case study that illustrates some of the issues an average Malaysian company faces and the way they react to existing technological and market forces. This is also supported by the current position Malaysia finds itself in today, which is not able to compete with China, India and Vietnam in cheap production bases, not it is able to rise to the level of Singapore as a high-end market and services provider. This is what Richard Vietor of Harvard Business School "HBS" describes as being stuck in the middle.

This book discusses and presents number of Malaysian companies from varying industries. The case study approach may be attributed to HBS as an example of effective methodology to examining not only a company, but an industry, which can put the learner in the decision making seat. Case analysis allows the reader not only to learn about a given company's activities, but to be able to compare, contrast and plan for course of strategies. The goal behind the case study approach is not to simply provide solutions, but it lies in the collective process of brainstorming, exchanging various point of views, providing the necessary reasoning for various positions held, interchange of perspectives, improving analytical abilities, exercising decision-making and developing leadership abilities, and most importantly building on various collective ideas presented in the process of discussion. It is important to mention that some of the companies discussed in this book did not allow the release of financial data, and so their wish was respected. Others however, are publically traded or allowed their financial statements to be shared, and hence, analyses were conducted to give the reader a cleared idea on the importance of financial structures. The data collected and presented in this book was through semi-structured interviews with the management, employees, review of program materials, available secondary data, direct observations and industry reviews. Some of the cases in this book purposely included a breakdown of the marketing 4P's, Porter's five forces and other models to illustrate how companies use such models in their daily assessment and analysis of their perspective organizations, their products and the industry. Such cases of real companies, serve as compelling examples for learners and practitioners alike, illustrating how powerful these tools can be for management in their decision-making and strategic corporate planning process.

Finally, the reader will see the word "Berhad" repeatedly next to a company's name. The word "Berhad" is used to indicate a private limited company in Malaysia. The suffix is "Bhd." Which is an abbreviation of the Malaysian word "Berhad," which literally means "private." This is an equivalent of the word limited "Ltd." as used in corporate America and Britain.

AirAsia

AirAsia Berhad was established in 1993, but began operations in Malaysia on 18 November 1996. It was originally founded by a Malaysian government organization known as DRB-Hicom. On 2 December 2001 the heavily-indebted airline was bought by former Time Warner executive Tony Fernandez company Tune Air Sdn. Bhd. for the token sum of RM 1 with 40 million worth of debts. However, Fernandez turned the company around, producing a profit in 2002 and launching new routes from its hub in Kuala Lumpur, undercutting former monopoly operator Malaysia Airlines with promotional fares as low as RM 1.

In 2003, Air Asia opened another new hub at Senai International Airport in Johor Bahru and launched its first international flight to Bangkok, Thailand. After that, it also added Singapore itself to the destination list, and started flights to Indonesia. In addition, flights to Macau began in June 2004, and flights to Xiamen, China and the Manila, Philippines in April 2005. The flights to Vietnam and Cambodia followed later in 2005 and to Brunei and Myanmar on 2006. Air Asia took over Malaysia Airline's Rural Air Service routes in Sabah and Sarawak in August 2006, but it is operating under the Fly Asian Xpress brand. After a year, the routes were returned to MAS Wings because of commercial reasons.

Tony Fernandez subsequently established a five-year plan to further enhance its awareness in Asia countries. Under the plan, Air Asia wanted to strengthen and enhance its route network by connecting all the existing cities in the region and expanding further into Vietnam, Indonesia, Southern China and India. In addition, Air Asia will focus on developing its hubs in Bangkok and Jakarta through its sister companies, Thai Air Asia. With increase frequency and the addition of new routes, Air Asia expects passenger volume to reach 18 million by the end of 2007. Functions of AirAsia is the first airline which introduced online booking system in Malaysia. Online booking system refers to making online, real time, Internet bookings for such things as flight, hotel rooms or even theater ticket. The number passenger of Air Asia has increased from 200,000 to 350,000 after Air Asia was introduced the online booking system to their clients. Furthermore, Air Asia also became the second largest airline in Asia to go completely ticket less after Sky mark Airline in Japan (AirAsia. 2015).

Brand Philosophy

According to Blackett, T. (2004), AirAsia went into escalated General notices and other prominent exercises, which contributed, to the high offering of their organization's picture. They accompanied a brand " Now Everyone Can Fly" These purposes of contact with their objective client help them to form their picture, which thus made faithfulness from their clients. Giving cash, administrations, and/or time can assemble trust and a positive picture for your business. Altruism contributes both toward your marking endeavors and toward your organization's inward prosperity. AirAsia set out on this to construct and draw in more clients. In mid 2005, AirAsia Sdn Berhad (AirAsia) declared that it would give away 10,000 free seats on its flights to choose Southeast Asian destinations. The carrier said that was its method for commending the fruition of three years of effective flying and of saying thank you to the general population for their backing. "AirAsia's achievements and achievement today is an impression of general society's trust and confidence in the organization," said Tony Fernandes, CEO of AirAsia. With this motivating force and altruism, more clients are pulled in to their business. AirAsia situated itself as the pioneer in its item class in Asia. It exhibits its capacity to lead and develop by putting resources into cutting edge innovations, new airplanes, sponsorship of worldwide brands and joint endeavor and vital organizations together to grow its image offerings. Accordingly, AirAsia can give a wide system of courses and destinations in the area and in addition around the world, helpful web booking and installment offices, imaginative travel bundles and spending plan inns. Its utilization of online offices for reservations and installment of airfares is a standout amongst the best in the locale.

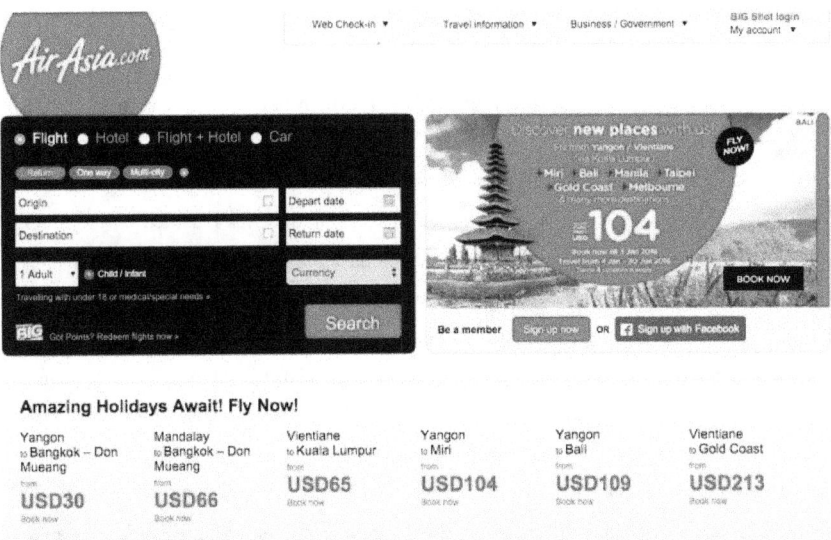

Product

King, B. E. (2013) stated that AirAsia works with the world's most minimal unit expense of US$0.023/ASK and a traveler breakeven load variable of 52%. It has supported 100% of its fuel prerequisites for the following three years, accomplishes a flying machine turnaround time of 25 minutes, has a group profitability level that is triple that of Malaysia Airlines and accomplishes a normal flying machine use rate of 13 hours a day. Air Asia as of now is the principle client of the Airbus A 320. The organization has put in a request of 175 units of the same plane to administration its courses and no less than 50 of these A320 will be operational by 2013. The main unit of the plane landed on December 8, 2005. As a spearheaded in ease air transportation in Asia, Air Asia has a few auxiliaries and partner organization to bolster its operation.

Subsidiaries

Thai Air Asia was set up as Subsidiaries of Air Asia Berhad on 8 December 2003 as joint endeavor with Shin Corporation. Flight operation was initiated on 13 January 2004 from its base in Don Mueang International Airport. Since 25 September 2006, the carrier is based at the new

Suvarnabhumi Airport. The other backup is Indonesia Air Asia. This aircraft is situated in Soekarno-Hatta International Airport. Air Asia obtained the then outdated Awair in 2004 with a 49% stake in the aircraft. Awair started administrations for the benefit of Air Asia in December 2004; full rebranding to Indonesia Air Asia was finished on 1 December 2005. The carrier is situated in Soekarno-Hatta International Airport. Thai AirAsia (TAA) was built up in 2003 as a joint endeavor between Asia Aviation and AirAsia Investment, and was recorded on the Stock Exchange of Thailand in May 2012. Thai AirAsia initiated its inaugural business flight on 4 February 2004 from Bangkok to Hat Yai, and now working from centers in Bangkok, Phuket and Chiang Mai. Philippines AirAsia (PAA) is an entirely claimed backup of AirAsia Inc., which is a joint endeavor organization between Filipino financial specialists; Antonio O. Cojuango, previous Ambassafor Alfredo M. Yao, Michael L. Romero, Marianne B. Hontiveros, and Malaysia's AirAsia Berhad. PAA works local and worldwide flights out of Manila, Cebu and Kalibo (passage to Boracay). It is, by a wide margin, the main nearby transporter that administrations the most number of universal flights from China and South Korea to Kalibo International Airport, with Fly-Thru administrations by means of Kuala Lumpur from Manila to different destinations in Asia, Australia and past. Philippines AirAsia is a piece of the AirAsia Group that has been honored the World's Best Low-Cost Carrier for seven back-to-back years, from 2009 to 2015, by Skytrax. Built up in 2013 as a joint endeavor between Tata Sons Limited, Telestra Tradeplace Pvt Ltd and AirAsia. The aircraft as of now works flights from its present base Bangalore to Chennai, Kochi and Goa, Jaipur and Chandigarh.

Associated companies

AirAsia Berhad additionally have partner organizations, for example, Air Asia X, Fly AsiaXpress, Tune Hotels and Tune Money. Air Asia X is an administration worked via Air Asia X sdn.Bhd. (already known as Fly AsianXpress Sdn.Bhd.) as an establishment of AirAsia. It has begun offering whole deal administrations from Kuala Lumpur to Australia and China utilizing Airbus A330. The inaugural flight was on 2 November 2007 to Gold Coast, Australia. The main AirAsia 'straightforward's inn, Tune Hotels, is prepared for inhabitance in Kuala Lumpur and Kota Kinabalu and later in Penang, Johor Bahru, KLIA, Miri, Kuching and Sandakan. Tune cash is Asia's first 'no nonsense's online monetary administration possessed by Tune Air Sdn.Bhd. Demonstrated aftaer Virgin Money, it involves life, home and engine vehicle protection and also prepaid cards.

Marketing Channels

According to Gunduz, F., & Pathan, A. K. (November, 2012) a marketing channel is a set of practices or activities necessary to transfer the ownership of goods from the point of production to the point of consumption. It is the way items and administrations get to the end-client, the purchaser, and is otherwise called a dissemination channel. Promoting tells potential clients what you are putting forth, and guarantees that your message is listened "over the jumble," Fernandes says. There is so much data being traded recently, that just depending on what he depicts as 'static, restricted channels' simply won't work. AirAsia's showcasing channel serves as a decent illustration of this rule. The Malaysian aircraft doesn't just promote on conventional mediums, for example, radio or TV, additionally on online networking channels. There are a few purposes behind the substantial utilization of online networking. Online networking channels permit AirAsia to straightforwardly associate with its clients and potential clients and to pick up criticism about its items and administrations. Since AirAsia has the vision of making air travel available for everybody, it actually offers lower expense admissions. Also, it is that part of its business which it underlines keeping in mind the end goal to separate it "from whatever is left of the field as far as cost, availability, flight frequencies, comfort, advancement and numerous others," Fernandes states. AirAsia needs to keep on driving as what he portrays as "world's best minimal effort carrier and as a pioneer making air venture out available to all." The aircraft couldn't separate itself from different aircrafts in the event that it didn't have the right advertising procedures set up. AirAsia has cultivated a reliance on Internet innovation for its operational and vital administration, and gives an online ticket booking administrations to voyager on the web. The accompanying demonstrates the landing page of AirAsia.com as the organization key channel of promoting and deals.

Pricing
Shavinina, L. V. (2006) claims, AirAsia's fares are significantly lower than those of other operators. This administration focuses on the visitors who will manage without the ruffles of suppers, preferred customer credits or air terminal parlors in return for tolls up to 80% lower than those as of now offered with identical accommodation. No complimentary beverages or suppers are advertised. Rather, AirAsia as of late present 'Nibble Attack', a scope of delightful snacks and drinks accessible on board at extremely moderate costs and arranged solely for AirAsia's visitors.

Visitors now have the decision of buying nourishment and drinks on board. Fernandes portrays Air Asia as a half and half. He led broad statistical surveying before setting the procedure of the aircraft, flying with low–cost transporters in Europe and the US. The bargain he has looked for the Malaysian local business sector is to hope to take the operational efficiencies of Ryanair, the worker relations of Southwest, the easyJet Internet system, and the marking ethics of Virgin Blue and Virgin Express. The aircraft works out of Kuala Lumpur's old Subang air terminal, a 30–minute drive from the focal point of Kuala Lumpur. The new air terminal at Sepang is over an hour's head out from the business focus of Kuala Lumpur, and Air Asia has connected to the Malaysian government to stay at Subang.

A choice is normal before the mid year. Regarding operations, Air Asia checks its travelers in physically and performs its own particular ground taking care of. On what Fernandes sees as a change on the Ryanair model, the pilots at the carrier do their own heap sheets. The three 148–seat 737–300s can accomplish normal turnaround times of 22 minutes. Air Asia utilizes a run of the mill low–cost aircraft level administration structure, and representative criticism is energized through casual get–together. Around 5% of the organization's value has been set–aside for the workers. The transporter is introducing the OpenRes reservation framework, which will empower it to receive the Internet as a deals apparatus. At present 80% of tickets are sold through travel operators and 20% through the aircraft's call focus. The short–term point is to accomplish a 50/50 split between commission bearing travel office deals and coordinate deals through the Internet and the call focus. The aircraft will utilize airasia.com as its image. Fernandes sees the brand including esteem in the way Virgin has possessed the capacity to utilize its image to offer a more extensive scope of products than just carrier tickets. The offer of tops, watches and T–shirts are all on the future motivation. The Internet webpage will in time permit bookings to be additionally taken for inns and auto contract. The carrier conveys travellers from three primary groupings, the VFR market (Malaysia has a vast transitory workforce), little/medium ventures, and the recreation market, both neighbourhood and outside. The monetary foundation is fairly reassuring: final quarter 2001 GDP fell by 0.5%, which analyses to a 7.0% fall in neighboring Singapore. Gross domestic product development for 2001 in general was 0.4%, and financial analysts expect that 2002 will see an enhancing positive development. Air Asia is looking to raise Ringgit 60m (US$16m) in new value to finance further development, with remote and neighborhood financial specialists being offered 25–30% of the organization's value. Before the corporate rebuilding, Air Asia was losing a normal of US$ 1.5m every month.

Promotion
It is widely believed that AirAsia always determine the customers as their first priority in every consideration. This can be seen into the first page of the AirAsia Website, which has expressed the part sign in catch. Client or potential clients can simply be joined with the AirAsia projects, for example, limited time booking offers, news overhauls, telephone fliers, flight changes information and others. Getting to be AirAsia individuals will convey clients to a development data that will guarantee individuals are forever one's progression ahead from others. These are the advantages that can be accumulated from getting to be individuals from the organization. All specific information of clients is secured and ensured for personalization by AirAsia.

Environmental Analysis
The environmental analysis will examine the external macro-environment that affects all firms. Here, we will examine the political, economic, social, and technological factors of the external macro-environment. This analysis was conducted based on AirAsia's Annual Reports and available industry data.

Political
The political impact on the avionics business is instrumental towards the development of the carrier, particularly, in the Asia-Pacific and the ASEAN district. Government support for national bearers and negligible limitations on relocation is appropriate for the development of a carrier. Moreover, security controls ought to dependably be kept up to mirror the respectability of the carrier. (AirAsia, Annual Report 2009).

Economic
On the financial front, the expanding local urbanization is relied upon to lead the improvement of new urban focuses, making new destinations for territorial travel. The expanding financial development rates of the ASEAN district would move the avionics business to more prominent statures. The GDP of the ASEAN economies measured a noteworthy USD 1.5 trillion as at 15 March 2010 (AirAsia, Annual Report 2009).

Social

AirAsia unmistakably could recognize the capability of the underserved market portion inside of the ASEAN district. More than half of the world's populace lives inside of a six hour flying range from Kuala Lumpur and a five-hour flying sweep from Bangkok, which highlights the potential size of the territorial flying business sector. The presentation of broadly accessible low air passages in Southeast Asia significantly diminishes the cost obstruction to air travel and makes a focused transport substitute for the ASEAN populace. The best medicinal consideration and instructive organizations are set inside simple achieve, sustaining the bodies and brain of an expanding populace (AirAsia Berhad, Annual Report 2009). Families are reinforced as parties turn out to be more normal and an ASEAN ethos is instilled because of the weaving of assorted societies into a beautiful local embroidered artwork (AirAsia Berhad, Annual Report 2009).

Technological

AirAsia's accomplishment in creating income from subordinate items and administrations lies in bridling the force of its e-business procedure and electronic Customer Relationship Management (Air Asia Berhad, Annual Report 2009). Also, AirAsia gives web booking framework, for example, "Go Holiday" and "Get A Room" that empowers AA to infer its income by joining an administration expense into the lodging rates (Air Asia Berhad, Annual Report 2009). AirAsia trusts that by bridling the force of the internet, the online networking gives a channel of correspondence to low admission advancements, new course dispatches, challenges, flight plans upgrades and visitor support administrations. Furthermore, it makes a stage to guarantee the brand picture of the gathering stays applicable through its site and differed online networking systems.

Challenges faced by Airasia

According to Shavinina, L. V. (2006), developing organizations confront a scope of difficulties. As a business develops, diverse issues and opportunities request distinctive arrangements - what worked a year back power now be not the best approach. Very regularly, avoidable errors transform what could have been an awesome business into an additionally ran. Perceiving and conquering the normal pitfalls connected with development is vital if your business is to keep on developing and flourish. Significantly, you have to guarantee that the strides you take today don't themselves make extra issues for what's to come.

Viable initiative will offer you some assistance with making the greater part of the open doors, making economical development for what's to come. The arrangement that appeared well and good for you a year prior isn't as a matter of course a good fit for you now. Economic situations persistently change, so you have to return to and overhaul your strategy for success consistently. See the page in this aide on staying aware of the business sector. As your business develops, your technique needs to advance to suit your changed circumstances. For instance, your center is liable to change from winning new clients to building gainful connections and augmenting development with existing clients. Existing business connections regularly have more noteworthy potential revenue driven and can likewise give solid income. More up to date connections might build turnover, yet the overall revenues may be lower, which may not be maintainable. See the page in this aide on income and money related administration. In the meantime, every business should be cognizant to new open doors.

There are evident dangers to depending singularly on existing clients. Enhancing your client base spreads those dangers. Taking after the same plan of action, yet greater, is not by any means the only course to development. There are other key choices, for example, outsourcing or franchising that may give better development opportunities. It's imperative not to accept that your present achievement implies that you will consequently have the capacity to exploit these open doors. Each significant move needs arranging similarly as another business dispatch. Here are a portion of the difficulties confronted via AirAsia from AirAsia faces challenges throughout Southeast Asia as competition continues to intensify. (2013, August 1), AirAsia faces challenges throughout Southeast Asia as competition continues to intensify. (2013, August 1); and Bearak, M. (2015, June 22):

Human Resources Management
According to Blackett, T. (2004), AirAsia's main challenges are controlling its Human Resource (HR). Ageing populations across the globe will continue to pose a challenge for AirAsia Berhad. From one perspective, experienced representatives are withdrawing the workforce, leaving an initiative void. Then again, numerous more established laborers, especially those in the US and

other industrialized nations, plan to bear on functioning admirably past the conventional retirement age. Numerous will basically need to keep winning, as social wellbeing nets, annuities and different advantages will never again be satisfactory or accessible. In any case, HR should set up more focused on motivation structures to keep less dedicated more seasoned specialists in the workforce. Organizations will likewise need to foresee and survey which new aptitudes and preparing more established workers will require, especially in the domain of innovation where they might feel less great than a considerable lot of their more youthful associates. Regardless of the fact that more baby-boomers can be influenced to stay around for more, numerous organizations will feel powerless as they leave the workforce by the thousand throughout the following couple of years.

AirAsia Berhad should deal with the effective exchange of experience and learning to more youthful eras at the beginning of their professions. On the off chance that request keeps on surpassing supply for specific positions, organizations will likewise need to reexamine how to contract junior laborers into positions requiring more residency and encounter, and figure out what extra preparing will be vital. Setting up the world's childhood for the work environment will surely introduce challenges. In nations with high youth unemployment rates, there are expanded worries that numerous youngsters will leave the workforce for all time, delivering a lost era. In the mean time, the aptitudes and training of the millennial who stay in the workforce should dependably be important and appealing to businesses. As we see underneath, governments, organizations and instructive establishments should make arrangements that change the instructive framework, and set up the future workforce for livelihood opportunities. Organizations have so far attempted to boost the capability of ladies, who are significantly under-spoke to at the highest point of real organizations. A negligible 13 out of the biggest 500 organizations on the planet by income had ladies CEOs in 2012, an extent of only 2.6 percent.

Populace decay, because of lower conception rates, alongside stagnant instructive change have provoked numerous associations to trepidation future aptitudes deficiencies, especially in specific parts. A 2012 Economist Intelligence Unit study of senior administrators all through the world uncovered that the most hazardous enrollment challenges, by a significant edge, identify with specialized/building parts, and to the procedure and corporate-improvement capacity. Vital vision and the capacity to handle multifaceted nature were referred to be the most troublesome aptitudes to discover among senior officials, probably likewise the motivation behind why vital parts are esteemed so risky to fill. Organizations are obviously attempting to enroll those with the evidently uncommon capacity to guide them through an erratic and aggressive outer environment.

AirAsia Berhad has tried to react to millennial's needs as per their size. Littler organizations, specifically, have cottoned on to the thought that cutting edge laborers will probably ache for flexibility from smaller scale administration. About portion of the specimen of the littlest organizations in a 2012 Economist Intelligence Unit review award self-governance to laborers as an ability administration instrument, a rate that declines as the organization gets to be bigger and more bureaucratic. One organization in this littler class is Zensar Technologies, who requests conclusions from an assorted cross-area of their workforce, not slightest as a way to expand representative engagement (see the Workforce inspirations segment for a contextual analysis on Zensar). The biggest organizations in the Economist Intelligence Unit study are liable to utilize the measure of their association as a motivational apparatus, offering shifted assignments in diverse parts of the world to laborers with high potential. This approach fills a double need. It permits organizations to connect any abilities crevices to specific parts of the world, while additionally giving open doors that numerous more youthful bosses are looking for. A 2011 PricewaterhouseCoopers (PwC) overview found that 71 percent of Generation-Y laborers anticipate that and need will finish an abroad task amid their vocation.

Innovation's advancing part in reclassifying what work means will oblige firms to think of new and imaginative techniques to deal with their undeniably versatile workforce. These procedures should offer portable specialists some assistance with remaining drew in and associated with the more extensive association they serve. An enhanced ICT base and expanded use in creating countries will absolutely keep on growing the accessibility of neighborhood ability for spotters and HR administrators in AirAsia Berhad. Be that as it may, difficulties will persevere, the same number of potential work market members will need access or sufficient innovative proficiency. HR offices inside of major worldwide firms should connect with nearby governments, colleges, junior colleges and professional schools to offer progressing preparing for all current and new representatives as advances change. With organizations now captivating with an adaptable and versatile workforce, execution measures should be patched up. When supervisors organize results, and not simply efficiency or process, new assessment models will be important. HR will likewise need to evaluate the best systems for overseeing and speaking with telecommuters, especially crosswise over outskirts.

Unfavourable market conditions
AirAsia has confronted testing economic situations over its home business sector of Southeast Asia since late 2013. Extraordinary rivalry and overcapacity has affected AirAsia's execution in for all intents and purposes the greater part of its business sectors. AirAsia likewise has dispatched three new partners subsequent to Jun-2014. Every one of the three of these bearers have confronted different administrative difficulties, prompting higher than foreseen misfortunes. Lower fuel costs have given a support in 1H2015 and have mostly determined the change in working results at four of the five unique bearers – MAA, TAA, PAA and MAAX. In any case, fences and USD thankfulness counterbalance the majority of the diminishment in fuel costs. The short-pull AirAsia Group supported half of its fuel in 1H2015 at a normal cost of USD93 per barrel. Although in 2015 oil prices experienced a sharp decline, this decline in oil prices immediately reflected on 2015's profit margins.

AirAsia is hopeful it will see upgrades over the portfolio in 2H 2015. Three AirAsia transporters have been rebuilding (IAA, MAAX and PAA) and are relied upon to be in any event earning back the original investment before the end of 2015. Two of the three new businesses(IAAX and TAAX) are additionally anticipated that would be at any rate make back the initial investment before the end of 2015. In any case, AirAsia still faces challenges in every one of its business sectors and it is impossible the greater part of the unbeneficial bearers will have the capacity to finish turnarounds in 2H2015 as trusted. Five AirAsia transporters had misfortunes per traveler of at any rate USD19 in 1H2015. This is clearly unsustainable and indicates how far several of the affiliates need to come before they are profitable.

Indonesia AirAsia still faces challenges
IAA additionally has its offer of difficulties as the aircraft rebuilds and recoils in an offer to come back to gainfulness. The aircraft has been doing combating troublesome economic situations and was affected in 1H2015 by the 28-Dec-2015 accident of one of its A320s. IAA finished 2Q2015 with 29 A320s. As CAPA beforehand dissected in Jul-2015, IAA wanting to

psychologist its armada to 25 A320s before the end of 2015 as the system is rebuilt. The AirAsia Group affirmed in its 2Q2015 results presentation that four or five A320s will be leaving the IAA armada before the year's over. The gathering said air ship would be expelled from the Bali, Bandung, Jakarta and Medan bases while the Surabaya base won't be affected.

IAA is fundamentally concentrating on household limit cuts as it sees more good conditions in the Indonesian universal business sector, which is additionally served by new medium/whole deal LCC IAAX. IAA wants to redeploy some local ability to the worldwide business sector in 2H2015. For instance more flights are being added from Surabaya to Johor and Kuala Lumpur in Malaysia while local administrations from Jakarta to Medan and Bali to Solo are being suspended. IAA is additionally taking after PAA in boosting air ship usage rates and executing self-taking care of at its bases. IAA's normal airplane use rate is relied upon to enhance from around 10hrs in 2Q2015 to 11.3hrs in 4Q2015 as the span of the armada is lessened. However, the viewpoint for IAA remains moderately shady given the extraordinary rivalry and slower monetary development in Indonesia. AirAsia is additionally as yet dealing with securing new capital for IAA. Until new shareholders are gotten and IAA succeeds at issuing new convertible bonds there will be waiting concerns.

AirAsia India faces challenging outlook
TAA and start-up AirAsia India (AAI) will be the main AirAsia short-pull bearers which will develop their armada in 2015. AAI as of now works five A320s, up from three flying machine toward the start of 2015, and arrangements to include no less than one more A320 before the end of 2015. In 2Q2015 AAI had the most elevated burden element among all AirAsia subsidiaries at 83%. AAI likewise reported a 13% diminishment in unit costs and expects further decreases in unit costs as it keeps on spooling up. Be that as it may, AAI still faces testing economic situations and an administration limitation denying worldwide operations until transporters are no less than five years of age and work no less than 20 airplanes. AAI was putting money on having the capacity to work global administrations so as to accomplish high air ship use. AAI at first expected the 5/20 guidelines would be abrogated by its one-year commemoration yet it is presently shows up confinements won't be evacuated under another common aeronautics strategy that is currently being drafted. AAI normal yield has been beneath household contenders, bringing about misfortunes in spite of high load components. The schedule second quarter is a

top travel period in India yet AAI stayed unbeneficial while even Jet Airways and SpiceJet, both of which posted extensive misfortunes in the financial year finishing 31-Mar-2015, were operating at a profit. AAI's misfortunes are relied upon to increment in 3QCY2015 because of overwhelming marking down and serious rivalry. Benefit is far-fetched in the close to medium term unless there is an adjustment in economic situations and government arrangement. AAI needs to date confronted a forceful reaction from its rivals and this is liable to keep on being the situation on new courses that it enters. The bearer will in this way require a more grounded war mid-section to withstand what can now and again be nonsensical valuing and limit organization, and will probably join IAA and PAA in requiring further recapitalization.

AirAsia A320 fleet to shrink by six aircraft in 2H2015
Overall AirAsia plans to shrink its A320 fleet in 2H2015 from 172 to 166 aircraft, driven by the sale of several older A320s and the leasing out of four A320s outside the group. AirAsia extended its A320 armada in 1H2015 by one and only air ship. AirAsia additionally has incorporated the deal or return of 72 A320s in its recently overhauled armada arrangement for 2016 to 2021. The gathering is slated to take 95 A320s (five A320ceos and 90 A320neos) amid this six year period, prompting a net development of just 23 airplane or 14%. That compares to normal per annum development of under 3%.

	A320ceo	A320neo	End of Lease / Lease Retirement	Sale of Vintage Acft (at 12 yrs)	Net Acft for Growth	Cumulative Fleet
2015	5		-3	-7 (3 from Zest)	-5	166
2016	5	4	-1	-1	7	173
2017		9	-4	-2	3	176
2018		11	-2	-8	1	177
2019		20	-3	-14	3	180
2020		22	-3	-19	0	180
2021		24	-13	-2	9	189

AirAsia Group fleet revised plan: 2015 to 2021

Diminishing the quantity of flying machine returns and deals could in any case effortlessly quicken armada development. However, AirAsia is unrealistic to resume twofold digit yearly armada development, which it reliably recorded since it was built up in 2002. As CAPA highlighted in the last portion, the AirAsia X Group is likewise altogether backing off extension of its A330 armada. AirAsia X is currently wanting to take just five A330s by the end 2018, giving it an armada of 31 air ship (29 A330-300ceos and two A330-900neos).

Accordingly the whole AirAsia family is presently slated to have an armada toward the end of 2018 of 208 air ship (166 A320neos, 11 A320ceos, 29 A330-300ceos and two A330-900enos). This is just 12 air ship more than the present armada of 196 flying machine, including 172 A320s and 24 A330-300s. Quicker extension is conceivable from late 2018 as AirAsia X takes the 55 A330-900neos it has on request. However, AirAsia X has not yet showed when it arrangements to return or offer its A330ceos, which gives it the adaptability to possibly take after short-pull sister AirAsia in seeking after humble armada development through 2021. (AirAsia X has 19 A330-900neo conveyances for 2019 to 2021.)

AirAsia passenger growth slows
As it slows down fleet growth, AirAsia will probably see a lull in traveler development. The eight AirAsia bearers joined transported 26.5 million travelers in 1H2015, speaking to a 6% expansion contrasted with 1H2014. Traveler development over the AirAsia portfolio was 9% in 2014, speaking to the first year development was in the single digits. Traveler development for 2015 will probably end a couple rate focuses lower and could dunk further in 2016.

	AirAsia Group	AirAsia X Group	Total AirAsia
2002	1.04		1.04
2003	2.09		2.09
2004	4.87		4.87
2005	7.37		7.37
2006	12.11		12.11
2007	15.34	0.02	15.35
2008	18.35	0.27	18.62
2009	22.70	1.03	23.74
2010	25.68	1.92	27.60
2011	29.86	2.53	32.39
2012	34.14	2.58	36.72
2013	42.61	3.16	45.78
2014	45.58	4.48	50.06
1H2015	24.28	2.19	26.47

AirAsia passenger (in millions): 2002 to 2014

Thai AirAsia records higher profit but drop in yields

Thai AirAsia turned a working benefit of THB517 million (USD16 million) in 2Q2013, an expansion of 124% contrasted with the THB231 million (USD7 million) working benefit in 2Q2012. The bearer's net benefit likewise multiplied from THB246 million (USD8 million) in 2Q2012 to THB499 million (USD16 million) in 2Q2013 (see foundation data). Incomes were up 21% to THB5.36 billion (USD168 million) as traveler activity expanded by 25% to 2.4 million. Thai AirAsia's seat load component enhanced by 3ppt from 79% to 82%, outflanking its Malaysian sister bearer which normally has had the most elevated burdens in the gathering. RPKs were up 25% while ASKs were up 18%. Thai AirAsia finished the quarter with a working overall revenue of 10% contrasted with 5% in 2Q2012. Not at all like the gathering's different members, Thai AirAsia has been reliably beneficial lately in spite of the fact that its working edge has never drawn closer the edge found in Malaysia. Be that as it may, traveler unit incomes were down 3% year-over-year in 2Q2013 and normal charges dropped 4% to THB1,877

(USD58.82). These were not as steep as the 8% unit income and 10% normal toll drops at the gathering's Malaysian short-pull operation however are disturbing as Thailand has not seen the same sort of emotional changes to the aggressive scene that Malaysia has seen for this present year.

Thai AirAsia faces new competitive threats in Thai Lion and Thai VietJet
Thailand's business sector as of now has only two nearby LCCs, Thai AirAsia and Nok Air. Situate Thai beforehand contended as a third LCC locally however has basically pulled back from this business sector, at first closing its LCC image One-Two-Go in 2008. In the course of the last couple of years Orient Thai has consistently decreased local limit and now just works two residential courses with a sum of 23 week by week flights, as per Innovata information. It has a bigger universal operation, with two booked courses and a few contract courses (basically to China), however this takes after a relaxation bearer instead of LCC model. Thai AirAsia, Nok and Thai Airways each right now represent roughly a 27% offer of seat limit in the Thailand residential business sector, as indicated by CAPA and Innovata information. Full-administration boutique bearer Bangkok Airways represents around a 18% share and Orient Thai represents under 2%.

AirAsia discovered the difficulties of doing business in India.
At the point when the quickly developing Malaysian bearer AirAsia needed to grow, India resembled the perfect wilderness. The nation had countless potential first-time fliers, numerous in second-and third-level urban areas that have only a couple flights a day. With restricted airfares as low as $20, AirAsia intended to catch colossal pieces of tourism and occasion activity from India's notorious however painfully moderate trains. At that point, AirAsia found the challenges of working together in India. While it profited from a late extricating of confinements on remote interest in aircrafts, AirAsia India has battled with a web of formality and regulations for new contestants that have added critical expense and multifaceted nature to its operations. Rivalry has likewise demonstrated furious, and tenacious cost wars cut profoundly into benefits.

After its first year in operation, AirAsia India has only 1 percent of the nation's residential traveler market, and the transporter is retooling its technique. While at first concentrating for the most part on littler, underserved urban communities in south India, the aircraft has now begun flying courses from the nation's biggest, Delhi. AirAsia India is taking after the way set by the bearer in different nations. Since an update in 2001, AirAsia has to a great extent concentrated on keeping costs low and selling so as to wring out additional incomes subordinate administrations like in-flight suppers and diversion, and also charging expenses for processed packs or situates with additional legroom. AirAsia sent out the model from its home in Malaysia to the Philippines, Thailand and Indonesia, attempting to gain by the quickly developing economies in the area. Among Southeast Asia's financial plan transporters, it represents more than 33% of all seat limit, as indicated by an investigation by the Center for Asia Pacific Aviation. Charges on avionics turbines are higher than anyplace else on the planet. Each carrier, even those with only a couple planes, is likewise required to fly frequently to remote districts, where flights regularly run half full. Also, new participants like AirAsia India are denied from flying lucrative worldwide courses until they are five years of age and have no less than 20 flying machine, the purported 5/20 guidelines.

AirAsia has additionally needed to clash with IndiGo. One of the first spending plan transporters to begin in the nation, IndiGo, with a strong notoriety for reliability and solace, now orders just about 40 percent of the business sector, as indicated by government measurements. It's one of only a handful few Indian aircrafts that has been reliably gainful. On each new course opened via AirAsia India, IndiGo has taken after, setting off a cost war.

AirAsia brand sustain challenge
From the organization's perspective, image, as specified via Landor (www. buildingbrands.com), is a guarantee that it makes to its clients. Characterized in this way it suggests that brand accompanies obligations and the failure to satisfy the guarantee can have extreme negative impacts. A brand must have the capacity to convey and make a positive commitment to have the capacity to support itself. The test to brands is to stay applicable with changing desires of shoppers because of changes in way of life, access to innovation and expansion of item decision. All things considered even fruitful brands need to continually advance and enhance with a specific end goal to stay important to the business sector. One of the markers of fruitful marking is when shoppers utilize the name of a brand synonymously to allude to an item, for example, Pampers for diapers or Kleenex for tissue papers, Colgate for toothpaste.

Keller (2002) proposed that there are four stages to follow in arranging a marking methodology. To start with, attempt an audit of the item keeping in mind the end goal to distinguish and fortify its worth which can be utilized to position its marking. This incorporates a push to augment the convincing so as to mark estimation of the item the purchasers the "additional items" that can be found in the item rather than its rivals. Second, arrangement for an exhaustive promoting so as to showcasing methodology of the item the marking esteem through a mix and incorporation of brand components and forceful advertising exercises. Third, survey and translate the brand execution as a consequence of the prior steps. At long last, advance and maintain the brand value, that is, the benefit and qualities connected to the brand that can increase the value of the item.

As per Davis (2002a) the best marking technique which has gathered a substantial piece of the pie for an item is the point at which an association regards its image as the most vital resource for the organization's long haul survival. At the end of the day, the association must be dynamic in advancing the brand and is willing to make significant interest in advancing, fortifying and managing the brand in the commercial center. Such speculation ought to incorporate the assignment of guaranteeing that the entire association comprehends its image and utilizes this comprehension to channel its worth specifically or by implication to the consumers.

1. **Keep prices low but not to sink below cost**

   There will be no more value war in the aeronautics business in this locale as carriers are sick of losing cash, said AirAsia Bhd bunch (CEO) Tan Sri Tony Fernandes. The value war is completion in Malaysia, as well as in Indonesia and the Philippines as (industry players) are sick of losing cash. AirAsia procedure (now) is to keep costs low however not to sink underneath expense. This can be a test for AirAsia.

2. **Faulty advertising strategy**

In 2008, Malaysia Airlines and AirAsia were condemned by the Malaysian Association of Tour and Travel Agents (MATTA) for promoting "zero toll" flights. MATTA said that such commercials were deluding and ought to be banned as they don't furnish clients with the full scope of costs to anticipate. Clients still needed to pay airplane terminal duties, fuel extra charges, and different expenses for the constrained "zero toll" tickets. While New Zealand, Australia and Europe have prohibited such publicizing hones, and the European Parliament had consented to another law to incorporate such expenses and charges in the promoted offer, such enactment has not been gone in Malaysia.

3. **AirAsia Indonesia crash**

Indonesia AirAsia Flight 8501 (QZ8501/AWQ8501) was a planned worldwide traveler flight, worked via AirAsia Group offshoot Indonesia AirAsia, from Surabaya, Indonesia, to Singapore. On 28 December 2014, the air ship working the highway, an Airbus A320-216, enlisted as PK-AXC, collided with the Java Sea amid awful climate, slaughtering each of the 155 travelers and seven group on board. Two days after the accident, trash from the air ship and human remains were discovered gliding in the Java Sea. Searchers found destruction on the ocean bottom starting on 3 January, and the flight information recorder and cockpit voice recorder were recouped by 13 January. The quest for bodies finished in March 2015 after recuperation of 113 of the 162 bodies. On 20 January 2015, it was accounted for that the air ship had slowed down amid a strangely soak climb and had been not able recoup.

Flying today is amazingly sheltered. It wasn't generally that way. In the good old days it was a dangerous business. However, right from the earliest starting point there was a comprehension among governments and industry that wellbeing was not a focused issue. What's more, there has dependably been extraordinary collaboration among all the business' partners in endeavors to make flying ever more secure. In 2013 there were somewhere in the range of 36.4 million flights and 16 deadly mischances. In the event that you were flying on a plane air ship, your odds of being included in a noteworthy mishap were one in 2.4 million. What's more, among the three billion travelers that flew (the likeness around 40% of the world's populace) there were 210 fatalities. There is no more secure approach to get from A to B than via plane. Be that as it may, mishaps do happen.

Surabaya Mayor Tri Rismaharini says her organization is prepared to sue AirAsia if it overlook the privileges of the groups of travelers on flight QZ8501, taking after the suspension of the carrier's flight license from the East Java city to Singapore. Risma said her organization had likewise counseled with legitimate specialists from Airlangga University on the reasons for alarm of most families in regards to the challenges in dispensing protection stores, after the Transportation Ministry respected the Surabaya-Singapore flight on Dec. 28 2014 as illegitimate. She said her organization kept on gathering information on the casualties, including their important possessions. The information would later be utilized for protection purposes and matters identified with the recipient privileges of the influenced families.

4. **High Operating Costs in Japan**

In June 2013, AirAsia chose to leave its interest in AirAsia Japan, making the organization an entirely claimed backup of ANA. The Nihon Keizai Shimbun reported that AirAsia Japan had the most reduced burden elements of the three new participant minimal effort transporters in Japan and noticed a few explanations behind the disappointment of the joint endeavor, including an internet booking framework that was not completely deciphered into Japanese and was along these lines baffling to numerous local clients, inability to use travel specialists circulation (which is still a noteworthy segment of household carrier deals in Japan), the disadvantage of its fundamental center point at Narita Airport, and the airplane terminal's serious confinements on right on time morning and late night flights.

On 1 July 2014, it was reported that AirAsia has joined forces with the online shopping center and travel organization Rakuten (to hold 18% of the stake), a Japanese beauty care products, caffeinated drinks and air ship renting firm Noevir Holdings (9%), the sportswear firm Alpen (5%), and private value firm Octave Japan (19%), to relaunch AirAsia Japan.[5] AirAsia will hold 49% of the stake. Its introductory is JPY7 billion

(USD69 million), with Yoshinori Odagiri, CEO from the past incarnation of AirAsia Japan, comes back to seat. The aircraft is relied upon to trade operation in summer 2015, from a center at Chūbu Centrair International Airport with 2 Airbus A320 planes, growing to 4 before the end of 2015. On 6 October 2015, it was declared that AirAsia Japan has gotten their air working permit to begin working flights, and also reporting Sendai, Sapporo, and Taipei, Taiwan as their initial three destinations from Chubu Centrair International Airport. Flights will start in Spring 2016.

More than 64 percent of air terminals' money related asset was secured by aeronautical charges, landing charges and fuel charges which are paid via aircrafts in Japan. For instance, the extent of landing charges of aggregate aeronautical expenses of easyJet is much lower (22 percent) than that of ANA (more than 60 percent) in 2004 in light of the fact that easyJet tried endeavors to lessen these expenses by arranging with air terminals and decreasing the base take-off weight of flying machine. In 2005, landing charges for a B747-400, an airplane broadly utilized by Japanese system bearers, added up to US$2,964 for a normal local flight and US$4,747 for a worldwide flight. On the way route charges for the same air ship on the Tokyo-Fukuoka highway (881 kilometers) added up to US$4,261 per part (0.9 US pennies for each seat kilometer) contrasted with US$827 (0.6 US pennies for each seat kilometer) for a B737-500. Japanese carriers are basically working extensive airplane, bringing about higher aeronautical charges contrasted with little estimated air ship. The distinction is particularly stamped when contrasting landing charges and worldwide center point air terminals in different locales.

The unit expenses of new participants in Japan are around 8.3 US pennies for each Available Seat Kilometer (ASK), contrasted with 13 pennies for JAL and 10.6 pennies for ANA. In Europe, Ryanair's unit expense is 4.3 pennies for each ASK contrasted with 7.4 US pennies for easyJet and 8.9 US pennies for British Airways in 2004. AirAsia's unit expense is just 2.5 US pennies for each ASK, the consequence of low capital speculation and low work costs. Generally, the work expense of Japan Airlines has been to a great degree high, including representatives' incidental advantages cost with its top around 1994 - 19964. Since 1997, all Japanese carriers have attempted to diminish their work costs however this has been extremely troublesome for them in view of solid unions. ANA effectively diminished their lodge group expense to US$42,400 in 2000 from the US$63,800 per head in 1994, by using low maintenance contract staff. These higher expenses have been secured by higher yields. Normal yield per Revenue Passenger Kilometer (RPK) of ANA and JAL in 2004 was around 15 US pennies and that of Skymark 14 US pennies. For chose aircrafts working in other deregulated locales, the yield per RPK changed from 5 to 9 US pennies. This higher yield of Japanese carriers is particularly noteworthy on residential courses. Interestingly, it has been higher secondary selling liberalization

Current financial conditions

Castillo-Manzano, J. I., & Marchena-Gómez, M. (2010) asserted that AirAsia is abating extension as it endeavors to pivot battling associates and restore benefit. Six of the eight AirAsia-marked bearers were unbeneficial in 1H2015 with just the since quite a while ago settled short-pull transporters in Malaysia and Thailand operating at a profit. Traveler activities across AirAsia family developed by just 6% in 1H2015 to 26.5million, and 2016 is anticipating a further slow down. 2015 experienced the slowest yearly movement development in AirAsia's 14-year history caused by the Chinese global economic slowdown. 2015 checked the first year AirAsia recoil its armada. AirAsia ended 2015 with 193 flying machine, including 166 A320s and 27 A330-300s, contrasted with 197 air ship toward the start of the year. To a great degree unassuming development is currently gotten ready for the following three years, bringing about an armada of 208 airplane (177 A320s and 31 A330s) toward the end of 2018. The first and biggest AirAsia bearer, Malaysia AirAsia (MAA), has reliably been exceedingly beneficial in the course of the most recent quite a long while with high twofold digit working edges. Be that as it may, MAA has seen its yearly net benefit decay for three back-to-back years and its yearly working benefit decrease for four sequential years. In 1H2015 MAA could enhance its working benefit from MYR401 million (USD123 million) to MYR517 million (USD142 million). However, the transporter's net benefit kept on dropping driven by account costs and remote trade misfortunes.

MAA (Malaysia AirAsia) reported a net benefit of MYR392 million (USD108 million) in 1H2015 contrasted with a net benefit of MYR507 million (USD155 million) in 1H2014. The benefit figure for MAA is additionally to some degree deceiving as some of its benefits have generally been created from flying machine leases to abroad partners. MAA reported MYR459 million (USD126 million) in flying machine working lease salary in 1H2015 contrasted with MYR393 million (USD120 million) in 1H2014. Thai AirAsia (TAA) has additionally reliably been beneficial in the course of the most recent quite a while despite the fact that it did see a huge lessening in benefits in 2014, incorporating a little misfortune in 1H2014, because of the common distress in Bangkok. TAA turned a net benefit of THB1.297 billion (USD39 million) and a working benefit of THB1.709 million (USD52 million) in 1H2015 contrasted with a net loss of THB73 million (USD2 million) and a working loss of THB82 million (USD3 million) in 1H2014. TAA has dependably been the second biggest AirAsia marked transporter after MAA in view of armada size and traveler numbers. In the course of the most recent year TAA additionally retook the refinement of being the second biggest AirAsia bearer taking into account incomes from Malaysia AirAsia X (MAAX) as MAAX cut limit. Every one of the six of the littler (and more current) individuals from the AirAsia family were unrewarding in 1H2015. The misfortunes at these six bearers totaled a disturbing USD214 million in 1H2015. At the point when likewise considering in the benefits at MAA and TAA, each of the eight bearers in the AirAsia family had a consolidated net loss of USD67 million in 1H2015.

Carrier	1H2015 net profit	1H2014 net profit	1H2015 op profit	1H2014 op profit	1H2015 revenues	1H2014 revenues
Malaysia AirAsia (MAA)	+108	+155	+142	+123	722	800
Thai AirAsia (TAA)	+39	-2	+52	-3	444	367
Indonesia AirAsia (IAA)	-79	-68	-58	-52	190	247
Philppines AirAsia (PAA)	-36	-62	-24	-64	99	100
AirAsia India (AAI)	-10	-1	-10	-1	30	0.3
Malaysia AirAsia X (MAAX)	-71	-43	-26	-46	393	435
Thai AirAsia X (TAAX)	-0.3	-11	N/A	N/A	N/A	N/A
Indonesia AirAsia X (IAAX)	-18	-0.6	N/A	N/A	N/A	N/A
TOTAL	**-67**	**-29**	**+76**	**-43**	**1,878**	**1,949**

Profit/loss (in USD millions) and revenues (in USD millions) for all AirAsia carriers: 1H2015 vs 1H2014

Note: *figures have been converted from MYR, THB, IDR, PHP and INR to USD using the average exchange rate for each period on Onada.com TAAX and IAAX do not report operating profit/loss or revenues. Totals for these categories therefore exclude TAAX and IAAX Source: CAPA – Centre for Aviation*

The combined net loss for this same group of eight carriers has widened slightly from a loss of USD29 million in 1H2014. Five of the carriers saw higher net losses or reduced profits compared to 1H2015 with TAA, Thai AirAsia X (TAAX) and Philippines AirAsia (PAA) bucking the trend. But on an operating level there has been a slight improvement over the last year, driven primarily by the higher operating profits at MAA and TAA. Excluding TAAX and Indonesia AirAsia X (IAAX), AirAsia carriers combined generated an operating profit of USD76 million in 1H2015 compared to an operating loss of USD43 million in 1H2014. AirAsia X Group does not provide operating profit/loss figures for TAAX and IAAX, which launched services in Jun-2014 and Jan-2015 respectively. Short-haul affiliate AirAsia India (AAI) also launched in Jun-2014 and therefore had a very marginal loss in 1H2014.

Conclusion

Because of increasing competition from other airlines and anticipated rise in the number of travelers, winners will be those willing to take challenges in delivering a better service and prices. According to Danial Chan (2000) in the future, many of the world biggest airline operators will and be acting players in Asian airlines industry.

As low cost carrier, AirAsia need to focus on cost reduction while ensuring effective operating activities and elimination of inefficiencies. So far, low global oil prices are helping in improving profit margins, but Airasia need to find creative ways to maintain profitability. More importantly, AirAsia is in an urgent needs to come up with strategy that focuses on gaining competitive advantage and differenciate their services from those of rivals. Furthermore, AirAsia, need to capitalize on their position as market leader of LCC in Malaysia, Thailand, and Indonesia, as they will face increasing competition from both existing and new players. In order to sustain its competitive advantage, AirAsia needs to leverage its competency in creating cost advantages across multiple value chains by taking advantage of low oil prices that significantly contributed to their profit margins in 2015.

Avialite

Avialite Sdn Bhd (Avialite), is a small sized Malaysian company established in November 2000 to produce specialized LED beacons for lighting towers. Avialite's primary focus is aviation lights used as markers for tall structures and obstacles with the height of 45 meters and above. Avialite also produces lights for microwave towers, transmission base stations, transmission lines for electricity company, mobile base stations, monopoles, stacks, chimneys and tall buildings apartments and even for houses.

A special feature of the lamps manufactured by Avialite is its waterproofing technology, which is incorporated into its products to withstand the very hot, wet and humid conditions of tropical countries. Thus the lamps are fully protected against ingress of dust and moisture and come with relevant certifications. The waterproofing technology developed by the company is patented. The waterproofing LED lamps technology is reliable and maintenance free, in addition to its heat dissipation ability to increase the lifespan of lights.

The Malaysian Investment Development Authority (MIDA) has recognized Avialite's unique and innovative design for aviation obstacle light by awarding them the Pioneer Status for their product in year 2006. It was noted that the award was given for being the first homegrown manufacturer in the field of aviation lighting technology using LED in Malaysia. With the support of other government agencies, namely MATRADE and SME Corp Malaysia, today Avialite has successfully exported their products to Indonesia, Philippines, Vietnam, U.A.E, Africa, Myanmar and many other countries. Now, more than 60% of Avialite's production is exported overseas. The change of technology in the LED lighting industry is ever-changing and because of this Avialite strives to improvise their products to ensure product's relevancy to the marketplace. Moreover, competitors with more advanced products are in existence mainly from China, making it a tough for Avialite to expand.

Company background
Avialite Sdn Bhd (Avialite) was incorporated in November 2004, a Malaysian owned manufacturer of LED Aviation Warning Light. The capital of this company to operate is about

RM500,000.00 with 32 workforces which comprises of both Malaysian and foreign workers. Avialite is a family business, led by Madam Hee Hwee Leng acting as the Chief Executive Officer (CEO), Ir. A.L Chew as the Chief Technical Officer (CTO), and two of their children, Chew Yein Sean and Chew Ein Li as directors. Below shows the Organization Chart of Avialite Sdn Bhd:

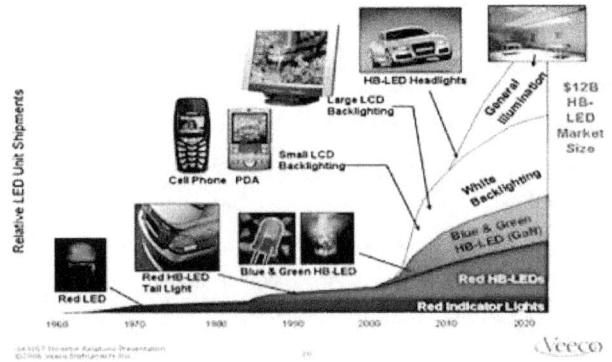

LED Technology Development from 1960s to 2020
Source: http://www.veeco.com

The company's goal is to be the main manufacturer as aviation light specialist in the next 5 years parallel in fulfilling Malaysia's national goal of "Vision 2020" and to dominate the global market segment by producing world-class products with a distinctive advantage and flair. In support of the Malaysian Government's effort in encouraging a 'greener culture' and the introduction of the Malaysian Green Policy, Avialite would like to contribute more to the environment in reducing carbon footprint as well as improve the lives of many.

It all started when Avialite came up with its first prototype model of low intensity LED aviation light Li-3280, which was designed and built in a small research setting in the middle of Kuala Lumpur. The initial idea of manufacturing aviation obstruction lights in Malaysia suddenly became a reality when imported aviation lights became ridiculously expensive and difficult due to the increase of Euro currency in 2000. During that time, the European market was quite slow in adopting new LED technology trends. Avialite's owner who is a qualified engineer in the

Electrical and Electronics (E&E) industry, Chew started to design and built his own version of LED aviation lights. A. L. Chew has a wide experience in the aviation light industry and was able to categorize and identify all types of issues and problems pertaining the conventional aviation lights. Malaysia's temperature is high in humidity all year long, which had always been a serious cause for moisture collecting inside glass covers of the imported aviation lights. Usually, neon type lights with silicone gel is used to prevent moisture from penetrating aviation lights. A. L. Chew came up with his own design of a new aviation lighting system with waterproofing technology that is incorporated into all of its products. With the unique and special features, it could withstand very hot, wet and humid conditions of the tropical countries.

Avialite's first waterproof product, a low intensity LED aviation light Li-3280 has unique design features, which addresses the shortcomings of other conventional lights. The lamps are fully protected against ingress of dust and moisture where it comes with IP67 certification. The certification is used to specify the environmental protection of enclosures around electronic equipment. The product itself by having waterproofing technology makes the LED lamps more reliable and maintenance free. The company aims to promote and ensure safer skies for the aviation industry, as aviation safety is crucial and becoming of foremost significance in the aviation sector. One of the current challenges is to mark all tall buildings, telecommunication towers and structures with the appropriate and approved aviation obstruction light for aviation safety purposes. Therefore, Avialite attempts to ensure that the quality of its lights to conforms to specifications.

Overview of the LED lighting industry
A brief history of LED technology industry level

Nick Holonyak developed the first of light emitting diode (LED) in 1962 when he was working for General Electric. The technology was created based on Gallium Arsenide Phospide (GaAsP) and through it led to the invention of orange, yellow, and green LEDs in 1967 by one of Holonyak's students, George Craford. Later in 1976, the world's first high brightness, high efficiency LEDs was created by Pearsall, which in turn formed the basis of fiber optical telecommunication that we all enjoy today. Nakamura, working with Nichia Corporation in Japan had created a blue LED based upon a new combination of elements, Indium Gallium Nitride in 1994 in a time that signifies the advancement of the use of LEDs illumination-purposes. Ultimately, it was noted that the blue LED was the basis of the white LED by combining it with phosphor.

The timeline of LED technology is summarized in the figure below. Some of the emerging applications of LED Lighting includes general residential lighting, cell phones, communication gadgets, architectural/ design, and general purpose street and flood lighting.

Technical Advantages

LED Technology for lighting applications has several advantages over conventional and compact fluorescent lights (CFL). The advantages include longer lifetimes, reduced in power consumption per lumen and reduced heat output. Features of the three main types of lamps are compared in Figure 2 below and it indicates that the features of LED are far superior to incandescent lamp and compact florescent.

Features	Incandescent Lamps	CFL	LED Lamps
Lifespan	1,200 hours	8,000 hours	25,000-50,000 hours
Wattage required for lumens of an average 60 W bulb	60 watts	13-15 watts	6-8 watts
Heat emission	85 BTU/hr	30 BTU/hr	3.4 BTU/hr
Light output of 1,600 lumens requires	100 watts	25-30 watts	16-20 watts
Temperature sensitivity	High	Medium	Low
Colour	Needs filters	Needs filters	Available in many hues
Toxic Materials—Mercury	No	Yes	No
Others	Abrupt failure and fragile to external shock	Sensitive to frequent on/off cycles	Dimming over time—no abrupt failure, more hardy, lights up faster, and immune to cycling

Comparison of the technical features of incandescent, CFL and LED lamps
Source: www.ledinside.com

LED Lighting Market

Figure 3 below illustrates the drivers and restraints in the LED technology market. The high growth rate is being driven by numerous factors, including supportive legislation, the technical advantages of LED lamps over existing lighting technologies, declining prices and the associated lower operating costs of LED lamps. The supportive legalization as a driver is also applicable to Malaysia as the government has enforced the use of LED lighting by the introduction of the Malaysian Green Policy in 2009. The policy stated that the Government will impose a ban on the sales and import of incandescent bulbs by the end of 2014 and priority is to be given to LED fixtures for lighting procurement of government buildings.

It is important to note that the driving forces are countered by a number of restrains which include the high initial investment required to purchase and install LED lamps, dominance of other technologies, and low market awareness.

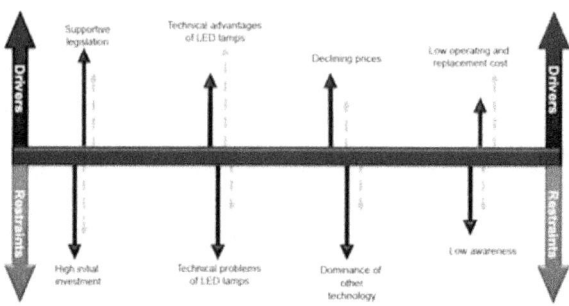

Drivers and Restrains for the LED Market
Source: www.ledinside.com

International Perspective

The LED lighting market was estimated to worth $3.6 billion USD, where North America comprised of 25.7% of this market, and Europe a further 28.1%. However, Asia commanded a 40% share and is the key engine for the revenue growth of the LED market since mid 2012. Europe and North America appear to be the more developed and saturated markets for LED lighting, as it was reflected in the higher market penetration by LED products in the general lighting industry. It is estimated that currently 7% of lighting installations uses LED sources; clearly a significant opportunity for displacement of existing conventional lighting technologies. In terms of absolute sales and revenue, Asia is the largest global market, generally considered to be because of the population (500 million live in South East Asia alone, additional 1.2 billion in India and about 1.5 billion in China). Although construction activities are roaring and government initiatives for energy efficient street lights going strong, yet with large number of Asian manufacturers competing in to low prices, the market is highly competitive.

Moreover, Latin America, Middle East and Asia remains an emerging markets and venerable to global economic shocks. Latin America has vast potential owing to increasing supportive legislation to phase out conventional lighting. Conversely, Middle East has high penetration, but limited potential, which is caused by a boom in real estate and tourism prior to the global recession of 2008. During this time, LED lighting is benefitting in the rise of retail and hospitality industries in the region. Figure 4 describes these geographic trends.

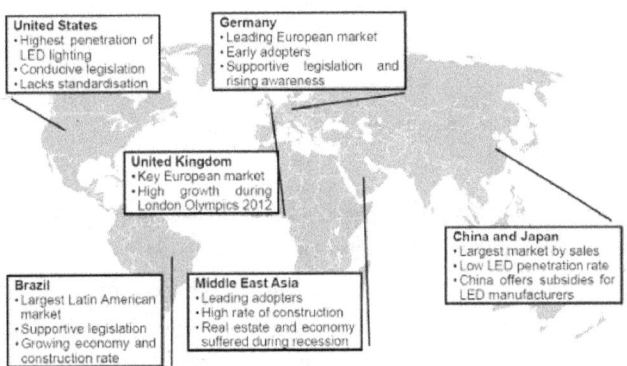

Geographic Trends in LED Lighting Adoption
Source: www.ledinside.com

Regional Perspective
As commonly known in the industry, Asia is the largest revenue contributor to the world LED lighting market with 40% contribution to the global revenue share. The market is concentrated predominantly in China, with South Korea, Taiwan and South-East Asia making significant contributions to growth. This revenue growth is being fuelled by legislative support and the growth in construction. Nevertheless, despite the larger revenue contribution, LED penetration in Asia remains lower than North America and Europe due to certain restraining factors.

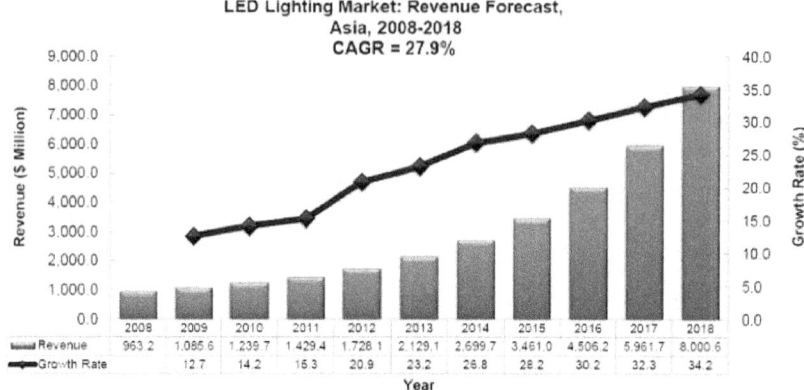
The Asian LED Lighting market – Revenue Forecast 2008 - 2018
Source: www. bizled.co.in

Based on Figure 5 above, growth trajectories of the Asian LED lighting market is doing well; the region is likely to remain the largest regional market for LED Lighting well beyond 2020. This fast pace of growth is driven by a number of factors including government and private initiatives, high rate of construction coupled with urbanisation and rising population density, and the overall economic growth of countries in the region. Additionally, energy efficiency is of an ever-increasing concern and the efforts of public authorities to save energy will accelerate the adoption of LED lighting for public buildings and street lighting. As major manufacturing centres are established throughout China, Japan, Korea and Malaysia, prices will fall further due to increasing competition.

Malaysia's Perspective
The LED industry was first established in Malaysia in the early 1970's. Today the industry is an emerging exporter of LED modules with several European and American companies, setting up a base in Malaysia to service the entire South East Asian market (Indonesia, Singapore, Thailand, Myanmar, Cambodia, Vietnam and the Phillipenes). Multinational companies such as Philips LumiLEDs Malaysia, Osram Opto Semiconductors (Malaysia) Sdn. Bhd, and also Malaysian-based companies are now in operation to cater for both the local and global LED market. Cheaper manufactoring cost in Malaysia allows European and American companies to increase profits, specially when selling their products in their home countries.

In the aftermath of the global financial meltdown of 2007-2008 and worldwide energy crisis, the Malaysian Government had come up with the *National Green Technology Policy* to lower carbon emission and achieve sustainable development economy as a byproduct of this policy. With regards to the green policy, a Green Technology Financing Scheme (GTFS) of about $495.97 million USD was established as an incentive for manufacturers of green products and developers to gain financial assistance. The Economic Transformation Program (ETP) was another government initiative to support the LED industry with the objective to motivate various sectors of the Malaysian economy to drive the country into a high-income nation. There are 15 Entry Point Projects (EPPs) that are specific to Malaysia's LED, solar, industrial electronics and home appliances sector and semiconductor. Such initiatives should help growth of Malaysia's LED industry.

Sectorial Perspective
Across the global LED lighting market, residential lighting offers the largest potential for revenue growth (Figure 6 describes the total LED lighting market by LED application). The following subsection describes the features and value drivers in the different LED lighting sectors.

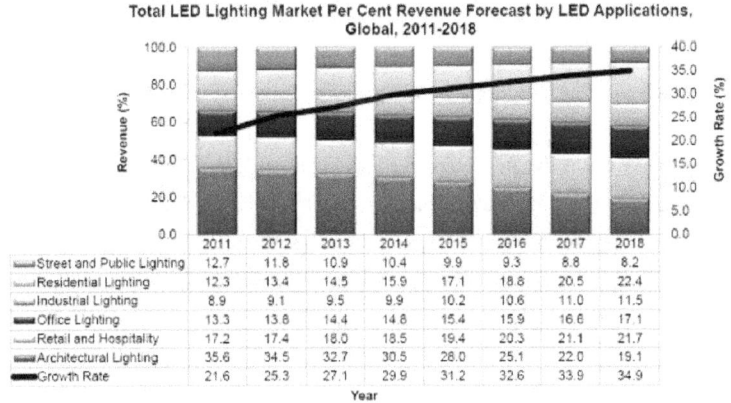

Total LED Lighting Market by LED applications (Global)
Source: Frost & Sullivan

Architectural Lighting
Key factors in the architectural lighting market include color tones, ease of control, directional lighting, ability to change lighting to suit moods and the quality of the light output; all of these features have helped contribute to product adoption in this sector. Since LED lighting used in high-end buildings, there is little price sensitivity associated with high-end LED. It is used as a key architectural design feature and is likely to continue as such well into this century, forming the basis for high revenue generation.

Retail and Hospitality
LED lighting is used both at higher and lower ends of the market. At the lower end however, large department stores and hotels are adopting LED lights. These are price sensitive markets, but very concerned with energy saving, longevity and maintenance costs reduction. These attributes are the key characteristics and advantages of LED lighting. In such applications, LEDs compete with linear and compact fluorescent lighting; since these have clear price differentiation. LED is still at a disadvantage in this market sector where adoption increases whilst prices continue to decline.

At the higher end of the retail/hospitality market, where LED used for display and spot lighting, in this segment LED competes with halogen and incandescent lighting. However, LED suffers from two disadvantages in this area; price and quality of light. The advantages can be seen in its long life span and energy saving, as well as a growing preference for the full colour spectrum light that LEDs producing.

Overall, the retail and hospitality sectors are expected to experience fast growth as prices fall.

Office Lighting
Although not a highly price sensitive market, product quality is a major driver and is cited as the predominant reason for LED lighting to experience low penetration in office building applications in Europe and North America. The main advantage however for LED lighting in office applications is its long life and energy saving features, however, directional lighting that LED is known for is not particularly useful for illumination of workspaces and therefore, is less favorable compared to fluorescent strip-lighting. Office lighting is considered as slow growth sector.

Street and Public Lighting

The key technologies preferred in industrial lighting are sodium vapour and metal halide lighting units. Although LEDs provide important advantages in terms of energy savings and longevity, which is directly associated with cost reduction, LED tends to be higher in cost performance. This is anticipated to change as better products are developed through R&D, and expected to be introduced to global market soon. Prices are also anticipated to drop over time.

Industrial Lighting
High intensity discharge (HID) and linear fluorescent lighting remain the best illumination sources in the industrial sector; although significant energy savings can be made with LEDs, better HID-replacement LED units need to be produced in order to compete in this sector. LED has low penetration in the industrial lighting sector due to high cost during the initial stage for example when doing renovation.

- Residential Lighting

Because of the high initial investment required, LED lighting has just started to be adopted in the residential lighting sector, making it a significant area for potential growth. Traditional incandescent bulbs have dominated the sector since the introduction of electric lights, only recently being challenged by CFLs. The phasing out of incandescent lighting in Europe and US is predicted to lead to greater penetration in these markets; however, price-sensitive regions like Asia and Latin America may not follow this trend, unless there is country-specific legislation discouraging the use of incandescent bulbs.

Financial analysis

A summary of Avialite's sales figures from year 2013-November 2015 is discussed as below. Only the sales figures and cost of goods sold were obtained and disclosed by Madam Hee Hwee Leng.

	2012 (Audited) RM	2013 (Audited) RM	2014 (Audited) RM
Sales	171,893.00	1,856,497.00	9,474,323.32
Cost of goods sold	1,369,216.00	1,805,456.00	3,531,078.00
Gross profit	-1,197,323.00	51,041.00	5,943,245.32

Summarized sales figures of Avialite Sdn Bhd for year 2012-2014

Based on sales and cost of goods sold figures, gross profit for year 2012-2014 can be determined. For year 2012, the company unable to make high sales due to focusing on the R&D process in developing new products. Therefore, higher cost was needed to purchase raw materials, shipping, air freight of imported electric components etc. While for year 2013, Avialite's sales jumped positively from RM171,893.00 to RM1,856,497.00. That year, the company was able to record a positive gross profit of RM51,041. 2013 was the year where Avialite's business started to pick up and assistance were also received from government agencies in the form of financial and marketing support. While 2014 marked a great year for Avialite's business with sales increased up to more than 500% with a gross profit of RM5,943,245.32. According to the CEO and CTO, government's assistance played a major role in supporting the company by linking them with the right parties such as the Public Works Department, Energy Commission of Malaysia, SIRIM Berhad (Certification Body) and Telekom Malaysia Berhad. Avialite succeeded so far to secure projects with government bodies and able to expand their business to Indonesia and the Philippines.

Early 2015 however, was quite a rocky quarter for Avialite due to the implementation of the Goods and Services Tax (GST) by the Malaysian Government. While August and September, during the Ringgit devaluation and increases in oil price, sales were only slightly affected by the torrid situations as 60% of sales is generated internationally, unlike other local LED companies main domestic market dominance. The CEO stated that their sales during 2015 might not exceed that of 2014 sales but it will likely touch forecasted figure of around RM8 million.

Products

Range

Avialite produces specialized LED beacons for lighting towers as such lighting towers may be one of the causes of air traffic obstruction. Such obstruction beacons are present on many different buildings and towers in the commercial sector as well as on airfields of height 45 meters and above. They also produce lights for microwave towers, transmission base stations, transmission lines for electric companies, mobile base stations, monopoles, stacks, chimneys and tall buildings apartments and even houses to mark the high structures to warn pilots of the impending dangerous situation with obstacles within the air space. Avialite's product range and model have increased over the past five (5) years. The CEO believes that the company's raw material are mainly local, while electronic components are from their main supplier "CREE" an

American based company which is currently the leading-market innovator for lighting-class LEDs, which also operates in China. Before being an LED lighting manufacturer, they were trading house, whereby they imported LED lights from Europe. With uncertainty in Euro currency during early 2000 and lack of marketing exposure, Ir. A.L Chew decided to design his own LED lights by hunting for local suppliers to reduce cost. With continuous Research and Development (R&D) to meet consumers' demand, A.L Chew have designed and created low intensity LED aviation obstruction lights, which have many additional features and is extremely compact and lightweight. With less than 1/3 of its competitor's product weight and able to provide the required luminous light output while complying with the International Civil Aviation Organization (ICAO) recommendations and specifications.

List of products:
- AVIALITE Li-1016A Series
- AVIALITE Li-3272 Series
- AVIALITE LS-3272 Series
- AVIALITE Mi-2KP Series AVIALITE MS-2KP Series
- AVIALITE MS – 20 KP Series

Certifications and Requirements

The implementation of quality management systems (ISO 9001:2008) and obtaining necessary product certifications are important to ensure direct entrance to market products internationally. A special feature of Avialite's lights is in its waterproofing technology as it comes with IP67 certification. This certification certifies that products are fully protected against ingress of dust and moisture. Before the implementation of ISO 9001:2008, the management of the company was slacking and the quality management was not at par with their customer's specifications. Subsequently, senior management decided to appoint a consultant to help them in improvising their managerial skills and expands business operations. As a manufacturer producing specialised LED beacons for the aviation industry, specific certifications and requirements are essential to attain in order to penetrate in certain markets and regions. Requirements such as the CE mark, a mandatory conformity marking to market certain products within the European Economic Area is vital. Avialite is targeting the European region but as of now, their main market remain local and withing the ASEAN region, with majority market share in Myanmar. The Malaysian and

Myanmar Departments of Civil Aviation have certified that the products manufactured by Avialite is in complience with the International Civil Aviation Organization (ICAO) requirements and currently used at various airports in Malaysia and Myanmar.

Freedom To Operate (FTO)

Another factor to go global is Intellectual Property (IP) where Avialite has done its part. It is important for companies with products to consider their IP alongside the competitors' IP for international markets to ensure they are free to operate (market and sell). Not to be missed is for the companies to identify any patenting opportunities that may exist. Clearly, careful management of IP can help secure market share, create additional revenue streams and build brand awareness.

Branding

Avialite uses its company's name as their product brand.
Their tagline and logo shows the company's character and its purpose in the industry.

Logo

Tagline

AVIA = Aviation;   **LITE** = Light / Lightweight
LED LIGHTING INNOVATION

There are three core components of their positioning:
- LED ; their core technology that is applied to their products
- LIGHTING ; encompass the nature of their business and its technology
- INNOVATION ; being smart, thoughtful, a step ahead of the marketplace through experience and understanding of industry's trends.

Avialite is a registered trademark in Malaysia, Singapore, Indonesia, Vietnam, Japan Philippines and Myanmar.

Marketing

Avialite's obstruction beacons are comparable to, if not better quality than the European and US LED manufacturers, since they have been designed to withstand local tropical weather conditions: waterproofed (IP rating of 60-70), surge proofed for rainfall and lightening, and is designed to avoid condensation. In addition, products are lightweight, which reduces cost during installation, solar powered, and highly reliable which reduces ongoing maintenance costs. Avialite offers customization and service that would not be available by big brands. While there is an up-front cost and effort required for customization, many features of the custom designs can be later incorporated into Avialite's standard designs improving their overall offering in the longer term. The company usually runs extensive marketing research before expanding into new market. The primary marketing focus currently is Asia and ASEAN region where travel costs can be kept to a minimum and easier to manage scaling up client visits and training new agents for product distribution. Long-term marketing plans set to branch out in Myanmar, Indonesia, and Philippines during 2016-2018 as market outlooks seems to be promising.

Avialite also utilize promotional online channel (website, social media and search advertising) as they know from experience the importance and power of online advertising. Their website is always being updated to ensure potential customers receive new and latest information of their products. Trade shows, conferences and attending local and international events is essential component of the marketing plans. Avialite is one of the participating LED companies in the "Creation of Home Grown SSL/LED Champions Programme", which is part of the Entry Point Projects 10 (EPP10) Programme under the Electrical & Electronics (E&E) New Key Economic Area (NKEA) of the Economic Transformation Programme (ETP). One of the benefits of being selected in this programme is to secure funding by government agencies such as MIDA, MATRADE and SME Corp Malaysia to local and international trade shows and events. This edge gives Avialite the opportunity to expose and introduce their products to potential customers.

Competitive environment and channels

Competitive Environment

McKinsey Consulting in 2011 stated the following "*The market is on a clear transition path from traditional lighting technologies to LED. However, world events over the past year have given clearer contours to the lighting industry's development, and some market parameters have shifted or accelerated*".

"LED lighting could see itself become the next solar, wind or other future opportunity that the U.S. will have given away by failing to address Chinese industrial policies and unfairly traded products." (Michael R. Wessel, a member of the U.S.-China Economic and Security Review Commission, a government advisory panel)

There are currently 5,000-6,000 companies in the LED lighting market with top tiered companies holding nearly half the market share, though this has in fact decreased with the emergence of Asian based companies. Along the way, the market is expected to consolidate non-organically, mostly through Mergers & Acquisition (M&A) and partnerships. Critical success factors for competing in the market includes strategic positioning, brand visibility, strong relationships in the distribution channels, complete solutions, technology and design, and providing financing for client projects. Many of these factors may be out of reach for the small and medium companies (SMEs), but could be addressed by partnering with one of the market leaders or established brands. With regards to competitive factors in varying regions, price is of utmost importance across all regions, as is performance. Where service and reliability are particularly important in North America and Europe, brand, capacity and track record seems to be more important in the Middle East & Asia (MEA). Malaysian LED companies need to grasp the fundamentals and aim at a particular region to expand business operations.

The competitive intensity and customer characteristics of major Asian countries, particularly the high level of price sensitivity amongst Malaysian consumers, and low degree of preference for local companies, entrance of lower cost foreign suppliers may pose a significant threat to Malaysian LED companies unless they are able to manufacture with sufficient economization of scale to compete with low cost Chinese manufacturers. The quality of low cost Chinese products will always be of top consideration. But, given the level of price sensitivity of buyers in the LED lighting market, higher-priced products with marginally differentiated quality will not be very competitive in Asian markets. However, low cost Chinese producers that have a reputation for low quality will be shaken out of the market and replaced by a smaller number of larger Chinese producers with better quality products and stronger brand recognition. With wages increasing in

China in an already crowded market the ability to exercise cost leadership will decline. The resulting consolidation within the Chinese market will allow larger Chinese producers to emerge. A perception is they may still adhere to a lower cost pricing strategy in an attempt to win market share away from established non-Chinese producers.

As for Malaysia's current LED industry situation, awareness of competition appears to vary between companies whereby most are aware about the major players in the LED lighting market, but may not have an understanding of the Intellectual Properties landscape or the need to perform freedom-to-operate (FTO) searches. While for forming a Management Team, which focuses on LED, nearly all companies have one or more of their executive management team with LED or semiconductor industry experience. It is unclear how much international exposure the executive management teams have had, nor their experience of international marketing and business development. Moreover development of competitive internationalization strategies for both products and or service appears to be patchy as is the knowledge of potential new markets.

Below is the list of the top competitors in Avialite's current market:

Competitor	Relative Market Share	Geography	Basis of competition
1 H&P (Huey & Philips) (Netherlands)	5%	Malaysia, Myanmar	On brand; Not a major competitor as they are exiting from the market due to high price
NanHua (China)	10%	Malaysia, Indonesia, Vietnam, Brunei	China brand, cheap price (up to 50% lesser); Some customers are ignorant on the International Civil Aviation Organization specs and they purchase based on the low price
InstaPower, Avaids Technovators (India)	10%	Malaysia, Myanmar	Indian brand; Cheap price Able to win against the Indian companies on larger tenders as Avialite could reduce their price slightly to compete head-on, their brand is also well known in Malaysia.
AVlite (Australia)	10%	Malaysia	Australian light and is a marine light; not up to specs, Avialite competes in quality and educating their customers on the

				specs needed.
Philips (Europe)	-		Malaysia, Brunei, Vietnam	Avialite often wins when competing both on quality and price; Able to compete due to tropical environment as European product does not have the design and Philips price is too high.
Honeywell (US)	-		Malaysia, Indonesia	Avialite often wins when competing both on quality and price; Able to compete due to tropical environment as European product does not have the design and Honeywell's price is too high.

Challenges

Avialite is currently constrained by manufacturing, sales and marketing capacity. They have a growing order in the pipeline in Malaysian local market, Indonesia and Myanmar. To help with the increasing manufacturing capacity their new factory in Kuala Terengganu will be in use by mid-year 2016 and the implementation of automatic machineries to produce their products might be able to manage the growing orders as currently, their products are being produced either manually or by semi-auto machines and customized orders will be subbed to third parties. Moving forward to 2020, they feel that human resource constraints are likely to be the biggest risk to the success of their business due to higher wages, difficulties to get workers and the dependency towards foreign workers.

As a Malaysian based SME, one major challenge with securing an international co-development partner is that most European based companies do not conduct any R&D. For the projects they manage, all design work is carried out locally while manufacturing and a Chinese LED company carries out production. The European based companies consider this approach to be the most cost effective and straightforward so long as quality control measures are put in place. It is difficult for the Malaysian SMEs to compete with China from a cost of production perspective. For Avialite, some of the potential partners either already in operation in the ASEAN region and therefore consider the SMEs to be a competitor, or they were not interested in co-development work. Some also lacks the capacity to expand their offering of products and services to accommodate the SMEs.

Going forward

Avialite is becoming a strong brand name in the aviation industry may it be locally or internationally whereby they successfully able to penetrate the international market and make their presence in the South East Asia (SEA) region. They have achieved the country regulatory requirement, which has assisted them to market their products abroad and currently in the process of qualifying their products for the CE mark to go for European market.

Avialite's main customers are mainly owners of mobile cellular towers (Telecom Towers) for the Aviation Warning Lights (AWL) also called Aviation Obstruction Beacons (AOB). Avialite's main focus is only on ASEAN markets as far as internationalization is concerned. The company needs to embrace the challenge of broadening their channels to other regions like Middle East and African regions. Signs of market demand coming from countries such as Namibia and Zambia that are becoming budding markets for LED lightings. The consideration to shift to other sectors is important as well, such as green buildings, utilities companies particularly wind turbines and construction projects (tall buildings etc.) and not just concentrating on communication towers.

Currently Avialite is participating in one of the government's initiative programs, that focuses on developing Solid State Lighting (SSL) Cluster in Malaysia, which is the "Creation of Home Grown SSL/LED Champions Program" under the E&E NKEA of the Economic Transformation Program with SME Corp Malaysia. Benefits of the program are; financial assistance in terms of grants (purchase of machineries and to get international certifications), exposures to international and local trade shows, workshops and trainings by industry experts etc. Other benefits to includes; tax exemptions from MIDA, testing facilities with other companies such as *SIRIM Berhad* and technical incubators with *MDEC*. It is also feasible that Avialite should not be too dependent on government assistance like grants as they will not have any wills to strive and move forward independently in the long-run. Government loans with lower interest rates or conventional loans from banks, with the ability to pay back will be more beneficial as they move forward.

Encorp

Encorp Berhad was incorporated on 2nd March 2000 and later was listed on the Main Board of Bursa Malaysia Securities Berhad on 11 February 2003. As one of the major property developer in Kuala Lumpur's Klang Valley, Encorp has been known for its forte in developing modern and sophisticated properties targeting high end buyers and investors. With the opening of The Strand in Kota Damansara in 2014, Encorp has added another portfolio into their business activity as a retail developer in order to remain strong and relevant in the property industry. However, in 2014, Felda Investment Corp Sdn. Bhd. (FIC), a wholly-owned unit of the Federal Land Development Authority (Felda) has acquired Encorp Berhad in order to allows Felda to venture into another dimension of land development and not just focusing on developing land for plantation. Currently, FIC holds 72.29 percent of Encorp shares. Previously, Encorp Berhad was owned and controlled by Datuk Seri Effendi Nawawi and his daughter through Lavista Sdn. Bhd.

Felda

Felda Investment Corporation Sdn. Bhd. (FIC) is wholly owned by Federal Land Development Authority (FELDA), an entity that was established in 1956. Was initially incorporated on 2 July 2013 under the name of Capital Protocol Sdn Bhd., it was later assumed its present name on 8 November 2013. The main objective for the establishment of FIC was to act as an investment arm of FELDA. FIC is responsible to undertake business activities, which are non-plantation related and at present FIC is involved in the areas of property development; hospitality; and other strategic investments. The main objective of FIC is to drive FELDA strategic businesses via acquisitions or collaborations that may benefit the company and FELD in the long run. At present, FIC has entered into several strategic dealings, including the investment in IRIS Corporation Berhad, Encorp Berhad and Barakah Offshore Petroleum Berhad.

Encorp

The acquisition of Encorp Berhad by FIC in 2014 has brought major changes in the management team and this has prompted FIC to execute strategic plan to revamp Encorp. During this tough period where sentiments of buyer and investors towards new investment has become low, the main priorities of Encorp are 1) to ensure that Encorp remain strong and dynamic 2) to secure more new projects despite slow down in domestic property market. Thus, in order to have a better outlook of the current position Encorp Berhad, a horizontal analysis will be conducted by evaluating its 10 year financial statements starting from 2005 until 2014. The aim is to understand and to determine the changes that had occurred in the past, whether increase or decrease, with regards to their financial performance and to suggestion a new proposal that may be useful in assisting Encorp to design a more comprehensive and robust business model for their future business.

However, choice in poor property buying and week investor sentiments has prompted a significant drop in property market in 2014 especially in Kuala Lumpur, Malaysia. This appears to be one of the main reasons for the slow growth in number of new properties being launched or introduced in 2014. Nevertheless, as potential buyers and investors started to feel the pinch of tight economic condition, this has also indirectly caused them to be more prudent in making further investment in properties. Apparently, the property market is still in the process recovering from a slow down caused by the sub-prime mortgage crisis that had affected the economy globally. Furthermore, as the pressure of tight economic condition has changed the buying behavior of Malaysian consumers, properties developers also share similar pain. In order to stay afloat, property developers are in the increasing pressure to find better ways to keep their development units attractive and profitable. As one of local property players that had the opportunity to experience the economic crisis, under new stewardship, Encorp Berhad is expected to weather the tough period successfully. Nevertheless, it is anticipated that Encorp without a new business model, Encorp will face few difficulties to continue staying ahead of the property market competition.

In evaluating Encorp's current business model, an approach introduced by Osterwalder in 2010 called "Business Model Canvas" will be applied for further discussion. In using this approach, Encorp will be dissected and analyze individually into 9 sections; 1) Value Proposition, 2) Customer Segments, 3) Customer relationship, 4) Channel, 5) Key Partners, 6) Key Activities, 7) Key Activities, 8) Cost Structure and 9) Revenue Streams. Evaluation will be done based on information that are available on public domain such as financial report, website, news paper, etc.

Value proposition

An organization that practice good work ethics, advocate trust and respect, strive for profitability and fast growing efficiently and uphold the idea of continuous learning and improvement.

Customer Segments

Based on the current offerings, Encorp serves buyers or investors who has interest in buying or owning residential properties e.g. landed, high rise unit or commercial properties who are looking to lease business space leasing or to invest/own individual business unit.

Customer relationship

In keeping relevant with the demand of the market, Encorp has identified few areas where they could reach their target customers or clients through custom-built initiatives. The four key areas that Encorp currently focusing on are:

Marketplace: As Encorp aspires to be recognized as an organization that committed towards delivering its value propositions, they have developed strategic procedures that aims to improves the existing quality management programs, investors relationship initiative as well as customer's relationship management.

Workplace: In maintaining positive work life balance while at the same time to encourage conducive working environment, Encorp will look into 4 key areas; recognition, training & development, work environment and volunteerism.

Community: In recognizing the importance of having a healthier society and communities, Encorp has initiated few Corporate Social Responsibility (CSR) programs to supports its cause.

Environment: Encorp inculcate the idea of preserving and creating sustainable environment philosophy via two channels; 1) property development and 2) Construction development.

Channel

Currently Encorp engages their clients, customers and suppliers through it's 16 subsidiaries.

Key partners

As one of the main players in property development, Encorp has set a strong foothold in properties market. Furthermore, with long experience in construction and property development, Encorp has built a strong network with *relevant ministries, state governments, local authorities, main subsidiaries, suppliers and contractors, real estate agencies as well as with advertising & promotion agencies.*

Key Activities

Although Encorp is being recognized through their business activity in property development and construction, there are five main activities that can be identified: *1). Property development, 2). Construction, 3). Marketing, 4). Advertising and promotion and 5). Real estate.*

Key resources

Current Ratio versus Quick Ratio

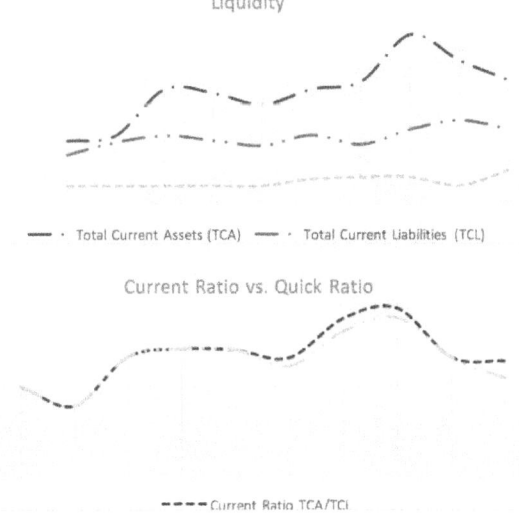

Current Ratio versus Quick Ratio

Encorp has been maintaining a remarkable business performance since 2005 when it was able to achieve a balance between its disposable assets and short term liabilities. Despite having slightly higher Current Ratio due to slow down in property market after 2009, Encorp has been able to offset the discrepancy in 2013.

It is worth noted that Encorp's inventories have been kept fluidly low since 2005, but as the economic recession in 2008 hits the property market in Klang Valley, Encorp had no choice but to hold to their completed development units for a longer period before being sold.

Since unsold completed development units are being classified as "Inventories" according to Malaysian Accounting Standard Board 2003, thus a prolong slow down in property market has created a negative impact on Encorp's quick ratio between the period of 2009 – 2013.

Account Receivables versus Inventories

As the country suffered from a severe economic crisis caused by US sub-prime mortgage crisis between the year 2007 – 2009, the adverse effect of the crisis had negatively injured domestic property market. Not spared from this crisis, Encorp saw its inventories increased by 981.2 percent from 2009 to 2012 due to the large volume of unsold completed residential units.

As a result, Encorp suffers a significant drop (-74.74 percent) in their account receivable within the same period. Subsequently, the impact of higher number of inventories has led to an increased of Encorp's Net Fixed Assets by 357.0 percent from 2009 until 2013.

Cost structure

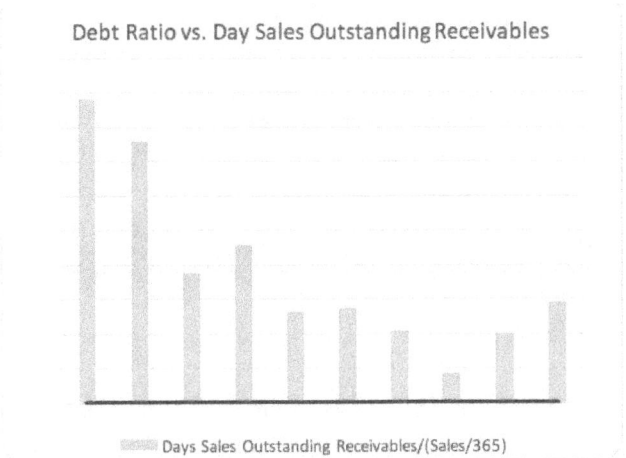

Days Sales Outstanding Receivables/(Sales/365)

Debt to Equity/Debt to Assets

Due to the poor transaction of their residential units between the period of 2008 - 2012, in order to remain afloat, Encorp has managed to improved their average collection of receivables from 226 days in 2008 to 41 days in 2012.

However, as a property developer, Encorp could not avoid from having high debt ratio due to the rapid movement of their fields operations e.g. labor, machineries, equipment as well as high turnover on supplies of raw material e.g. bricks, sands, cements, etc.

In the period of 2010 – 2014, few property developments and constructions were carried out by Encorp that may lead to higher debt ration such as The Strand Kota Damansara, Seremban-Gemas Electrified Double Track Rail Project and Sarawak Schools Projects.

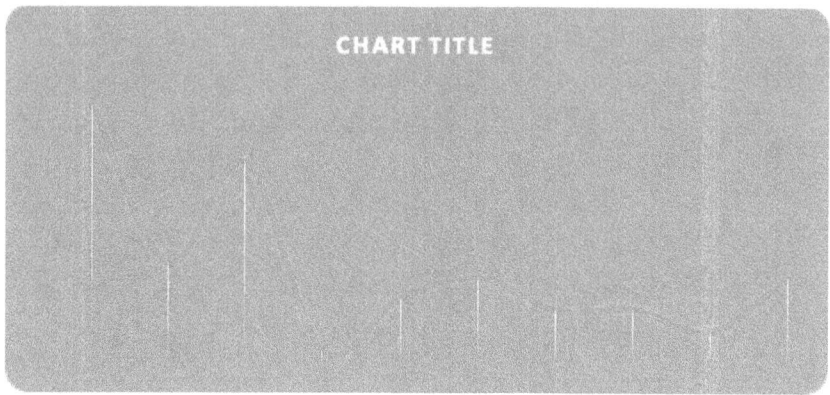

Cash flow ratio

As property market in Kuala Lumpur's Klang Valley seems to suffers from low appetite, Encorp appears to be holding back their forwards movement by not introducing or launching any new property products into the market in 2014 (Kaur, The Star Online, 2015). This has immediately improved Encorp cash flow ratio in 2014 after a long streak of low cash flow ratio since 2008. Currently, Encorp's appears able to generate sufficient positive cash flow to maintain and grow its current operations, with less requirement for external financing.

Revenue streams

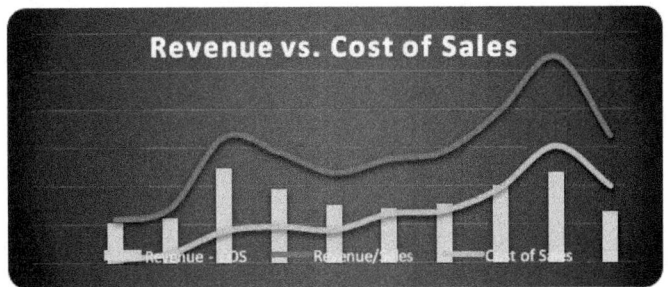

Revenue growth

After five years in operation, in 2005, Encorp recorded its revenue at RM114,545,999. Soon after, Encorp saw a more positive revenue growth from 2005 until 2013 despite experiencing a downward slope in 2008. As the property market recovered from the worldwide economic crisis caused by the sub-prime mortgage in the US after 2009, Encorp's sales had increased steadily by 129 per cent in the span of 5 years. In 2013, the revenue growth was 368.3%, equivalent to RM536,435,000. Nevertheless, in 2014, Encorp saw a decline in its revenue to RM330,385,000 (-38.41%) as the property market in Klang Valley suffers from market slowdown.

However, it must be noted that in 2013, Encorp underwent a management buyout that saw the exit of Tan Sri Effendi Norwawi, the founder of Encorp Berhad. Group Chief Executive Officer, Yeoh Soo Ann and Chief Operating Officer, Mohd Ibrahim who together acquired 30.55 percent equity interest from Tan Sri Effendi Norwawi later sold Encorp to Felda Investment Corporation (FIC) in 2014 which currently holds 72.29 per cent of Encorp Berhad shares.

Existing development

Currently, Encorp has few flagships property development with high Growth Development Value:
- Encorp Strand in Kota Damansara (GDV: RM1,372 million)
- Encorp Cahaya Alam, in Shah Alam (GDV: RM1,100 million)
- Encorp Marina Puteri Harbour in Nusajaya, Johor (GDV: RM656 million)
- The Residence on McCallum Lane in Perth, Australia (GDV: RM82.5 million)

In 2014, Encorp reported that they have not secured any new development project which could leave the newly entity acquired by FIC to be in a difficult situation. Furthermore, within the same financial year, Encorp has sold its construction arm due to poor performance.

	2005	2006	2007	2008	2009	2010	2011	2012	2013	2014
Profit Margin	2%	-84%	34%	25%	15%	5%	4%	12%	22%	8%
Return on Assets	0%	-7%	6%	4%	2%	1%	1%	2%	6%	1%
Return on Equity	1%	-53%	39%	24%	11%	4%	3%	17%	35%	7%

Net Income vs. Sales

----- Net Income

Net income growth

In measuring Encorp's profitability trend for the past 10 years, it is worth to look into how well has Encorp invested in their operations and investing in the past 10 years.

The growth rate for Encorp's profit margin, ROA and ROE for the year ended 2010, 2011, 2012 and 2013 appears to be relatively corresponding (starting from low to high) as this is the period where most property development or construction project were at its erection stage.

However, it must be taken into consideration that as Encorp spent average 3-5 years to complete one development project, the return from their operational activities may take 1-1.5 year to materialize.

SWOT analysis
- a. Strength
    - i. Since Encorp is now owned by Felda through FIC, this will give Encorp access to land capital that belongs to Felda nationwide.
    - ii. With long experience in property development and construction, Encorp has a strong brand name in domestic property market.
    - iii. Despite not having new property development projects, this will allow Encorp to capitalize on their current cash flow.

- b. Weaknesses
    - i. With the delay in announcing its new management team, this will slowly lead to a decay of investor's confidence.
    - ii. With Felda as the owner of Encorp, the prospect of investor to doubt Encorp's capability to deliver is medium to high since Felda is being seen as a new entrant into property market.
    - iii. Encorp appears to have less aggressive sales and marketing team that can push for more property transaction.

- c. Opportunity
    - i. With the current economic challenge, Encorp has more room to maneuver into property development serving mid-low income segment.
    - ii. With an increase of mid-low income earners size, this would allow Encorp to tap the new market since it can overcome the barrier to entry into this new segment.
    - iii. FIC and Felda has multiple portfolios under their entity which may provide opportunity for Encorp to penetrate new market segments.

- d. Threat
    - i. Prolong low transaction in residential units.
    - ii. Fluctuation of price for raw materials as well as labor
    - iii. Uncertainty on consumer's sentiments towards property market

iv. As access to financial capital becoming difficult, this may create domino effect of the entire property market value chain
v. Residential property market may suffer from speculations and thus would distort the supply-demand curve

The residential construction industry and factors influencing the growth
The Malaysia Property Market in 2014

According to report by Valuation & Property Services Department, Ministry of Finance Malaysia, the overall property market in 2014 has witnessed a slight growth as compared to 2013. As there are 5 sub sectors under property market namely; residential, agricultural, commercial, development land and industrial, the top performer among the 5 sub sectors is the residential sub sector which recorded 64.4 percent contribution to the overall market. The total market size for residential is RM82.06 billion and it remain the as major contributor to national property market. In primary market, positive sentiments among developers can be observed where 68,351 units of new launches were recorded. Almost half of the new launches are condominiums and service apartments. Outlook for 2015 appears to be positive however, buyers and investors may delay their purchase until May 2015. Moreover, as house price remain as the main concern among young professionals, this will continue to downplay the consumer's appetite towards making any purchase.

The residential construction industry in Klang Valley:
According to a market assessment prepared by VPC Asia Pacific "Property County Report: Malaysia" (2014), Klang Valley recorded RM72.06 billion worth of transaction in 2013. As value per transaction increased by 6.3 percent in 2013, however, volume transacted during the same period was down by 9.7 percent. Raine and Horne (2014) reported that average price per transaction in Putrajaya is RM837,007.00 while Kuala Lumpur is at RM673,249.00. Nevertheless, as the overall economy appears to be contracting, further adjustment on consumer's buying appetite will be observed and thus this will have an impact on the price of properties in the future.

Key issues and considerations

After the key management changed in 2014 following to acquisition by FIC, Encorp Berhad had to face few issues relating to reorganizing the top management, setting up new business direction and looking for new way to navigate Encorp so that it remains relevant in the property market. Below are some of the issues currently faced by top management:

Absence of robust and cohesive management team
After the departure of key management personnel in 2014, Encorp has been struggling in structuring a solid management team. Currently, Encorp is being managed by the executive committee chaired by Datuk Zakaria Nordin, who is also an Encorp director.

The need to immediately sell completed investment properties
Currently, Encorp is about to complete all their existing residential development with zero new projects acquired in 2014. However, as the property market in Klang Valley currently running slow which can be one of the main factor that contributes to low sales of Encorp properties in 2015, Encorp has to find new revenue streams. As the current property market remains unattractive to investors or new buyers for next 12 to 18 months, Encorp either has to remain prudent in keeping their property development attractive or they will get left out from the competition.

The need to revisit marketing strategies
Encorp seriously need to look into their marketing strategies as currently they have high number of properties which has not been successfully sold or rented out in the past 12 months. In order to tackle this, Encorp may want to revisit their marketing strategies in order to accommodate the current slowdown in property market. Furthermore, with the current economic slowdown, Encorp may need to gather new information in order to better understand consumer's buying pattern and their investment appetite.

The need to consider new business model
After the departure of previous management team, FIC has been continuously in the process of restructuring and streamlining Encorp's operation in order to maintain its presence in the property development market. Nevertheless, as the restructuring is currently ongoing, FIC should

also consider developing a new business model that suites the capability of the new Encorp management team.

ENCORP: The proposed business model

In Encorp's current business model, Encorp has proven it s capability in weathering the slowing down yet highly competitive property market due to 1) robust financial management and 2) cohesive management team. As suggested earlier, further proposal will be presented based on the 9 sections in the Business Model Canvas. Nevertheless, not all sections will be discussed here since there are sections where this study strongly feels Encorp should retain its values such as 1) Key Partners, 2) Key Activities, 3) Key Resources, 4) Channels and 5) Customer Relationship. The rational of not discussing these 5 segments:

- It is capital intensive exercise if Encorp decides to revamp the 5 segments before working on the proposed solutions.

- For the past 10 years, Encorp has been in operation employing the current resource structure. Thus, Encorp should leverage on the current resources and try to get the general buy in.

- Encorp has been in the industry for quite a while and the industry understand the position held by Encorp in the property market. Should Encorp decide to execute sudden change in their behavior in the industry, this may disrupt the long term relationship and trust that Encorp has built with other industry players.

Thus, after analyzing Encorp's present Business Model Canvas, the new proposed business model for Encorp would covers:

1) **Value proposition**

    FIC and FELDA must take the initiative to redefine Encorp's value proposition. This is to streamline the business and marketing strategies of all three entities focusing on three key factors: corporation, customers and competition.

2) **Customer Segments**

    Encorp should analysis their market segmentation in order to identify new leads that will bring them to new customer segments. As property buyers and investors are more cautious with their investments, perhaps Encorp should design, for example, a financial instrument that is unified with properties or create a customized development that caters young generations, small families or aging societies.

3) **Cost Structure**

Encorp proves to be sound in managing its financial commitments and requirements. Nevertheless, as the demand is being overtaken by the supply, perhaps Encorp should start to identify what actually their key variables that helps Encorp to sustain in the current property markets.

4) **Revenue Streams**

Since its inception, Encorp has been relying on residential and commercial products as their revenue streams. Nevertheless, Encorp must find other revenue stream that will bring fuel its journey in the next 10 years. As property market are becoming more dynamic due to the technological advances, Encorp perhaps should attempt to invest in new technology.

Conclusion

In order to tackle the key issues that have been presented earlier, Encorp through FIC, should immediately initiate strategic negotiations with FELDA and other stakeholders where the objective should be to identify and prioritize key issues based on the level of importance and urgency and to decide whether to tackle them separately or concurrently. Below are some of the key issues that this study has found:

1- In order to remain relevant and competitive in the domestic property market, how can Encorp maintain its earning while addressing the increased of inventories.

2- If Encorp decides to expand it business elsewhere, what kind of new revenue opportunities that can be created if Encorp could shift its emphasize on property development to, for example, real estate.

3- In order to weather the highly competitive yet slowing down property market, what other new resources do Encorp need to acquire or develop in order to respond to consumer's unrealized buying behaviour.

Felda Global Ventures Holdings

Plantation Industry Overview

Malaysia's position as the World's leading Palm Oil producing country has allowed the industry to flourish in the way it has never been before (MPOC, 2015). By continuous effort in R&D, we are churning out a wider variety of by- products making the downstream manufacturing into an industry itself. This leads Malaysia to remain heads and shoulders above its other competitors. According to the Malaysia Palm Oil Council, Malaysia currently accounts for 39% of world palm oil production and 44% of world exports. If taken into the account of other oils & fats produced in the country, Malaysia accounts for 12% and 27% of the world's total production and exports of oils and fats. Being one of the biggest producers and exporters of palm oil and palm oil products, Malaysia has an important role to play in fulfilling the growing global need for oils and fats sustainably. The palm oil industry has been embarked by the Malaysian Government as a critical player in its aspiration of becoming an industrial nation (Vision 2020).

Bala et al, 2005 reported in their journal under the third National Agricultural Policy (1992-2010), various policies have been made formulated to ensure that Malaysia's position in the world's oils and fats market is not only sustained, but also enhanced and its competitive edge maintained. To pursue this goal the palm oil sector has been identified as a focus area for consolidation and restructuring. The government's aim are : (a) to create the world's largest oil palm plantation company thereby leveraging economies of scale and hopefully become an efficient model for others to follow, (b) to enhance investors' interest and increase tradability of the stock, and (c) to spearhead efforts in creating large capitalization stock. Plans to merge PNB-owned plantation companies and the listing of FELDA on the Bursa Malaysia were mooted in the budget 2004 speech, reported by *The Star*, September 13, 2003 (Bala et al, 2005).

Company Background of Felda Global Ventures Holdings Berhad

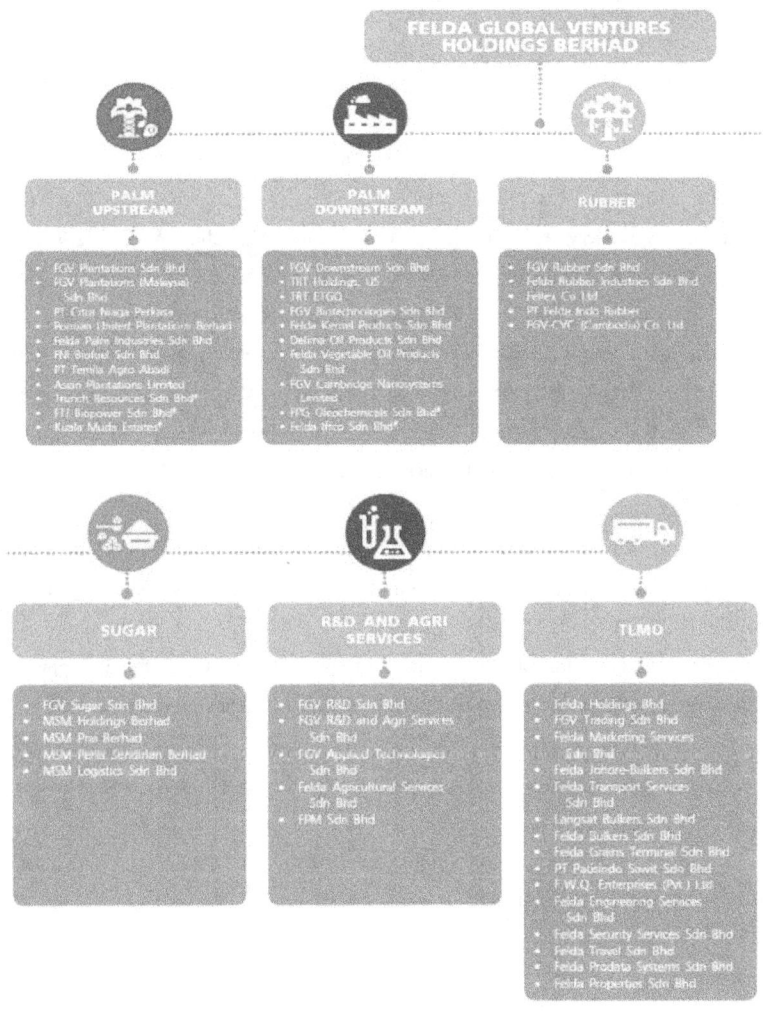

Felda Global Ventures Holdings Berhad Business Structure
Source : FGV Annual Report, 2014

Felda Global Ventures Holdings Berhad (FGV or the Group) incorporated in Malaysia as a private limited company 2007, FGV initially operated as the commercial arm of Federal Land Development Authority (FELDA). On 28th June 2012, the company was listed on the main market of Bursa Malaysia Securities. FGV is one of the Malaysia's leading global diversified agri-business operating under six main businesses. These six main businesses under six core Clusters. There are Palm Upstream, Palm Downstream, Sugar, Rubber, Research & Development and Agri Services and Transport, Logistics, Marketing & Others (TLMO). Operational business of Felda Global Ventures Holdings Berhad been organised into Clusters to allow greater converge of core capabilities and to orchestrate more opportunities for collaboration and innovation. Currently, FGV is the world's largest producer of crude palm oil (CPO) and the third largest oil palm plantation operator. FGV's operate in more than 10 countries across North America, Europe, Asia and the Middle East, by the 2020 FGV aspires to be one of the top 10 conglomerates agribusiness in the world. There are 19,000 people in the group, together with all subsidiaries.

The Palm Upstream Cluster is FGV's largest revenue earner and the forms the core of the company. With the total land banks of more than 450,000 hectares, Palm Upstream is responsible for FGV's status as the world's largest CPO producer which produces more than three million tonnes of CPO annually (FGV Annual Report, 2014). FGV is the only plantation company in Malaysia that adopts the Land Lease Agreement (LLA) business model.

The Downstream Cluster aims for a leading position globally in industrial fats, and regional heavyweight status in palm- based consumer goods. FGV strives to diversify further into downstream activities, in order to create additional revenue streams. The Downstream Cluster is organized into three sub clusters, namely :

i. Processing
ii. Oleo chemical and others
iii. Fast Moving Consumer Goods

The Rubber Cluster aims to transform FGV's current rubber processing operation into a leading integrated rubber business. The cluster sells latex concentrate, Standard Malaysian Rubber (SMR), Standard Indonesian Rubber (SIR), Cambodian Standard Rubber (CSR) and 'Green Rubber' products. In Malaysia, the rubber processing operations are managed by Felda Rubber

Industries Sdn Bhd, which controls 7 factories. While in Thailand, Indonesia, Cambodia and Myanmar FGV manage to have control in respective countries and also established a strategic partnership.

Sugar Cluster is operated by MSM Malaysia Holdings Berhad (MSM). Incorporated on 10 March 2011, is Malaysia's leading sugar producer. MSM produces, market and sells refined sugar products. MSM also own their logistic company, known as MSM Logistics Sdn Bhd. Annual production of MSM and its subsidiaries is 1.1 Million tones of refined sugar products.

R&D and Agri Services Cluster was Incorporated on 10 September 2014 which its main focus being in Research and Products & Services. The cluster consists of FGV R&D, FGV Applied Technologies Sdn Bhd, Felda Agricultural Services Sdn Bhd and FPM Sdn Bhd Fertilizers. The cluster devotes significant resource to oil palm breeding and selection program over the last 40 years and have an R&D team dedicated to improving both Fresh Fruit Bunch (FFB) and yield per hectare. High Yielding seedlings was produces which is award winning DxP Yangambi, is being used in palm upstream group replanting program of 15,000 hectare per annum which can improve the overall crop profile.

The Transport, Logistics, Marketing & others (TLMO) was set up due to the FGV goals to be globally diversified and integrated agri-business. The cluster's business are strategically divided into three main sub-Clusters under the core business:
 i. Transport & Logistics
 ii. Storage
 iii. Trading Sub- Cluster

Long established marketing arm, Felda Marketing Services Sdn Bhd (FELMA) has traditionally carried out trading of palm oil, acting as a principal agent to FGVPM (Plantations), FPI (Mills), FVOP (Refineries), FKP (Kernel Processing). In becoming more integrated and competitive as well as other players, FGV driving towards and transforming FELMA to FGV Trading (FGVT).

SWOT Analysis of Felda Global Ventures

SWOT Analysis allows us to identify and highlight favorable and unfavorable factors concerning both external and internal operations. Thereafter, determinations of factors relating to business model can be developed accordingly.

    i.   Strength - Internal ability that leads company
    ii. Weakness- Internal lacking of the company that can be harm to business
    iii. Opportunity – External elements that can contribute to expansion of business
    iv. Threats-External element that possible shrink down the business

Strength

FGV bargaining power gain from the big amount of scale of FGV itself' s in negotiating for contracts and purchases. Parties doing business with FGV tend to secure in contracting activities since FGV is a Good Pay Master.

Low hanging fruits as the losses at its downstream division could mean stronger earnings growth compares to its peers.

Weakness

FGV Group comprises subsidiaries with complex business operation. The structures of stakeholders of FGV, comprises Felda Holdings as 49% as associate stakeholders giving higher tendency of profit leakages among subsidiaries and cost inefficiency.

Opportunity

FGV huge cash hoard post-listing in 2012 gives FGV the flexibility and bargaining power to potentially acquire large assets or even already profitable plantations assets, which other companies may not be able to digest.

Threats

New Rules and regulations governing land bank acquisition or expansion in Indonesia could limit long term growth. In addition, if FGV continued scrutiny on the palm oil industry by the environmental groups it could have a negative effect on the company.

Porter Five Force Analysis

The competitive rivalry within the oil palm industry can be more clearly seen by analyzing the five competitive forces facing the oil palm player. The critical points in plantations sector are in refineries. In FGV, under downstream cluster, there are major buyer involve and exporters of palm oil. Any weakness in competitive position against the foreign buyers/importers is a weakness to the Malaysian palm oil industry.

Porters Five Force Analysis

Threat of new entrants

Entry into the refining sector is not easy. In a meantime, where the crude palm oil production is now in unfavorable condition, it is unlikely the government will issue new refining license.

Bargaining power of Suppliers

Because of the FGV, had becomes a large plantations company, it gives FGV as a suppliers has a strong bargaining power.

Bargaining powers of buyers

The large numbers of refineries give ample choice of suppliers for buyers too choose. The buyers of palm oil are therefore in a very strong position bargaining position.

Threats of Substitutes

Threats of substitutes are high. Palm oil faces competition from at least 16 major edible oil and fats in the international markets. It has to compete with the soybean and other subsidized oil, as such its price performance is currently limited by the supply and availability of the other edible oils.

Intensity of Rivalry

The refining sector is faced with high intensity of rivalry. The results from rivalry are high threat from substitutes, poor bargaining position against foreign buyers and local suppliers and high exit cost. In summary, the above analysis has identified the following weakness in the structure of the oil palm industry. FGV Upstream cluster in a strong position against refineries and the refineries are in a weak position to compete against other producer countries and edible oils and fats. The position of the refineries does not give downstream the strength to market and promote the oil aggressively in the international market. This is because marketing of palm oil overseas require large amount of financial resources and a strong bargaining against international buyers.

Felda Global Ventures Holdings Berhad Challenges

FGV group of companies face the challenges in operating and expanding their business. Both upstream and downstream cluster encountered difficulties and challenges in their way of growing, domestic and international.

Resource Scarcity and Climate Change

Anti-palm oil sentiment, Deforestation Issues

Palm oil has become under attack in some countries as it has elsewhere for its links and believe in with deforestation in Southeast Asia, loss of habitats and biodiversity and been told high levels of saturated fat. The palm oil sentiment was already evidence in some European Country, where some food manufacturers had already placed 'no palm oil label' on their products (Quartz Business, 2015). This will tarnish the image of oil palm industry. This continuous pressure might affect the wellbeing of this industry & FGV main business in the future.

Land Limitation in Malaysia

With 3.5 million hectares already planted with oil palm, the shortage of prime agricultural land for the cultivation of the crop and the strong pressure from non-governmental organizations against further clearing of tropical forestland, limits the land area for expansion (Khoo & Chandramohan, 2002). Most of the agriculture land has been converted to palm oil plantation; hence there is unavailable agriculture land for expansion. Expansion has been stagnant due to limited land. In some areas in FGV estates, there are marginal areas with poorer soils, terrain and rainfall. Inevitably, such plantings will cost more to develop, will lead to higher production costs. To be the largest plantations, FGV acquire more land in neighbouring countries as Indonesia, Myanmar and Africa.

Labour

Plantations are stripped of their most productive labor as the younger better-educated workers are enticed by the attractions of working in the modern controlled environment of new manufacturing plants (MPOB, 2002). Recruiting labor from neighboring countries has provided a lifeline for the plantation industry. MPOB report that the reliance on foreign workers has become a serious issue where Malaysia has employed 1.5 million workers by various industries. Frequent abrupt changes in policy and inconsistent application of the laws by the various authorities have and continued to confusion and difficulties to employers as well as to the foreign workers. New challenge for FGV in reducing the total cost per hectare, FGV try to minimize the contract- based operation by doing the daily operation such as harvesting, evacuating fresh fruit bunch to the mill by its own labor. The shortage and difficulties to get permits and quota from authority's body urge plantations division to outsourcing the operation, which leads to increase the cost. New challenge regarding the labor, The World Street Journal reported FGV had being unfair to the one of Bangladesh worker. This report tarnishes the FGV image as the largest oil palm player.

Global Economic Condition

Fall in commodities prices and devaluation of Ringgit

International Monetary Fund (IMF) forecasting a slowdown in global growth rates. The decline in commodity prices of the edible oil segment has put the agricultural commodities business under pressure. FGV struggles in high pressure to stay competitive in the market. The fluctuated of Crude Palm oil (CPO) prices of 32 % from 2011 until 2014 (MPOC, 2015). The price continued fluctuated in 2015. In the other hand, sugar and rubber priced also dropped. Until now, as CPO remains a core commodity for FGV, prolonged price depression, coupled with recent economic uncertainty, have significantly impact the business.

CPO Local Price (RM)

	JAN	FEB	MAC	APR	MAY	JUNE	JULY	AUG	SEPT	OKT	NOV	DIS	AVERAGE
2014	2,534	2,635	2,862	2,696	2,605	2,436	2,404	2,174	2,059	2,179	2,219	2,155	2,382
2015	2,302	2,272	2,244	2,164	2,166	2,268	2,191	1,975	1,988	2,213			

Source : MPOC Website, 2015

Figure 3: Monthly Average Prices Of CPO in Malaysia for Year 2014 & 2015.

With the CPO prices depressed and far from RM3,000.00 level FGV are likely to have decreased in revenue and operating in a high cost input since the fertilizer cost will increased in 15%-30% affected by the exchange rate of ringgit.

Geopolitical Uncertainty and Regulatory Burden

FGV's mission in expanding the plantations sector in the neighboring country especially in Indonesia become a hardship due to the potential revision of plantation regulations by Indonesia's Ministry of Agriculture (MOA), which might lead to a possible 30% cap on foreign ownership of plantation land in Indonesia. The implementation of stricter plantation regulations might potentially restrict the expansion and impact the existing holdings of landbanks by FGV.

Company	Malaysia	Indonesia	Others
Sime Darby	59.5	39	1.5
IOI Corporation	93	7	-
Kuala Lumpur Kepong	44.3	55.7	-
Felda Global Ventures	95.7	4.3	-
Genting Plantations	47.6	52.3	-

Source : iFAST Research Team, 2014

Figure 4: Planted Areas by Country

An international palm oil industry analyst suggests that India should impose at least 10% import tax on crude palm oil to protect its own farmer. If the tax implement by India Government, Malaysia should increase the export price of crude palm oil. The higher costs will drive less demand for CPO as the price will shoot up, and consumer will go for the alternative vegetables oil for cheaper price. Less in demand will increase the inventory level of CPO. CPO tax policy in palm oil producer countries also plays a part in setting the crude palm oil prices. Plantation Industries and Commodities Ministry has proposed to cut the palm oil tax rate from the current 23% to between 8% and 10%. Decreased of palm oil tax will help strengthen exports and reduce the inventory level.

Supply and demand of CPO to the largest importers, which are China, India and Europe seems to have a downturned trend. Euro zone debts slow the import of CPO. In India and China, the slowing food demand contributes to the low demand in CPO trade.

Conclusion

Developing strategic business expanding plan

Because of the uncertain of policy in acquisition of landbank in Indonesia and others outside country, FGV should focus to maintain good investments to local landbanks. Buying the brownfields is the easiest way to get yields in short term periods. FGV can form Joint Ventures with local small holders. By doing so, the imposed complicated legal issues are minimized or eliminated. Legislation issues are clear in Malaysia and manageable. Buying the small competitive company would be a strategic planning move in expanding business operations.

Explore and expanding business in Indonesia through acquisition of landbanks. FGV need to explore additional opportunities in Liberia, following the footsteps of major revelries such as Sime Darby, which expanded it plantations into Liberia in 2011. As at 30 June 2013, Sime Darby landbanks ownership in Liberia is totaling 8,025 hectares (iFAST, 2014). Another rivalry is Kuala Lumpur Kepong who's rehabilitates and develops oil palm plantations in Liberia is totaling 25,547 Hectares (iFAST, 2014).

Strengthen the Downstream Cluster

FGV should focus on FGV Trading and initiates a new business strategy on how to market the Crude Palm Oil (CPO) since FGV is experiencing high level inventory of CPO. As a result of lower demand on CPO, the increase stock of CPO will results in higher cost. FGV Trading is now serving as marketing arm for FGV in selling and market the CPO. Before FGV Trading emerged, Felda Marketing (FELMA) doing the marketing for the Felda Plantations and Felda Palm Industries. It was a good long-term plan but not reliable in open market like FGV been listed in since 2013. FGV trading should actively mitigate new plan and actively doing penetration into the international market. FGV need to further emphasize the creation and development of new products by engaging product development technology (R&D) into downstream activities. Many opportunities await FGV to explore and widen the demand base for oil palm. Moreover, minor components in palm oil can be produced to nutraceuticals, pharmaceuticals and food applications. According to MPOB, at present, only palm-based carotenes and vitamin E are produced in Malaysia. The ultimate potential in producing health related industries is presenting opportunities to prospective investors in creating value added downstream to produce and market Oleochemical products, in non-food category such as shower cream, soaps, and detergents, and toiletries with high growth potential. Products from subsidiary companies of FGV Group should capitalize on existing market segments. Re-branding and a new marketing approach will boost the sales of Delima Oil Products Sdn Bhd.

Diversified Sources of Income

Prior to the price downturn and demand for CPO, others subsidiary companies in FGV Groups should initiates new strategies. For instance, Felda Engineering Services Sdn Bhd, need to be a separate business unit and out of the direct control of FGV Group to explore new business opportunities. Presently, Felda Engineering Services Sdn Bhd relies on the intercompany business in construction and consultation for engineering projects. If Felda Engineering Services Sdn Bhd manages to successfully become independent entity, this would make Felda Engineering more competitive and major challenger in the constructions & engineering sectors in addition to the property development segment. By diversifying business operations and exploring new revenue streams, FGV will help to weather the slowdown segments in plantations sectors. The table below illustrates the lesser effect of FGV's main competitor mainly because of diversification of business sectors.

Company	Plantation	Resource-based Manufacturing	Property	Others
Sime Darby	46.8	-	13.0	40.2
IOI Corporation	43.9	25.2	30.9	-
Kuala Lumpur Kepong	46.2	46.5	4.2	3.1
Felda Global Ventures	69.0	-2.5	-	33.5
Genting Plantations	-6.5	-	19.8	86.7

Source: Latest Annual Reports of Respective Companies

Breakdown of FY2013 Operating Income by Segment (%)

Source: iFAST Research Team, 2014

Eco World

Introduction

Eco World Development Group Berhad (Eco World) is a relatively new company in the Malaysian property industry. After launching a reverse takeover of Focal Aims in Sept of 2013 in a deal that worth RM 230.7 million. Despite that, Eco World is already the 5th largest developer in Malaysia with an estimated market capital of RM 4.8 billion. Eco World currently has 15 ongoing projects that are spread out over three key economic regions, namely Klang Valley, Iskandar Malaysia and Penang. The Group presently has approximately 4216.3 acres of landbank with remaining gross development value of RM 51.2 billion. The story of Eco World shows how a relatively new company could survive and excel in the current sluggish property industry as well as to compete with other well established property developers.

Eco World has property development activities across three economic regions in Malaysia, namely Klang Valley, Iskandar Malaysia and Penang. The Group presently has approximately 4216.3 acres of landbank which are geographically diversified and remaining gross development value of RM 51.2 billion as of Feb 2015. [5] Eco World currently has 15 ongoing projects that are spread out over the three key economic regions as aforementioned. There are also numerous upcoming developments pending launching in the next couple of years, namely the infamous downtown of Kuala Lumpur "Bukit Bintang" City Centre which is a joint venture with UDA Holdings Berhad and Employees Provident Fund Board (EPF), Eco Business Park II, Eco Meadows, Eco Marina and Eco Forest. Its product range includes affordable as well as luxury homes, integrated high-rise developments and green business parks. Through Eco World International Berhad (EWI), the brand has also gone global by extending its presence in London, United Kingdom and Sydney, Australia. In Oct 2014, Eco World proposed to list EWI as a property Special Purpose Acquisition Company (SPAC), the first property SPAC in Malaysia. However, the application was withdrawn in June 2015 and instead EWI would be listed under initial public offering (IPO) whereby EWB would take 30% stake in the proposed listing.

Eco World is helmed by a solid management team whereby many of them are extremely experienced and respected industry players in the Malaysian property sector. A large number of the key management team in Eco World is previously directors and executives from SP Setia. SP Setia was taken over by Permodalan Nasional Berhad (PNB), a government-linked Bumiputera fund management company after PNB increased its stake in the company and triggered a mandatory offer. Thus Eco World is believed by many to be the new property vehicle by the previous management team from SP Setia after the hostile takeover. Currently, Eco World is led by Tan Sri Liew Kee Sin as the Chairman who is one of the most prolific corporate figures in Malaysia. The other established industry professionals who are among the board of directors are Tan Sri Abdul Rashid, Dato' Leong Kok Wah, Dato' Chang Khim Wah, Datuk Heah Kok Boon, Tan Sri Lee Lam Thye and also Liew Tian Xiong who is the son of Tan Sri Liew.

Driven by its vision of *Creating Tomorrow & Beyond* and steered by a top-notch management team with vast experience in the industry, EcoWorld has already seen its strong branding translates into high take-up rates for its projects launched so far with more than 80%. Albeit a relatively new property developer in the industry, Eco World is already the 5th largest developer in the country with an estimated market capital of RM 4.8 billion, ranked after SP Setia, UEM, Sunway and IOI Property Group.

Industry background

The real-estate and property industry in Malaysia has gone through various cycles of up and down since its independence in 1957. Rapid development of the property sector has largely occurred in the urban areas and as expectedly *Klang Valley* has been the focus of development over the years whereby Kuala Lumpur is the capital city. Since the days of independence until today, the skyline of Kuala Lumpur has been totally transformed and the building of skyscrapers notably the once world's tallest building "Petronas Twin Towers" are evidence of the robustness of the property industry in Malaysia. The urban migration towards the city for better living and job opportunities as well as the development of ample amenities and public infrastructure are among the factors contributing to the rapid development. The other urban areas in the country, namely Penang, Johor Baru and for the past one decade Iskandar Malaysia which has received huge attention in view of its strategic location in proximity to Singapore and the determination by the government to attract foreign direct investment, as well as Kota Kinabalu in the East Malaysia have all gathered pace in tandem with the capital city.

Malaysia is a relatively young nation with a growing population. As of date, Malaysia has

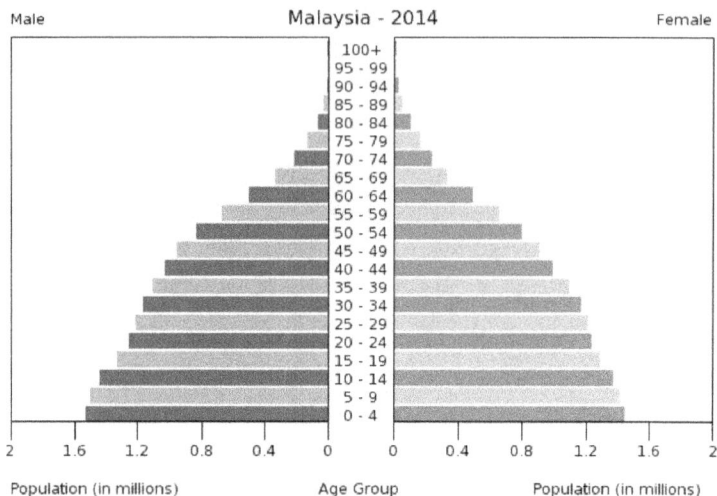

Source: Department of Statistics, Malaysia 2014

Malaysia is a relatively young nation with a growing population. As of date, Malaysia has a total population of 31 million with about 87% below the age of 55 years old. These favorable demographics renders the property demand to be high. Coupled with the steady development of the country striving towards achieving its target of being a developed nation, the demand for properties be it residential, commercial or industrial has been resilient.

There are 813 companies listed on the Main Market in the Bursa Malaysia out of which 82 counters are listed under the property industry classification. UEM land is the largest property counter in term of market capital amounting to RM10 billion followed by SP Setia at RM 7.3 billion.

In the past decade, the local housing prices have risen at a rapid rate due to the increasing inflows of foreign investment seeking for higher returns after the United States of America started Quantitative Easing in 2008, low interest rate with lax lending requirement by the local financial institutions as well as low cost entry barrier with the introduction of Developer's Interest Bearing Scheme (DIBS: a scheme whereby developer will pay for the monthly bank installment on behalf of the house owner during the construction period of the unit). Throughout these years, property developers have enjoyed high sales and decent profit margin. The house price index for Kuala Lumpur, Selangor, Johor and Penang has all increased markedly from 2008-2014 as shown in graph 2. However, in order to curb property speculation and prevent possibility of property 'bubble' from forming, government has intervened by abolishing DIBS

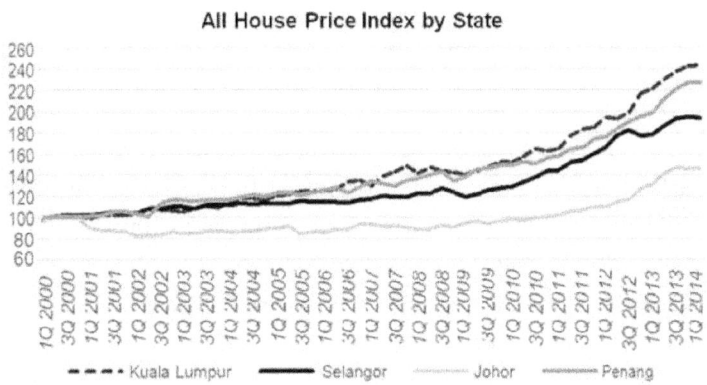

Graph 2

and introducing real property gain tax in 2014. The central bank, or called Bank Negara in the native language, has also set out measures tightening the lending rules for instance 70% loan-to-value ratio for the third property as well as approval of housing loan based on disposable income rather than gross income. Foreigners are also not allowed to buy properties below RM 1 million. This has in turn slowed down the property industry in the country and makes the business environment more challenging especially for the past two years. House price growth has also gradually tapered off. There is a visible reduction in the number of residential property transacted as shown in graph 3. The value of property transacted still increases even though the transacted volume is reducing in trend most probably due to the inflated house prices from the years earlier.

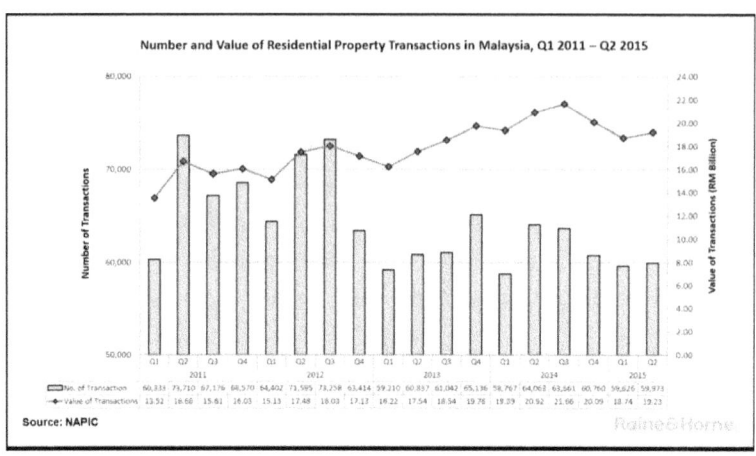

Graph 3

Moving forward, it is expected that the property industry in Malaysia is set to be subdued due to the tightening measures as aforementioned. The impact can already be seen by the poor take-up rate among the house buyers for the recent new residential project launches. Properties in the affordable range (below RM 500,000) will still have considerable demand despite the slowdown mainly from genuine house buyers rather than from investors, but it may not be the same case for the higher end properties. The outlook for the property industry in Malaysia at its current state appears gloom and conservative.

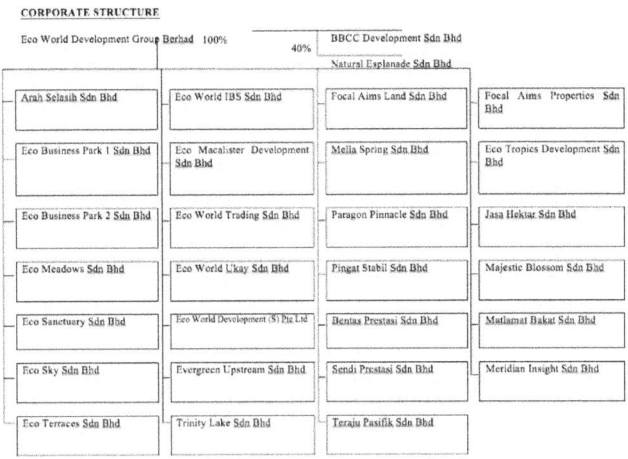

Financial Statement Analysis

	2012	2013	2014
Revenue (RM)	65,793,018	156,751,448	138,701,858
Operating Income (RM)	7,897,077	29,013,540	11,187,771
Net Income (RM)	7,201,675	24,267,813	6,625,877
Gross Profit Margin	34.19	31.08	29.40
Operating Profit Margin	12.00	18.51	8.07
Net Profit Margin	10.95	15.48	4.78

	Return on Assets	1.55	4.94	1.13
	Return on Equity	2.44	7.89	2.06
	Total Assets (RM)	491,272,244	491,089,331	686,856,296
(RM)	Total Liabilities	192,418,185	169,867,337	360,995,411
	Total Equities (RM)	298,854,059	321,221,994	325,860,885
share	Book value per	0.48	0.52	0.53
	Debt Ratio	13.04	10.62	35.04
Ratio	Debt to Equity	21.61	16.36	73.86
(EPS)	Earning Per Share	0.01	0.04	0.01
	Dividend Yield (%)	2.78	0.52	0
	Price-Earning Ratio	9.52	20.25	171.83

Source: CIMB iTrade

Stock Information:
Market Cap   : RM 3467.6 million
Total shares issued   : 2364 million

Major Shareholders:
Syabas Tropikal Sdn. Bhd   32.02%

Eco World Development Holdings Sdn Bhd	21.29%
Liew Tian Xiong	13.66%
Employees Provident Fund	9.02%

Weekly Stock Price Performance of Eco World Development Group Berhad from May 2013 to Dec 2015

Source: CIMB Itrade

ECOWLD Project Details (as at Feb 2015)

Project	Total GDV (RM'b)	Remaining GDV (RM'b)	Total Landbank (ac)	Remaining Landbank (ac)	Land Use	Tenure
Eco Central						
SaujanaGlenmarie	0.1	0.05	25.9	0.0	Landed Resi	
EcoSky	1.0	0.4	9.6	0.0	Integrated Commercial	Freehold
EcoMajestic	11.1	10.1	1073.1	818.0	Mixed Dev	Freehold
EcoForest	3.5	3.5	492.7	492.7	Mixed Dev	Freehold
EcoSanctuary	8.0	8.0	308.7	308.7	Mixed Luxury Dev	Leasehold
BBCC	8.0	8.0	19.4	19.4	Mixed Dev	
	31.7	30.1	1929.4	1638.8		
Eco South						
EcoBotanic	3.8	2.8	325.1	209.3	Mixed Dev	Freehold
EcoSpring	5.9	5.3	613.8	449.2	Mixed Dev	Freehold
EcoTropics	3.4	3.2	743.6	743.6	Mixed Dev	Freehold
Eco Business Park I	3.8	3.4	612.0	453.4	Industrial	Freehold
Eco Business Park II	3.0	3.0	383.6	383.6	Industrial	Freehold
Eco Business Park III	2.0	2.0	248.0	248.0	Industrial	Freehold
	21.9	19.7	2926.1	2487.1		
Eco North						
EcoTerraces	0.3	0.3	12.8	12.8	High Rise Resi	Freehold
EcoMeadows	0.9	0.9	76.5	76.5	Mixed Dev	Freehold
EcoMacalister	0.2	0.2	1.1	1.1		Freehold
	1.4	1.4	90.4	90.4		
	55.0	51.2	4945.9	4216.3		

Table 1
Source: Ecoworld Development Berhad

Challenges in the current property industry

As aforementioned, there are 82 listed property companies in Bursa Malaysia and Eco World is ranked 5th in term of market capital. This excludes many private property developers as well as other public listed companies which have non-core activities in property development. Hence, the competition in the property industry in Malaysia is very much intense. The situation is made worse with the entry of large property developers from China especially in Iskandar Malaysia which saturates the market with huge supply of properties.

The operation and success of a property company depends largely on the size of landbanks it owns for future development as well as the location of the landbanks. Thus it is not uncommon to see local property companies having high gearing ratio in order to purchase suitable landbanks sometimes at a premium price as land is considered to be a scarce asset. This situation is especially common after the recent property price surge following the global financial crisis in 2007 leading to escalation of the selling price of lands. Property developers are also not competing on equal footing because some companies are able to convert plantation estates from parent companies into residential or commercial development zone for instance Sime Darby Group Berhad and IOI Corporation Berhad.

The property industry in Malaysia is made even more challenging as the local property buying sentiment has turned bearish since the year 2014. In order to curb property speculation, the government has intervened by abolishing DIBS and introducing real property gain tax during the Budget 2014. The central bank has also set out stringent lending rules for instance 70% loan-to-value ratio for the third property as well as allocation of housing loan based on disposable income rather than gross income. Foreigners are also not allowed to buy properties below RM 1 million. This renders property buyers and investors to adopt a "wait-and-see" approach which translates into poor take-up rate for new launches and reduction in the transaction volume for the secondary market.

Property companies are also expecting a huge reduction in their profit margin. This is partly due to the increasing operating and construction costs caused by the marked depreciation of the Malaysian ringgit which causes imported building materials to increase in price. The introduction of Goods and Services Tax (GST) also leads to increased operating expenses. The recent increase in electricity tariff as well as the implementation of minimum wage with the latest increment to RM1000 per month further shrinks the profit margin.

Company SWOT analysis

In this section, SWOT analysis are used to illustrate how Eco World being a relatively new company could survive and excel in the current property market.

Strength:

Experienced management team:

The key management team in Eco World has vast experience in the property industry whereby many of them had been with SP Setia for more than 10 years before the company was taken over by Permodalan Nasional Berhad (PNB). The recent appointment of Tan Sri Liew as Chairman to helm the operation of Eco World in March 2015 gives a major boost to the company as he is believed to be one of the prominent figures previously in SP Setia who led to its successful transformation. Having an experience management team also eases the operation of the company as they have already established good working relationship and reputation with the banks, raw material suppliers and various government agencies as well as having an extensive distributive and sales network.

Geographically diversified and strategically located landbanks

Eco World has landbanks in 3 different states, namely Klang Valley, Johor and Penang. Its size of total landbanks owned as of February 2015 is 4945.9 acres with a gross developmental value of RM55 billions. Eco World has the largest landbank in Johor (59%), followed by Klang Valley (38.9%) and Penang (2.1%) as shown in Table 1 above. These various landbanks are strategically located in areas which are the focus of investment and commercial activities and hence strong take-up rates are expected for these projects. Besides being in prime location, the landbanks owned by

Eco World also have good connectivity to nearby highway which will be able to spur for higher sales.

Weakness:

High gearing ratio

As shown in the financial statement, the debt ratio as well as the debt to equity ratio are on the increasing trend over the years. Eco World has been aggressively expanding its landbank since its inception in 2013. Its debt ratio currently stands at 35% and its debt to equity ratio stands at 73.8%. On 22 September 2015, Eco World made another stunning announcement that it plans to acquire 2198.4 acres of leasehold land in *Ijok, Kuala Selangor* in a deal worth RM 1.181 billions. This undoubtedly would further increase its net gearing to exceed the comfort level of 0.5 times. Eco World might have a tight operating cash flow in case of long bearish property cycles and persistent poor buying sentiment.

Relatively new brand

Being a relatively new company in the property industry, Eco World has worked hard to promote its brand in the market. The company is positioning itself to be a brand targeting towards the higher-end market whereby most units are priced above the affordable range. Eco World has allocated a considerable amount of money for advertisement expenditure (ADEX) in the media, which can be seen especially during the festive seasons. It has also advertised aggressively in the local newspaper for instance The Edge Financial Daily. The show galleries are exquisitely decorated as well. Coupled with its established management team who commands a high respected profile among property buyers, so far Eco World has seen a strong take-up rate for its new launches.

Opportunities:

Opportunity for landbanking

The bearish property cycle currently presents an opportunity for Eco World to acquire new landbanks for future development. After half a decade of steep increase for the pricing of properties, the pace has slowed down due to both microeconomics and macroeconomics factors. The flight of foreign capital in anticipation of the hike of interest by the Federal Reserve System of US as well as the tightening measures by the government to prevent inflation of the housing prices are among the contributing factors. The land prices are believed to have stabilized as land owners will be more realistic with their asking prices taking into consideration the current circumstances.

Major transportation plan

The government has been allocating huge amount of its budget for the development of public infrastructure. The construction of public infrastructure is always believed to have positive impact towards the property sector in terms of sales performance and value. [8] In the Klang Valley, the ongoing construction of Mass Rapid Transit (MRT) Line 1 as well as the soon-to-be-built MRT Line 2 and Light Rail Transit (LRT) line 3 would definitely help boost the property sector in the region. The highly anticipating Kuala Lumpur – Singapore High Speed Rail which is in the midst of tendering process would also contribute positively towards the property sector in the Southern Region of Malaysia, mainly Johor and Iskandar Malaysia. The recent completion of Second Penang Bridge and the hotly debated Penang Transport Masterplan are also set to transform the property landscape in Penang. Eco World being a company with landbanks in these three highly happening and robust regions would only stand to benefit from these developments.

Threats:

Poor Sentiments

The local property buying sentiment has turned bearish since the year 2014 after the government and central bank have announced various measures to curb property speculation following years of steep house price escalation. DIBS has been abolished which makes the entry cost for property ownership higher. The central bank has also set out stringent lending rules for instance 70% loan-to-value ratio for the third property as well as allocation of housing loan based on disposable income rather than gross income. The introduction of real property gain tax during the Budget 2014 also depletes the interest in property investment.

Increased operating cost

Property developers are set to experience increased operating and construction costs due to the marked depreciation of the Malaysian ringgit over the past 1 year. The introduction of Goods and Services Tax (GST) also leads to increased operating expenses. The recent increase in electricity tariff as well as the implementation of minimum wage with the latest increment to RM1000 per month further shrinks the profit margin.

Competition from other more established property developers
According to the market cap, Eco World is the 5th largest developer in Malaysia. As the local property buying sentiment remains sluggish, Eco World has to face stiff competition from other more established developers for example SP Setia, UEM land and Sunway for the reduced market demand.

Risk of venturing to overseas
Eco World is tipped to acquire a 30% stake in Eco World International (EWI) should EWI apply for initial public offering (IPO) as expected in first half 2016. EWI already has projects in both United Kingdom and Australia. It plans to expand its overseas venture after the IPO. With the recent marked depreciation of the Malaysian ringgit, the expansion of operation overseas possesses a certain amount of risk and may further worsen Eco World's balance sheet.

Strategies applied by the company
Since its inception, Eco World has performed tremendously well out of the expectation of most analysts and even exceeded the company's own sales target. It has a record breaking year in 2014 whereby the sale of RM 3.2 billions exceeded the company's target of RM 2-3 billions. Eco World has expanded aggressively by acquiring various prime landbanks and launching new projects despite a general slowdown in the property sector. This may be attributed to its strength of having an experienced management team and thus the confidence to prosper. The management team also commands a good reputation since its time in SP Setia previously for delivering work on time and of the highest quality. Hence it comes as no surprise whereby most of its launches have a strong take-up rate among property buyers. Eco World has also successfully built its branding of quality, environmental-friendly and trendy through effective advertising and exquisitely decorated show galleries aligned with its vision of "Creating tomorrow and beyond".

Although most of the projects are priced above the affordable range, Eco World has done considerable market research to know that there is still market demand for properties within such range which translates into high sales. In order to contain its net gearing ratio, Eco World has also smartly established joint-venture (JV) partnership with other companies in order not to be burdened by the full land cost. The Bukit Bintang City Centre (BBCC) Project with an estimated GDV of RM 8.0 billions is a good example whereby Eco World will be subscribing a 40% stake in the JV. Eco World has also planned for similar JV partnership should its recent proposal to acquire and develop a township on the 2198.4 acres of leasehold land in Ijok, Kuala Selangor is approved. Apart from that, Eco World may be able to set foot on the international arena if Ecoworld International (EWI) successfully applies for initial public offering in 2016 whereby Eco World will acquire 30% stake in EWI.

As of the writing of this paper, EWI is a private vehicle of Tan Sri Liew and his partner Datuk Voon with projects in London, United Kingdom and Sydney, Australia. It is worth noting that Tan Sri Liew has served previously as the Chairman of Battersea Project Holding Company Limited in London during his tenure with SP Setia and already has ample experience in conducting property development overseas. As the local property market still remains bearish for uncertain duration, the venture into overseas property market may well be a good strategy for Eco World to counteract the sluggish property sentiment back in Malaysia. However, Eco World should exert extra caution with its operation overseas especially with the recent marked depreciation of Malaysian Ringgit.

Outlook and Conclusion

Looking forward, the Malaysian property market is expected to remain conservative and sluggish. There is no sign that the government or the Bank Negara is going to reverse its actions to curb property speculation anytime soon as the ratio of household debt to gross domestic product (GDP) still stands at 87.9% in 2014.

Nonetheless, Eco World is believed to be able to survive the current bearish property cycles based on its strong performance since its inception in 2013. The experienced yet ambitious management team will continue to drive the company forward barring any major setbacks. The group still possesses huge landbanks that it can work on for the years to come with remaining GDV of RM 51.2 billions. Eco World may well also set foot and venture overseas as soon as next year once Eco World International (EWI) goes for the initial public offering.

As a conclusion, Eco World will soon be a force to be reckoned with in the Malaysia property industry as well as at the international stage provided it continues with its current growth trajectory.

Southern Coated Peanut "A Better One"

Desa Southern Food Products (DSFP) is a food products packaging company and is one of the pioneers in the food products repacking industry in Malaysia. It started off as a packaging division within its parent company, Desa Southern Agency Sdn Bhd (DSA). As the volume of sales grew substantially over the years, it was finally split from its parent company and was registered as Desa Southern Food Products Sdn Bhd in 1986. Initially the products that were repacked were mainly biscuits, as biscuits were sold in tins and inconvenient to consumers then. Other products included pillow snacks, peas and nuts. Subsequently activities expanded to include preserving fruits imported from China & Thailand, and slowly increased their products line. Dried fruits preservation included dehydrated mangoes, guava, pineapples, raisins, pitted prunes and cranberries joined the products range. The introduction of pitted prunes, raisins and cranberries prompted DSFP to come up with the concept of "Your Healthier Choice" in their effort to promote dried fruits product line.

In 2009, in an effort to upgrade and to improve its operation systems, DSFP has undergone ISO-9001:2008 and HACCP certification to ensure all their products are produced according to the stringent requirement set by international standards and certification bodies. In doing so, they were able to secure contracts as OEM suppliers of preserved fruits and dried fruits for prominent retail chain stores, such as 7-11, Tesco, Giant, Aeon Big, cold storage in Hong Kong and Singapore. To gain wider acceptance in the Muslim market of Malaysia, all products supplied by DSFP were Halal certified.

Over the years of operation, DSFP started off with the primary function of supplying packed products to their parent company DSA, goods were then distributed to all retail outlets accross Malaysia, including convenient chain stores like 7-11, minimarkets, supermarkets and hypermarkets. At a later stage, DSFP started to set up its own van-sales teams to distribute packed products to minimarkets, petrol stations and kiosk, sundry shops, medicinal stores and tourist resorts in Johor region. When this was proven workable, the parent company DSA started to set up branches in various parts of Malaysia, thus helping Desa Southern Food business grow steadily.

By 2012, DSFP have entered into a new area of business by engaging themselves into the hot beverage segment of the market, such as the instant 3-in-1 white coffee, instant milk tea, instant hot chocolate and instant cereals were launched to both the local and export market.

By 2014, DSFP moved from re-packing to nuts manufacturing. A new machine line was invested in manufacturing roasted coated peanut. Products were introduced to local markets at first, then expanded marketing activities to foreign markets through exports. Desa Southern Food Products is originally a professional re-packaging company, and was seen as a pioneer in their industry. The repacked product line included various types of preserved fruits, dried fruits and nuts with wide distribution throughout Malaysia. In recent years however, management was looking for opportunities to further expand marketing activities globally. In Feb 2014, DSFP has received an enquiry from Chinese distributor, to develop a new series of coated peanut, by benchmarking 'Koh Kae', a Thailand based brand, which its coated peanut has been selling well in Chinese markets.

Seeing the opportunity in penetrating the export market with the introduction of coated peanut, management has invested heavily in developing Southern Coated Peanuts. Extensive R&D activities have been conducted, new machineries were purchase, and extra manpower was recruited. In six-month timeframe, Southern Coated Peanut with four flavors, which is Chicken, BBQ, Hot & Spicy and Seaweed Wasabi was successfully developed and launched into both domestic and export market on August 2014.

In September 2015 during the quarterly meeting with sales & marketing department, managing director of Desa Southern Food Products Sdn. Bhd. (DSFP) Mr. Ch'ng Poh Tee talked to Mr. Lee, the sales and marketing manager about his concern over the poor financial performance of DSFP with sales and profit declining year-on-year since 2014. Mr. Ch'ng Poh Tee was anxious to find solutions to improve sales and overall profitability of the company. He requested Mr. Lee to come out with a comprehensive report, by which identifying the root causes of the drop in sales and finding out how investment in the newly coated peanut line can further improve the sales.

Overview of the local & global snack food industry

Snack Food Industry Revenue

With an abundance of industry players from small to large, the market for snack food has always been fragmented and intensely competitive. According to Nielsen retail sales data, global snack sales have reached $374 billion annually ending March 2014, with an increase of 2% year-on-year. Europe ($167 billion) and the US ($124 billion) are the largest markets; Latin America ($30 billion), Middle East/Africa ($7 billion) and the Asia/Pacific ($46 billion). Asia is the fastest growing snack food markets, with year-on-year increase rate of 9%, 5% and 4% respectively. According to Euromonitor International, sales of sweets and savory snacks in Malaysia were recorded with an average growth of 3% between 2011 to year 2013. Extruded snacks took up a 32% of sales, followed by nuts (24%), chips/crisps (12%), fruit snacks (5%), popcorn (2%) and others.

Snack nuts and seeds launches

In H2 of 2013, 33% share of the global snacks category tracked launches came from the snack nuts and seeds. Between 2008 and 2012, snack nuts and seeds launches witnessed a compound annual growth rate (CAGR) of 29%, which had outperformed the snacks category CAGR of 26%. Except Australia and New Zealand, all regions have seen a year of year increased in the snack nuts and seeds launch activity. Asia and Europe are the top two regions in terms of snack nuts and seeds launches, which is about 900 and 800 products respectively. The top seven companies account for only 5% of the total H2 2013 snack nuts and seeds launches, indicating a highly competition in the market between the giants (Kraft, Lidl, Carrefour, Pepsico, Paramount Farms, Intersnack and Tong Garden).

The table below shows the percentage of consumers who said they ate snack nuts/seeds in 30 days, based on the Nielsen Global Snacking Survey, which polled 30,000 online consumers in 60 countries. The study was conducted between Feb 17 and March 7, 2014. Results are tallied with the report by Innova Market Insights with Asia and Europe are the top two regions in term of snack seeds and nuts launches. Peanut is the top flavor in Europe, Asia and Latin America, while consumers in North America and Australia/New Zealand prefer Almond.

Region	%
Global Average	41
Asia Pacific	49
Europe	34
Middle East/Africa	N/A

| Latin America | N/A |
| North America | N/A |

Percentage of Consumers who Ate Snack Nuts/Seeds in Last 30 days (Nielsen, 2014)
N/A = nuts/seeds snack wasn't rated as top 10 favorite snacks

Sales of nut snacks products in Malaysia have been growing constantly, from RM226.7 million in 2008 to RM 243.2 billion in 2013, with an average 2% of growth annually. However, CAGR of nuts category in Malaysia was relatively low in comparison with other snack categories, with an average of 8% volume growth between 2008 and 2013. The key players in Nuts category in Malaysia are Tong Garden Snack Foods Sdn. Bhd who accounted for 7.3% of retail value in year 2013, followed by Ngan Yin (3.3%), Pagoda (3.0%), NOI (2.7%) and Camel (0.8%) for sweet and savory snacks market. It is forecasted that the percentage of value growth for nuts category in Malaysian market is at 0.7% for CAGR where 3.8% total.

Consumer snacks preference & buying behavior

Based on Neilson's study, respondents around the world prefer the absence of ingredients rather than addition of them. There were 20 health attributes included in the study. Snacks with all natural ingredients are rated as the highest percentage, where 45% of global respondents rated very important, 32% rated moderately important. This is followed by absence of artificial colors (44%), genetically modified organisms (43%) and artificial flavors (42%) which was also rated as very important. 30% to 34% of respondents rated that it is very important that snacks has to be low in calories, fat, salt and sugar (in ascending order).

Based on Innova Market Insights research, top five positions identified for snacks nuts and seeds are as following: vegetarian is the leading claim in Asia (14%), Europe and Latin America more emphasize on Ethical Packaging (22%, 25%), low cholesterol for North America Market (17%), no additives/preservatives for Australia/New Zealand market (17%), and Halal for Middle East/North Afria (21%). (Exhibit 3) Innova's Market Insights research highlighted several opportunities in the snacks nuts & seeds launches. Ethnic flavor launches (eg. Matcha Green Tea Almonds, Jalfrezi Flavor jumbo peanuts), yogurt & wasabi based launches, grilled and smoked nuts launches, versatile combinations (eg. Tropical mix & berries mix with nuts & seeds).

Snacking apparently is not just for the experiences of leisure and pure enjoyment. According to Neilson's study, a big group of respondents are snack planners. 76% of global respondents eat snacks to fill the hunger between meals, while less than 45% use snacks as a meal replacement. 79% of people enjoy snacks at home, where 68% eat snacks with family and friends. 63% of people tend to have a few snacks that will be kept for rotation.

Distribution Channel

In addition to the awareness of consumers' buying behavior, it is imperative to identify the right distribution channels to reach the target consumer. This task however is challenging in global marketing, since distribution channels and consumption habits could vary tremendously from one region to the other. In Asia-Pacific for instance, online respondents according to Neilson's study showed that they would purchase snacks from hypermarkets (47%), grocery stores (44%) and convenience stores (36%). In Europe however, respondents preferred to shop at grocery stores (53%) than hypermarkets (41%), followed by convenience stores (22%). In Middle East & Africa, respondents tend to purchase snacks from grocery shops (48%) and hypermarkets (37%).

Future outlook

The Asia Pacific region is viewed as largest growing market in the next 25 years since the increased per capita consumption in relation to population percentage. The Chinese market is the highest growing market in Asia due to increased income. However, there are increased concerns in China over food security issues arise from international but more so arising from national/local Chinese manufacturers. Bridging the gap between nutritious and indulgence of tasty will be a challenge, but brings along tremendous opportunities of snacks manufacturers. It is essential here to note that local preferences for taste can't be ignored.

Industry Competitiveness

Overall Sales Performance

In manufacturing business, re-packing is rather simple process and requires less investment than other operations. This allowed for more new markets players that resulted in intense competition and highly fragmented industry. As a result, local sales of the DSF were highly affected; sales figure declined from RM16, 789,994 to RM14, 992,274 between 2011 and 2014. However, export sales have increased from RM854, 479 in 2011 to RM2, 384,608 in 2014. The increase in export sales is mainly attributed to the introduction of dried fruits, instant beverages and the coated peanut into the Chinese market. Higher expenses offset growth in sales and caused stagnant profit as DSFP decreased year-on-year to RM345, 991 in 2014.

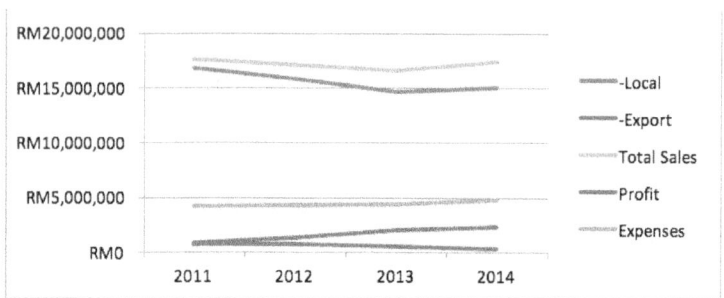

	2011	2012	2013	2014
-Local	RM16,789,994	RM15,821,902	RM14,606,522	RM14,992,274
-Export	RM854,479	RM1,349,735	RM2,039,789	RM2,384,608
Total Sales	RM17,644,473	RM17,171,637	RM16,646,311	RM17,376,882
Expenses	RM4,256,646	RM4,350,462	RM4,406,421	RM4,800,266
Profit	RM716,941	RM712,721	RM518,702	RM345,991

Financial Performance of DSFP (Local vs. Export)
Year 2011- 2014

Company Sales Performance by Product

Products sold by DSF can be categorized into three major groups, these are: repacked products with contribution of 76% of sales, self-manufactured products (4.6% of sales), and third party products (19.4% of sales). The table below shows the net contribution of each product to the total revenue of DSF.

Repacked products

The repacked product category includes preserved fruits, dried fruits, nuts, confectionery and festive item. All the raw ingredients are either sourced locally or imported from China, Thailand or U.S.A. The table below shows that revenue contribution by repacked product category has been decreasing year-on-year. The industry for repacked products has become more competitive than ever before due to low investment requirements and lack of entry barriers. Domestic markets are extremely saturated with companies supplying similar products. Opportunities for expanding sales locally are limited. In addition, consumers are more health conscious than ever before, which limits the consumption of preserved fruits containing preservatives and coloring. Since raw materials for repacked products are sourced globally and subject to exchange rate fluctuation, DSFP has limited control over the cost of raw material. Profit margin of this product line has been decreasing solely because of the weakening Malaysia Ringgit, which caused a 25% increase in the cost of raw material. Dried fruits however are an exception since it's selling to both domestic and global markets. Other types of repacked products can only be sold in local market because of competitive pricing and the fact that preserved fruits ingredients cannot meet the food regulations of global markets. This lack of global competitiveness stems from the fact that used preservatives are either exceeds the allowable limit or the product contains preservative or additives that are banned in foreign markets. The chances of revenue growth for this product line locally or globally are slim.

Type of Products	2011	2012	2013	2014	Total	%
Repacked						
Preserved Fruits	RM6,987,140	RM7,041,308	RM6,844,509	RM6,614,821	RM27,487,778	39.9%
Dried Fruits	RM2,841,245	RM3,090,600	RM2,527,956	RM2,384,884	RM10,844,685	15.8%
Nuts	RM2,433,432	RM2,413,978	RM2,187,688	RM2,088,986	RM9,124,084	13.3%
Festive Product	RM767,066	RM795,134	RM620,027	RM393,869	RM2,576,096	3.7%
Confectionery	RM433,300	RM345,104	RM656,056	RM831,252	RM2,265,712	3.3%
Sub Total	RM13,462,183	RM13,686,124	RM12,836,236	RM12,313,812	RM52,298,355	76.0%
Self-Manufactured						
Southern Coated Peanut	-	-	-	RM825,296	RM825,296	1.2%
Beverage	RM284,024	RM536,478	RM809,288	RM713,981	RM2,343,771	3.4%
Sub Total	RM284,024	RM536,478	RM809,288	RM1,539,277	RM3,169,067	4.6%
3rd Party						
Extrusion Snacks	RM1,966,204	RM1,725,165	RM1,532,451	RM1,558,453	RM6,782,273	9.9%
Open Market Item	RM1,102,905	RM871,636	RM1,046,497	RM1,389,010	RM4,410,048	6.4%
Others	RM829,157	RM352,234	RM421,839	RM576,330	RM2,179,560	3.2%
Sub Total	RM3,898,266	RM2,949,035	RM3,000,787	RM3,523,793	RM13,371,881	19.4%
Total	RM17,644,473	RM17,171,637	RM16,646,311	RM17,376,882	RM68,839,303	

DSFP Sales performance based on type of product
(Financial Year 2011-2014)

Self-Manufactured Product

The decreased demand for preserved fruits, and lack of control over the cost of raw material for other types of repacked products, caused management to move DSF from being a re-packer to a manufacturer. Instant beverages product line was introduced to local markets in 2012, while coated peanuts were introduced in year 2014.

Instant Beverages

The instant beverages product line consists of six products, these are; hot chocolate, 2 in1 White Coffee (no sugar added), 3 in 1 White Coffee, Hazelnut White coffee, Milk Tea and Ginger Milk Tea. All the above products come in three different type of packing, which are 15 sachets in a bag, 8 sachets in a box, and 6 sachets in a bag. They initial introduction was limited to the southern region of Malaysia "Johor" for market testing purposes with some exports to the Chinese market. Since 2012 the distribution and promotion method locally is done through the van sales team of DSFP. Instant beverage market is highly fragmented and intensely competitive. Consumers are very brand sensitive when it comes to beverage. As a result of being new brand in the market with minimum marketing activities taking place to promote the product, revenue streams for southern instant beverage are slow, with only 3.4% contribution to total sales.

Coated Peanut

The investment in the coated peanut product line was initiated by the constant requests made by the Chinese agent. The agent noticed a good response in the market for coated peanut brand named 'Koh Kae' in China. Therefore, the agent requested DSF to develop similar type of products to penetrate the Chinese market. Hoping the development of this product range would allow DSF to expand export activities, management invested heavily in new product development. Six months of extensive research and development activities yielded four flavors of coated peanuts. The introduction of Hot & Spicy, BBQ, Chicken and Seaweed Wasabi Flavored coated peanut was very successful since its inception in August 2014. These new flavors require only one type of packing, a 70g of aluminum foil packing is used for both domestic and export markets.

Repacked Industry vs. Coated Peanuts Manufacturing

DSFP utilized Porter's Five Forces model to assess current business situation of the repacked industry and analyze the strength of coated peanuts product line.

The Bargaining Power of Supplier

Repacked Industry	Coated Peanut Manufacturing
- Price are easily driven up by supplier especially preserved fruits range due to the limited supplies from both local and export market (-) - Suppliers having a strong power as there are only a few who are able to supply product that are free of cyclamate (a sweetener which is banned to be used in Malaysia) (-)	- There is quite a numbers of trading house that imports raw peanuts into Malaysia which DSFP can approach can stronger position to ask for a better quality and price of peanuts (+)

The Bargaining Power of Buyer

Repacked Industry	Coated Peanut Manufacturing
- DSFP repacked products have been in the market for more than ten years, and somehow have generated some brand awareness among consumer. Buyer would rarely switch to other product/service as long as their profit is maintained. (+)	- There's a variety of nuts product outside the market. As a product and brand which is new to the market, buyers are rather reluctant to purchase it. (-) - As the product is self-manufactured, DSFP has more bullets in offering special price or promotion to both retailer and end consumers in promoting the product. (+)

Competitive Rivalry

Repacked Industry	Coated Peanut Manufacturing
- There's a lot of new market entrants in the re-packing industry due to the relatively low	- There's a lot of nuts manufacturer out there, but nuts manufacturer that produce coated

investment and simple process involved (-) - Competitors normally offer cheaper price (-) - Price war are always encounter in repacked industry (-)	peanut is nonetheless very little due to its process involved is more complicated than other type of nuts products (eg. Fried peanuts, fried peas) (+)

Threat of Substitution

Repacked Industry	Coated Peanut Manufacturing
- As the content of the repacked products are more or less the same in comparison to the other brand, the threat of substitution is high. Product substitution can be achieved by changing the weight of product, size of packaging and design of the packaging (-)	- The chances of substituting the product is hard due to the manufacturing process of coated peanut are rather complicated, and the formulation of product is not known by others. Product imitation and substitution is not easy. Competitors can hardly create a product that is similar to ours product, due to the product itself consists of its unique crunchiness and flavors, which is made up by various type of ingredients. (+)

Threat of New Entry

Repacked Industry	Coated Peanut Manufacturing
Repacked industry can be entered easily due to its simple process and hence relatively low investment is required (-)	Coated Peanut Manufacturing involves more investment on machineries. Technical expertise is required to develop the product as it involves of several type of process and combination of different kind of ingredients (eg. Coating, roasting, seasoning etc.) (+)

Summary of Porter's Five Forces

Factors	Repacked Industry	Coated Peanut Manufacturing

Bargaining Power of Supplier	Negative	Positive
Bargaining Power of Buyer	**Positive**	Negative
Competitive Rivalry	Negative	**Positive**
Threat of Substitution	Negative	**Positive**
Threat of New Entry	Negative	**Positive**

Based on porter's five forces analysis, it was clear for management that the repacking industry is unattractive at the moment. This has been supported by DSFP financial performance of the year 2011-2014. It would be risky if DSFP continues to rely on this range of product to boost its sales. In contrast, the newly invested coated peanut line was more attractive since more opportunities facing the product line than threats. In conjunction with continuous growth of sales for the nuts segments in local and export market, it is therefore a good idea for the company to move from repack industry gradually to nuts manufacturing.

Marketing effectiveness of Southern Coated Peanut in Malaysia
Product

Southern Coated Peanut was developed by benchmarking against 'Koh-Kae' coated peanut, a product of Thailand that is sold internationally. Four flavors of Southern coated peanut were introduced. A sensory evaluation has been conducted to compare consumer preferences between Koh-Kae brand vs. Southern Coated Peanut. All flavors were compared except for Hot & Spicy flavor since Koh-Kae doesn't sell this flavor of coated peanut. Four parameters were assessed during the evaluation process, which covers the following criteria; appearance, aroma, crunchiness and taste. Results show that Southern has scored higher on BBQ and chicken against Koh-Kae. However, as for seaweed wasabi flavored coated peanut, Southern scored relatively lower against Koh-Kae. Further improvement on the seaweed wasabi flavored coated peanut is needed.

According to a survey conducted by Nielson on consumer's preferences for snacks, findings shows that consumers prefer snacks to have natural ingredients, free of artificial color and flavors, low in cholesterol and fat. Therefore, the absence of artificial coloring is a unique selling point that differentiates Southern Coated Peanut from Koh-Kae's Coated Peanut. This advantage will be highlighted during the marketing campaign.

Koh-Kae's Coated Peanut is sold in a metal canister with a weight of 240g to 265g. The cost of the metal canister is relatively high, thus, Southern Coated Peanut is packed in an aluminum foil packaging with a weight of 70g to improve its cost advantage. In Malaysia's snacks and nuts market, the packaging of nuts is normally done in smaller sizes (weighted 30-50g), or larger sizes (weighted 128g-140g). Southern Coated Peanut's 70g product is ranged somewhere in between. This could be beneficial if consumers tend to appreciate this uniqueness; however, it could backfire if consumer doesn't accept the differences in the size of packaging.

Place

Neilson's study further shows that consumers in Asia-Pacific tend to purchase snacks from hypermarkets (47%), grocery stores (44%) and convenience stores (36%). Currently, Southern Coated Peanut has been selling only at one of Malaysia's largest hypermarkets "Giant". The rest of sales are done through grocery shops and mainly distributed by DSFP own van-sales teams. Unlike repacked products, which could be found in most Malaysian hypermarkets such as Aeon big, Giant, Tesco, Econsave, Mydin, Southern Coated Peanut products are sold in small grocery stores, petrol kiosk (Shell, Petronas, BHP etc.) and convenience stores such as 7-11. The distribution channels of Southern Coated Peanut are relatively poor.

Koh-Kae Coated Peanut can be found in any super/hypermarket in Malaysia, in addition to smaller grocery shops. However, convenient shops and petrol kiosk stations are not penetrated yet by Koh-Kae, which is probably attributed to lack of sufficient resource by the importing agent inside Malaysia. To reach smaller grocery shops, kiosks and gas stations, only Van-sales team can do such a job by taking the product directly to each outlet.

Price

Koh Kae Coated Peanut (metal canister) of 240g to 265g is sold for RM 9.95 at hypermarkets. This price will drop to RM7.5 or RM 8.3 during promotions. While prices of Southern Coated Peanut in 70g (Aluminum Foil) is set by DSFP at RM2.9 in hypermarkets. Prices are dropped to RM 2 to RM 2.5 during promotions. 100g of

Koh-Kae Coated Peanut (Aluminum Foil) is sold for RM 4.05. If based on the price of similar type of packaging, Southern Coated Peanut is slightly over-priced.

As a key player in snacks nuts and seed market, Tong Garden has most of their products packed in a smaller size of packing, which is 40g and is sold at a price of RM 1.59. Coated peanut in smaller packing size is not available in the market yet. DSFP should consider the possibility of introducing smaller size of packing at a price in the range of RM1.59 to grab market share from Tong Garden.

Promotion

DSFP has taken part in the trade shows, mainly in the Southern region of Malaysia to promote its Southern Coated Peanut brand. Sampling activities take place at selective outlets such as Giant hypermarket. No advertisement campaigns are conducted of Southern Coated Peanut because of the high cost associated to such campaigns. It is highly advisable that DSFP considers the promotion of its product on billboards due to the relatively lower cost when compared with TV or radio advertising campaigns. Social media can be a very viable tool for advertising DSFP product, especially in distinguishing their no artificial coloring and roasted products. Both Tong Garden and Koh-Kae doesn't conduct any advertising events in Malaysia, including the utilization of social media as an effective channel to reach new segments of the market in addition to existing consumers. The only form of promotion of utilized is offering price-offs and discounts. This is also done by DSFP from time to time to keep up with price competition. It has been observed that with promotional selling prices of RM 2, product sales highly increased. This may also be done in conjunction with product sampling promotions in hypermarkets.

Conclusion

Financial performance of DSFP has been plummeting since 2011 largely because of higher expenses. As a company with major revenue from repacking, DSFP is facing a difficult time in further boosting sales and revenues. Management is considering to further expanding its business operations to coated peanut manufacturing, based on their analysis, which shows where the existing opportunity are in the market place. Product line expansion is needed and may prove to be a good decision made by management to improve overall financial performance. However, considering that new product lines are new in the marketplace, it is advisable for Southern Coated Peanut to improvement on the recipe of *Seaweed Wasabi* flavored coated peanut, to further improve the marketing channels. Increase promotional campaigns to include social media, billboard and tradeshow in conjunction with price-off promotion and products sampling in selective outlets. Introduce smaller packing size of Coated Peanut (30g – 40g) at a lower price in the range of RM 1.60, by benchmarking against Tong Garden products. To stress product uniqueness "no artificial coloring, non-frying products and roasted products during promotion campaigns. Improving local sales of Southern Coated Peanut, by exploring opportunities in global markets, starting in Asia. To reduce operational cost, DSFP management should consider outsourcing alternative suppliers for repacked products, and constantly look for new and innovative solutions to reduce expenses and improve product offerings.

Exhibit 1: Sales of Sweet and Savoury Snacks by Category (Malaysia):
Value 2008 – 2013 (RM million)

Type of Products\Year	2008	2009	2010	2011	2012	2013
Chips/Crisps	101.6	102.6	105.7	109.4	112	114.8
Extruded Snacks	253.1	256.9	268.4	283.2	297	309.1
Fruit Snacks	43	44.1	45.9	47.2	48.4	49.3
Nuts	226.7	227.8	231.2	233.5	238.2	243.2
Popcorn	14.3	14.4	15.1	15.8	16.7	17.5
Pretzels	-	-	-	-	-	-
Tortilla/Corn Chpis	56.9	57.7	59.7	62.1	64.7	67.2
Other Sweet and Savoury Snacks	138.9	141.7	145.3	149.6	153.2	156.3
Sweet and Savoury Snacks	834.5	845.3	871.3	901	930.1	957.6

Source: Euromonitor International fromo official statistics, trade associatoins, trade press,
company research, store checks, trade interviews, trade sources

Exhibit 2: Sales of Sweet and Savoury Snacks by Category (Malaysia):
% Volume Growth 2008-2013

% volume growth			
	2012/13	2008-13 CAGR	2008/13 Total
Chips/Crisps	1.5	2.1	10.9
Extruded Snacks	2.5	3.2	17
Fruit Snacks	1.5	2.5	13.1
Nuts	1.7	1.6	8
Popcorn	4.7	3.8	20.2
Pretzels	-	-	-
Tortilla/Corn Chips	3	3	15.7
Other Sweet and Savoury Snacks	1.5	2.1	10.7
Sweet and Savoury Snacks	1.9	2.3	12.2

Source: Euromonitor International official statistics, trade associations, trade press, company research, store checks, trade interviews, trade sources

Exhibit 3: Positioning types as % for Sanck Nuts & Seeds product launches tracked per region (H2 2012- H2 2013)

Region	Total Products	Vegetarian	Halal	Ethical-Packaging	No Additives/ Preservatives	Low Cholesterol
North America	913	7%	1%	3%	14%	17%
Europe	2135	14%	0%	22%	10%	1%
Asia	2501	14%	13%	8%	7%	6%
Austrlia/New Zealand	155	0.07	0.06	0.02	17%	10%
Latin America	448	0%	0	25%	5%	0.08
Middle East/North	327	0.08	0.21	20%	0.06	0.12

Exhibit 4: Sensory Evaluation Result (Preference Test) of Coated Peanut (Southern vs. Koh Kae)

	Apperance		Aroma		Taste		Crunchiness	
	Southern	Koh Kae	Southern	Koh Kae	Southern	Koh Kae	Southern	Koh Kae
Chicken Flavoured Coated	27%	73%	50%	50%	64%	36%	59%	41%

Peanut								
BBQ Flavoured Coated Peanut	85%	15%	67%	33%	56%	44%	56%	44%
Seaweed Wasabi Flavoured Coated Peanut	6%	94%	25%	75%	31%	69%	44%	56%

Boustead Heavy Industries Corporation (BHIC)

Introduction

Boustead Heavy Industries Corporation (BHIC) of Malaysia was established in 2005 with the merger of two local maritime companies, Boustead Naval Shipyard Sdn Bhd and Penang Shipbuilding and Construction, and Naval Dockyard Sdn Bhd (PCS-ND). Since the merger BHIC had a tough times to survive in the SBSR industry. In 2014, BHIC had RM747.2 million in assets including three shipyards in Lumut (Perak), Pulau Jerejak (Pulau Pinang) and Langkawi (Kedah). In 2015 BHIC managed to record RM332.8 million in revenue while profit after tax (PAT) were RM17.9 million.

Fortunately, one of the sub-sector currently being supported by the government of Malaysia through the Economic Transformation Program (ETP) is shipbuilding and ship repair (SBSR). In March 2012, the industry was accepted as one of the Entry Point Project (EPP). Support for such key industry is believed to contribute towards the overall growth of the economy. BHIC is one of the top performers in shipbuilding and ship repair. BHIC with its subsidiaries are the champions of an initiative to become Malaysia's first company to design and build offshore support vessel (OSV). With the collaboration from organizations such as design expert Macduff Ship Design and Marine Technology Centre of Universiti Teknologi Malaysia (MTC-UTM), BHIC is banking on such strategic alliance to pay off within the next couple of years.

Challenges

In order to grow their businesses with the objective of becoming a conglomarate in their sector, BHIC management planned for organizational transformation program. The set target is to reach RM180 million PAT by 2020. This may be achieved according to management by supporting growing demand from the defense & security sector, energy sector and through the repositioning of the commercial sector. However, to achieve the set targets, BHIC realized that they must deal with pressing issues first to pave the way for successful realization of their plans.

Based on recent financial performance, the management felt that company's profitability is in decline, which could put them financially at risk. Historical look at the company tells us that they their cost always experienced over runs and delays in projects delivery. In terms of human capital, BHIC's assessment is that they're facing ineffective project management, whith lack of experience and lack of control and integrity issues. BHIC management thinks that now is the right time to transform the company and build distinctive capability in design, engineering, project, contract and supply chain management, leasing & financing, business development & marketing in addition to competative talent management to "Boustead" customer's experience.

Ship Building & Ship Repair (SBSR) Industry Analysis

Malaysia's economy was growing till mid 2015 when oil prices experienced sharp decline that caused sharp budget tightening. However, the maritime sector has always been a corner stone of the economy. In accordance to the 3rd Industrial Master Plan, the shipbuilding and ship repair (SBSR) industry rose to be one of the major contributors to Malaysia's GDP, primarily due to transportation. Support for the industry dates back to late 2011, when Malaysia's Prime Minister Najib launched SBSR industry 1st blueprint with the title of 'Malaysian Shipbuilding/Ship Repair Industry Strategic Plan 2020' (SBSR 2020). The blueprint was developed to guide the industry moving to the right direction in order to steer Malaysia into becoming a maritime hub. It is the group effort of the Association of Marine Industries of Malaysia (AMIM) and the Malaysian Industry Government Group for High Technology (MIGHT). The SBSR 2020 blueprint has listed seven (7) main strategies and 40 action items to be taken up in order to achieve industry's objective:

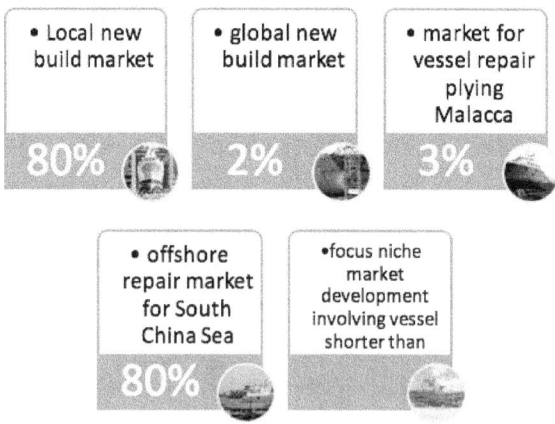

The objective of Malaysian Ship building & Ship Repair Industry Strategic Plan 2020 (SBSR 2020)

The seven (7) strategies that have been identified and to be executed by 2020 are as the following:
- a. To strengthen the institutional framework;
- b. To establish business friendly policies that support the growth of the industry;
- c. To reinforce regulatory frameworks to assure the integrity of SBSR companies and the quality of their products;
- d. To attract and prepare adequate and capable workforce;
- e. To apply local design and adopt new shipbuilding/ship repair technologies;
- f. To improve financial & incentive packages and promote inward investment; and
- g. Upgrade competency and level of sophistication of the industry.

With the determination to attain the above objectives through strategic planning, the industry targeted contribution to the overall Gross National Income (GNI) is RM3.65 billion, and to create about 55,000 new jobs by 2020 in Malaysia.

Industry Performance

The Malaysian maritime industry has been affected during late 2015 and early 2016 by the global economic slowdown and decreasing performance in shipping trades worldwide. Decrease in demand for this service sector is considered as a key indicator that SBSR industry is declining. Traditional the local SBSR industry is driven by Oil & Gas sector as a major driver. The core business activities for shipyards are Oil & Gas sector, with demand driven by structure fabrication, conversion of ship (i.e. Floating Storage Unit (FSU), Floating Storage Offloading (FSO), Floating Production Storage and Offloading (FPSO)), building of rig, maintenance and repairing of platform and ship charter activities.

The industry managed to record RM8.36 billion in terms of revenue in 2013, the increment more than 10% compared to the previous year. The following graph mention about the revenue by SBSR industry between 2011 to 2013:

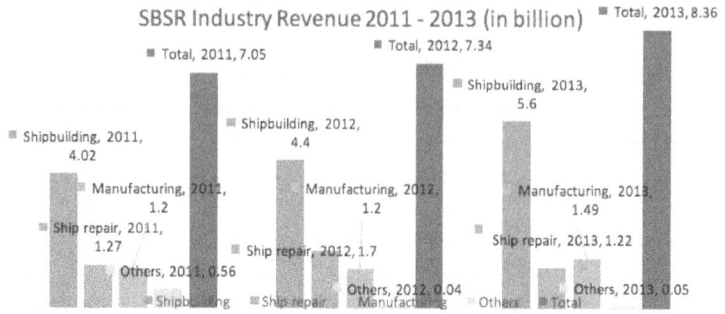

Ship Building & Ship Repair (SBSR) industry revenue 2011 to 2013

In line with the above revenue recorded, the industry managed to create about 35,000 jobs. In terms of investment, Foreign Direct Investment (FDI) and Domestic Direct Investment (DDI) are key investment factors for SBSR. However, the Malaysian Investment Development Authority (MIDA) report stated that investments in SBSR industry were slowing down since 2012, with four approved SBSR projects valued at RM415.6 million. While only two approved projects in 2013 with an investment value of RM33.5 million, both situations are completely contradicting investment records shown in the graph below with total investments of RM6 billion, including 10 projects approved for shipbuilding, ship repairing and engineering works. Such contradictory data reporting is not unusual in Malaysia and other Asian countries.

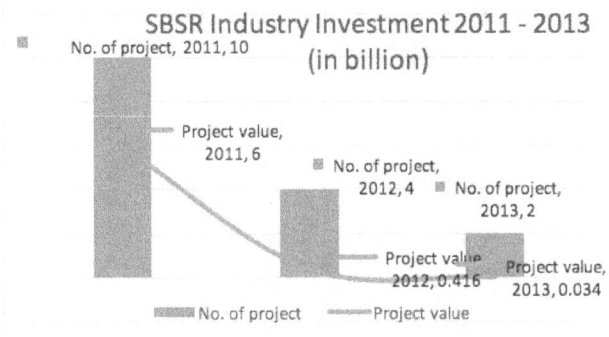

Ship Building & Ship Repair (SBSR) industry investment for 2011 to 2013

One of the main factors for industry investment trend shown above is partially caused by the prevention of SBSR industry from the Promotion of Investment Act passed in January 2011. In order to overcome this situation, the Malaysian Investment Development authority (MIDA) planned to enhance the promotion of SBSR industry and encourage FDI and DDI investments.

Shipbuilding & Ship Repair (SBSR) Industry Supply Chain

The major activities for shipbuilding and ship repair (SBSR) industry in Malaysia are shipbuilding, ship repair and marine equipment manufacturing. This industry is fragmented, with majority of companies being small-sized shipyards. SBSR industry is divided into three main components. There are currently 104 industry players for shipyard activities, while 85 players for non-shipyards with ship building activities with major revenue contribution to the SBSR industry. In 2013, with a total of 93 shipyards nationwide, there were 234 ships produced that generated revenue of RM5.6 billion. This revenue was mainly generated through Boustead Heavy Industries Corporation (BHIC), through the building of Littoral Combatant Ships (LCS) for the Royal Malaysian Navy. Among other type of ships being built were passenger vessel, specialty ship, offshore and coastal type of vessel. As far as the capacity for shipbuilding, Malaysia has the capability to build vessels up to 30,000 Deadweight tonnage (DWT).

Type of vessel build or repair by Malaysian companies

As for the ship repairing activities, the revenue for this segment was mainly from the activities related to maintenance and repairing of special purpose vessels such as liquefied natural gas ship, tankers, bulk carriers and containers that majorly done by Malaysia Marine and Heavy Engineering (MMHE) Sdn. Bhd. Other domestic shipyards contribution to the repair of small size boats such as tugs, barges and fishing boats. In terms of prospect, the states of Sabah and Sarawak have the largest potential to develop their capacity as major hubs for ship repair activities. However, major investments are required to overcome the geographical obstacles exist such as shallow river depth and rough sea. The domestic ship repairing capacity has the potential to grow up to 450,000 DWT.

As for the marine equipment-manufacturing segment, this part of the supply chain has been developing steadily. In 2013, this segment of the industry has contributed RM1.49 billion in revenue. The quality of products produced by Malaysian manufacturers was able to satisfy global demand. However, to further improve quality and gain global recognition, SBSR industry players need do lots of work (marketing, branding, advertising, and active participation) to get global product recognition.

Category	Activity	Major Companies
Prime	Shipyard–Facilities & Project Manager	Malaysia Marine & Heavy Engineering (MMHE) Sdn Bhd, Nam Cheong Dockyard Sdn Bhd, Shin Yang Shipyard Sdn Bhd, Labuan Shipyard & Engineering Sdn Bhd,

Tier		Boustead Heavy Industries Corporation (BHIC) Berhad
Tier 1	Platform & Payload Integrator, Shipbuilder	JRM Services Sdn Bhd, **Boustead Heavy Industries Corporation (BHIC) Berhad,** Contraves Advanced Devices Sdn Bhd, Criterion Maritime Sdn Bhd, Teknik Padu Sdn Bhd
Tier 2	Sub-system Manufacturer/ Assembler	Matrix Power Network Sdn Bhd, SIMPAC Marine Sdn Bhd, Kewpum (M) Sdn Bhd, MTU Services (M) Sdn Bhd, Bintang Manjung Sdn Bhd
Tier 3	Sub-system Component / Manufacturer	Jotun (Malaysia) Sdn Bhd, TECO Electric & Machinery Sdn Bhd, Bintang Manjung Sdn Bhd,
Tier 4	Raw Material and subcomponent for sub-system	Amalgamated Metal Corp (M) Sdn Bhd, Prima Metals Ind Sdn Bhd

Supply chain category of SBSR Industry in Malaysia

Boustead Heavy Industries Corporation Berhad Company Description

Boustead Heavy Industries Corporation Berhad (BHIC) is a company that specialized in shipbuilding, ship repair, naval engineering and vessel-related services, and is listed on the Main Board of Bursa Malaysia Securities. As at 10 February 2015, the major shareholders of BHIC is the parent company itself Boustead Holdings Berhad with a 65%, followed by Lembaga Tabung Angkatan Tentera (LTAT) with an 8.15% of shares and Lembaga Tabung Haji (7.64%). The remaining shares own by minority shareholders such as Amanahraya Trustees Berhad, B & A Family Holdings Sdn Bhd, few private individuals and other organisations. BHIC is the umbrella for 1,787 employees across Malaysia.

BHIC was formed in 2005 when the Government of Malaysia enforced a merger between Boustead Naval Shipyard Sdn Bhd (Boustead Holdings Berhad's business arm for commercial shipbuilding) and the problematic company, Penang Shipbuilding and Construction - Naval Dockyard Sdn Bhd (PCS-ND). PCS-ND was a company based in the area of Lumut, Perak with primary business activities to maintain Royal Malaysian Navy (RMN) vessels as well as RMN dockyard. The mismanagement happened in the company in the early 2000 resulting of the merger of PCS-ND and BHIC. Since then, they have expanded and became one of the largest shipbuilding and ship repair companies in Malaysia.

BHIC Financial Performance

Under the leadership of Ahmad Ramli Hj Mohd Nor, as managing director, BHIC made a sound financial results in 2014, with a revenue of RM332.8 million and profit after tax (PAT) of RM17.9 million compared to RM319.1 million revenue and PAT of RM3.2 million in the previous year. At the end of 2014, BHIC's net assets were at RM1.21 per share and shareholders' funds were at RM300.6 million. In order to expand businesses further, BHIC invested in multiple streams of sub-business sector within the SBSR industry by forming subsidiaries such as Boustead Penang Shipyard Sdn Bhd, BHIC Marine Carriers Sdn Bhd, Boustead Naval Shipyard Sdn Bhd, BYO Marine Sdn Bhd and others. The table below provides synopses of BHIC's financial performance .

RM'000	2014	2013	2012	2011	2010
Revenue	332,823	319,051	257,668	302,653	403,590
Profit/(Loss) before taxation	20,218	7,395	141,133	6,230	78,443
Profit/(Loss) after taxation	17,850	3,161	138,982	22,236	69,740
Profit/(Loss) attributable to Shareholders	17,850	3,161	139,132	21,146	69,805
Shareholders' equity	300,557	282,707	281,259	435,419	430,304
Total equity x	300,557	282,707	281,259	435,419	430,304
Total assets	747,232	733,176	875,259	958,701	682,717
Sen per share					
Earnings/(Loss) per share	7.18	1.27	-56	8.51	28.1
Net dividend per share	–	–	6	6.5	6
Net assets per share	1.21	1.14	1.13	1.75	1.73

BHIC financial highlight for 5 years between 2010 - 2015

Competitive environment for BHIC

Initially, it was predicted that demand for vessels building will increas beyond 2015. However, this estimate has to be revived because of the global economic slowdown of 2015-2016. The vessel associations of Malaysia projected that hundreds of new vessels are required to cater for activities in the oil and gas industry in Malaysian waters by the year 2020. Local maritime companies were expecting steady growth prior to the economic slowdown. However, if demand proves to be true, this poses a big opportunity to expand BHIC's present in the local SBSR industry scene.

Moreover, BHIC as a major player tends to view this differently. BHIC looked at economic trend of instability in 2015-2016 in global oil prices, with the view that the slowdown will significantly impact their industry and the company. If the economic trend continues throughout 2017, the result is massive uncertainty and instability in SBSR industry due to oversupply of vessels in the marketplace, which will cause a spillover of lower profits for all shipyard operators. This in turn will increase competition amongst domestic and regionally players in the industry. Ship operators increasingly prefer sophisticated new vessels with the latest computerized technology to decrease their operational expenditure (OPEX). BHIC see this as headwind challenging. Regionally, competition coming from Chinese ship builders is intensifying because of the mass new vessels production capabilities, lower cost, and short time delivery. This defiantly give China a competitive advantage as numerous oil and gas companies tend to employ younger vessels in their daily operation to maximize profit and reduce expensive repair cost.

While Japan and South Korea shipbuilders provides fierce competition for their ability to provide their customers the latest technology. Their ability to build vessels with multi-function adds to the Japanese and South Korean competitive edge over BHIC where as some local ship operators increasingly rather to purchase new vessels from Japan and South Korea. The Cabotage Policy policy by neighboring Indonesia attempts to restrict foreign vessel from operate in Indonesian waters. This has increased tension between both countries. Additionally, Indonesia is undergoing policy formulation of 'local built' as essential component of the Cabotage program. BHIC looks at the Indonesia threat as a killer competition once the program implemented, and future orders will significantly drop and substantially affects SBSR industry in Malaysia the very existence of BHIC. Locally, numbers of companies may be considered as direct or indirect competitors to BHIC. All of which are facing same competitive issues as BHIC. Below is a list of BHIC's major competitors.

BHIC major competitors
a. Malaysia Marine and Heavy Engineering Holdings Bhd (MHB)

Malaysia Marine and Heavy Engineering Holdings Berhad (MHB), through its subsidiary Malaysia Marine and Heavy Engineering Sdn Bhd (MMHE), is a globally trusted name in quality marine and offshore solutions engineered for a wide range of ships and offshore rigs. Backed by 40 years of reliable experience and a rapidly growing track record of over 3,700 vessels, MHB has the proven expertise to recognize your every requirement and deliver safely, on time and at cost. A leading one-stop solution center for repair, refurbishment, upgrading and conversion works, MHB is known for its excellent services dedicated to hundreds of clients from over 20 countries worldwide, thanks to its highly skilled workforce and strategic technical partnerships with the industry's leading experts such as Samsung Heavy Industries for LNG cargo containment system works, and Technip for hull engineering.

b. Muhibbah Marine Engineering Sdn. Bhd. (MME)

Muhibbah Marine Engineering Sdn. Bhd. (MME), a 100% owned subsidiary of Muhibbah Engineering (M) Bhd. (A main board Public Listed Company at KLSE, Malaysia), from a humble beginning since 1996, MME operate as a shipyard with the objective to complement Port Klang as a maritime hub in West Malaysia with core businesses in ship building, ship repair, ship conversion and marine engineering fabrication. Since 2002 riding on the market boom in the oil and gas industry, MME had successfully built and delivered more than 60 OSVs (Utility vessels, Straight Supply Vessels, AHTS, Accommodation Work Boats). More than 15 of which were with DP1 and DP2 capability. MME had also delivered the first built in Malaysia a 77M Diesel Electric Propulsion Platform Supply Vessel in 2013. MME is the largest offshore support vessels builder in Malaysia now.

c. Nam Cheong Dockyard Sdn Bhd

Nam Cheong Dockyard Sdn Bhd operates as a shipbuilder of offshore support vessels. It focuses on the construction and engineering of offshore support vessels for use in the offshore oil and gas exploration and production. Its vessels include platform supply vessels, safety standby vessels, anchor handling tug supply vessels, accommodation barges, multi-purpose support vessels, and landing crafts. The company also provides vessel chartering services, such as bareboat and time charters. It offers its products and services in Singapore, Indonesia, Vietnam, China, the Netherlands, India, Tunisia, the United States, and the Middle East. The company was incorporated in 1962 and is based in Kuala Lumpur, Malaysia. Nam Cheong Dockyard Sdn Bhd operates as a subsidiary of Nam Cheong Limited.

d. Labuan Shipyard & Engineering Sdn Bhd (LSE)

Labuan Shipyard & Engineering Sdn Bhd (LSE), a subsidiary of Radimax Group Sdn Bhd and SapuraKencana Petroleum Bhd, was incorporated on 26 September 2005 and took over the facilities, operations and all business activities of Sabah Shipyard Sdn. Bhd. The yard itself has been in existence since 1972 and has built up an extensive and proven track record in oil and gas engineering and fabrication, shipbuilding, ship repair and construction of power barges. LSE is also actively involved in the refitting, modernization and scheduled maintenance of naval crafts. Tank coating services has recently been introduced and is offered to ship owners for their new or existing ships. LSE's main operations are located in the Federal Territory of Labuan, Malaysia, an idyllic duty-free island lying in the opening of the Brunei bay.

BHIC Nature of Business Activity
BHIC is a corporation with assorted business activities and interests ranging from maritime, aerospace (defense), enforcement, and energy sectors. The main BHIC business can be classified into the following segments:

    a. shipbuilding;
    b. ship repair;
    c. heavy engineering fabrication; and
    d. defence related.

As for shipbuilding business stream, BHIC enjoys top facilities with experienced manpower in shipbuilding. Among their business streams is naval and patrol vessels for Royal Malaysian Navy, commercial vessel, small ship, yatch, high speed boat including personal boat up to 120 meters in length. They also have the capability to do in-house design by using sophisticated modular technology. BHIC offers most types of shiprepair activities such as ship and engine repair, electronic/electrical test, non-metal trade as well as defense equipment's maintenance and overhaul. They also offered services such as outfitting, painting and varnishing of yatch. Amongst BHIC's customers are clients from France, New Zealand and Australia.

BHIC heavy engineering fabrication businesses supports multiple fabrication activities for oil and gas as well as civil engineering industries. BHIC defense related activities, they managed to secure contract for with the Malaysian through the Royal Malaysian Navy (RMN). Services provide range from simple maintenance of RMN fleets to high quality work including electronics and communications related activities. In order to support their maritime business activities, BHIC has three shipyards situated in:

    a. Jerejak, Penang;
    b. Lumut, Perak; and
    c. Langkawi, Kedah.

Shipyard	Services offered
Lumut Shipyard (Perak)	• build and maintenance of naval and commercial ships such as patrol vessels, yachts, tugs and offshore ships • fabrication works for container cranes and steel structures for the oil & gas • operated by Boustead Naval Shipyard Sdn. Bhd
Jerejak Shipyard	• shipbuilding, repair and servicing. Ship services

(Penang)	include anchor handling tugs, cargo ships and other commercial ships • operated by Boustead Penang Shipyard Sdn Bhd	
Langkawi Shipyard (Kedah)	• expertise in the repair of luxury yachts and has a 100-meter berthing facility • expertise for painting and blasting, mast repair, fabrication, electrical/Electronic activities • operated by Boustead Langkawi Shipyard Sdn Bhd.	

Service offered by shipyards own by BHIC

BHIC Transformation Plan

To realize the transformation plan, BHIC needs to grow their involvement in supporting activities related to the energy sector bt repositioning their commercial sector as well as capitalizing on their defense & security contracts. BHIC also need to quickly develop and improve in-house human capabilities and relations with vendors and contractors. This will assist in the realization of the planned transformation.

6.1   Growing the energy sector and repositioning the commercial sector

Energy and commercial sectors are the key components to the transformation journey, since both sectors may increase by 30% by 2020, with a Compounded Annual Growth Rate (CAGR) of 24% annually. As for the energy sector, BHIC is planning to acquire existing strategic fabrication yard across Malaysias well as building new yard for the planned expansion. By enhancing the company's networking in the industry, they will be better positioned to compete. Diversifying into integrated maintenance and operational support by becoming a total offshore service provider will further enhance their competative position. To this end, BHIC could form a joint ventures and collaborate with others in the industry.

While the commercial repositioning exercise is a key component, BHIC would consolidate their current products and services to expand customer base. BHIC understand that most customers are looking for new product such as vessel and yatch with latest technology, since customers and ship owners well aware of the fact that technologically sophisticated vessels reduce their overall operational cost. BHIC need come to the realization that this is the time to start building new generation of vessel that can compete in the marketplace. One way to achieve this is by upgrading all machineries, equipment, tools, ship yards and invest in research & development. BHIC further need to plan for re-alignment of business activities at their existing shipyards in Lumut, Pulau Jerejak and Langkawi. This would be based on the existence of major customers near by, such as naval related activities at Lumut Shipyards while commercial related maritime industry at Pulau Jerejak and Langkawi ship yards.

Transfer of technology with leading ship building companies such as Mitsubishi Heavy Industries, Hyundai Heavy Industries, China Shipbuilding Industry Corporation and Samsung Heavy Industries is a viable option to consider. Furthermore, BHIC should benefitting from their cooperation with design expert Macduff Ship Design and Marine Technology Centre of Universiti Teknologi Malaysia (MTC-UTM) to become first company in the country to design and build offshore support vessel (OSV). With the success of the cooperation that could be seen in the next few years, BHIC should capitalize on this the opportunity benefitting from their ability to locally design and build OSV themselves through patented and commercializing it in the future.

Conclusion: Strengthening defense & security sector

BHIC is one of the main companies that gained SBSR related contracts from the government of Malaysia, strengthening maritime defense and security sector. This is largely becauseof BHIC's major shareholders, which are Government Linked Company (GLC) such as Lembaga Tabung Angkatan Tentera (LTAT) and Lembaga Tabung Haji. BHIC is also the owner of the biggest ship yard in the country situated in Lumut, Perak where the major customer is Royal Malaysian Navy (RMN). Naval shipbuilding and maintenance, repair and overhaul (MRO) for defense industry highly depending on governmental budget allocation. Unlike the commercial shipbuilding industry, international trade for naval shipbuilding is very low because of the sensitivity and confidentiality of defense technologies and information.

Since the industry as a whole involves the manufacturing of products for use in aerospace, maritime, defense related equipment, therefore it provides vast opportunities in the area of technology development, skills enhancements and export. The spillover effects from these activities will accelerate the development of other supporting industries. BHIC need to cease such opportunities to increase capabilities and undertake activities in the area of maintenance, repair and overhaul, upgrades and modernization in certain areas as well as the capability to manufacture parts and components for both local and foreign markets.

| Royal Malaysian Navy | Marine Operation Force | MMEA | Marine Department of Malaysia |

By leveraging on this advantage, BHIC is focusing to secure more contracts from the Malaysian government, especially non-RMN related contracts. There are other governmental agencies that also own and operate vessels and boats for their day to day activities. Agencies such as Marine Operations Force of Royal Malaysia Police (RMP), Malaysian Maritime Enforcement Agencies (MMEA) and Marine Department of Malaysia as BHIC's new potential customers.

Conclusion

Ship building and ship repair (SBSR) industry will continue in the positive trend in Malaysia despite the slowdown of oil and gas sector globally. This is because of the support of government of Malaysia through initiatives under the Economic Transformation Program (ETP) as well as improving the regulatory framework for the industry, emphasizing on developing locally design and build of Offshore Support Vessels (OSVs). While the SBSR industry players themselves must play such big roles to embark on diversifying services and products in order to keep competitive domestically as well as regionally. They need to compete globally by securing some contract from the regional market. With the right collaboration with international players such as Mitsubishi Heavy Industries, Hyundai Heavy Industries, China

Shipbuilding Industry Corporation and Samsung Heavy Industries could proof beneficial in terms of technology transfer, global market insight and global business opportunity.

Boustead Heavy Industries Corporation Berhad (BHIC) as a well-known conglomerate in SBSR industry in Malaysia must leverages their abilities, facilities, experience as well as governmental networks to cultivate future business. With BHIC's top management is on the transformation mode, it is the right time act utilizing distinctive capabilities in design, engineering, project, contract and supply chain management, leasing & financing, business development and marketing to provide a competitive advantage to their customers. Given current global slowdown and government budget deficit, it is unlikely that BHIC reaches the planned target of RM180 millions in profit after tax (PAT) for the year 2020.

BHIC Bofors Asia

Co-author: Adlan Bin Ariffin

This case explores the market in South East Asia for BHIC Bofors Asia Sdn Bhd venturing into South East Asian market. BHIC Bofors Asia Sdn Bhd has been solely depended on Malaysian market since the day it commenced operation. This sole dependency on Malaysian market has resulted in declining profit margin and negative financial trend despite increasing revenue since overhead cost growth outpaced revenue growth. BHIC Bofors Asia Sdn Bhd needs to increase the revenue growth and reduce dependency on Malaysian market by venturing into South East Asia market. The market potential in South East Asia has been identified in Brunei, Indonesia and Thailand. The market volume and value for each of the market potential have also been determined. The global trend for naval maintenance, repair and overhaul market is increasing on annual basis. The countries that have been identified in the market potential are not excluded from this global naval maintenance, repair and overhaul trend. The global trend of increasing maintenance, repair and overhaul market is not only limited to naval but also army and air force too. The trend of increasing global maintenance, repair and overhaul is contributed mainly by the collapse of the Soviet Union and exaggerated even further by the global economic recession where countries around the world reduced their defense budgets. This caused the security forces around the world to focus their limited resources and budget on their core business, which are combat and law enforcement. The increase of global naval maintenance, repair and overhaul trend has created opportunities for BHIC Bofors Asia Sdn Bhd to increase revenue by venturing into potential market in South East Asia.

BHIC Bofors Asia Sdn Bhd is a joint venture company between BHIC Defence Technologies Sdn Bhd and BAE Systems Bofors Holdings Sdn Bhd. BHIC Defence Technologies Sdn Bhd is a holding company of Boustead Heavy Industries Corporation Bhd involved in defence. BAE Systems Bofors Holdings Sdn Bhd is a subsidiary of BAE Systems Bofors AB, Sweden.

BHIC Bofors Asia Sdn Bhd was established on April 2004 with corporate office in Kuala Lumpur and operation office in Lumut, Perak and Kota Kinabalu, Sabah.

BHIC Bofors Asia Sdn Bhd was setup to provide through life support for Bofors guns in Malaysia and Asia Pacific region, and to produce Bofors guns parts and components in Malaysia. Through life support for Bofors guns provided by BHIC Bofors Asia Sdn Bhd includes Bofors guns spare parts supply and delivery; Bofors guns maintenance, repair and overhaul, and Bofors guns trainings for operators, maintainers and instructors. BHIC Bofors Asia Sdn Bhd had solely depended on Malaysian market since commencing operation. BHIC Bofors Asia Sdn Bhd had succeeded in monopolizing the Malaysian market. There is only one competitor to BHIC Bofors Asia Sdn Bhd, which is Waris Bumi Gajah Sdn Bhd.

BHIC Bofors Asia Sdn Bhd was having steady revenue growth since commencing operation as a result from monopolizing the Malaysian market. The steady revenue growth has generated profit and growth for BHIC Bofors Asia Sdn Bhd.

However, Bofors guns through life support market for Malaysian is already exhaustive as a result of monopoly by BHIC Bofors Asia Sdn Bhd. BHIC Bofors Asia Sdn Bhd is forecasted to experience declining profit from the year 2015 onwards despite annual increment in revenue due to overhead cost growth rate exceeds revenue growth rate. BHIC Bofors Asia Sdn Bhd is forecasted to experience loss from the year 2020 onwards when overhead cost exceeds revenue. The declining profit margin trend is contributed by the shrinking of Bofors guns through life support market in Malaysia. The shrinking of Bofors guns through life support market in Malaysia in Malaysia is contributed by shrinking number of Bofors guns population in Malaysia.

The declining profit margin and the threat of loss for BHIC Bofors Asia Sdn Bhd has jeopardize the growth and sustainability of the company. In the wake of declining profit margin and the threat of loss has leave BHIC Bofors Asia Sdn Bhd with three options. The first option is to increase the revenue of BHIC Bofors Asia Sdn Bhd by exploring new market for Bofors guns through life support. The second option is retrenchment in order to reduce the overhead costs, where BHIC Bofors Asia Sdn Bhd needs to scale down the operation, reduce the number of staffs, reduce the size of the office space, and reduce the size of the workshops space. The third and final option is to close down BHIC Bofors Asia Sdn Bhd. The Board of Directors of BHIC Bofors Asia Sdn Bhd during a strategic meeting on 11th of November 2015 has selected the first option. Therefore BHIC Bofots Asia Sdn Bhd needs to increase the revenue of the company by exploring new market for Bofors guns through life support.

The closest and the most feasible market for Bofors guns through life support is in South East Asia. BHIC Bofors Asia Sdn Bhd has identified several market potential in South East Asia. The market potential in South East Asia that has been identified by BHIC Bofors Asia Sdn Bhd are Brunei, Indonesia and Thailand. The Bofors guns through life support market volume and value in the identified market potential have also been determined. BHIC Bofors Asia Sdn Bhd has solely depended on Malaysian market since commencing operation. BHIC Bofors Asia Sdn Bhd has even monopoly the Malaysian market. BHIC Bofors Asia Sdn Bhd has enjoyed steady revenue and profit growth since commencing operation. However, BHIC Bofors Asia is forecasted to experience declining profit from the year 2015 onwards due to overhead cost growth rate exceeds revenue growth rate despite steady revenue growth. BHIC Bofors Asia Sdn Bhd is forecasted to experience loss from the year 2021 onward. Figure 1.1 on the next page illustrates the negative financial trend for BHIC Bofors Asia Sdn Bhd. The decline in profit for BHIC Bofors Asia Sdn Bhd is contributed by the shrinking of Bofors guns through life support market in Malaysia. The shrinking of Bofors guns through life support market in Malaysia in Malaysia is contributed by shrinking number of Bofors guns population in Malaysia. The shrinking number of Bofors guns population in Malaysia is contributed by two factors. The first factor is when Royal Malaysian Navy decommissioned (retired) their old ships, they do not replace the decommissioned ships with brand new ships on one-to-one basis. Royal Malaysia Navy is the main customer for Bofors guns through life support in Malaysia. The second factor is when Malaysian Maritime Enforcement Agency decommissioned their old ships, they do installed Bofors guns onboard their brand new ships instead they have installed a different brand gun of a smaller calibre onboard their brand new ships.

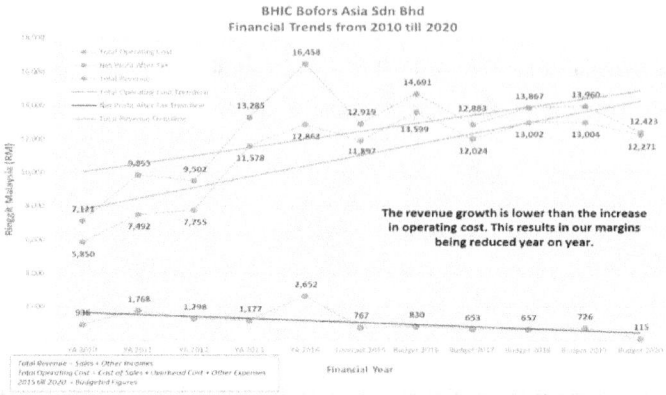

Financial Trend for BHIC Bofors Asia Sdn Bhd from 2010 until 2020

The declining profit margin and the threat of loss for BHIC Bofors Asia Sdn Bhd has jeopardize the growth and sustainability of the company. In the wake of declining profit margin and the threat of loss has leave BHIC Bofors Asia Sdn Bhd with three options. The first option is to increase the revenue of BHIC Bofors Asia Sdn Bhd by exploring new market for Bofors guns through life support. The second option is retrenchment in order to reduce the overhead costs, where BHIC Bofors Asia Sdn Bhd needs to scale down the operation, reduce the number of staffs, reduce the size of the office space, and reduce the size of the workshops space. The third and final option is to close down BHIC Bofors Asia Sdn Bhd. The Board of Directors of BHIC Bofors Asia Sdn Bhd during a strategic meeting on 11th of November 2015 has selected the first option. Therefore BHIC Bofots Asia Sdn Bhd needs to increase the revenue of the company by exploring new market for Bofors guns through life support.

The closest and the most feasible market for Bofors guns through life support is in South East Asia. BHIC Bofors Asia Sdn Bhd has identified several market potentials in South East Asia. The market potential in South East Asia that has been identified by BHIC Bofors Asia Sdn Bhd are Brunei, Indonesia and Thailand. The Bofors guns through life support market volume and value in the identified market potential have also been determined.

Company Profile

The history of establishment of BHIC Bofors Asia Sdn Bhd began when the previous Prime Minister, Tun Dr. Mahathir Mohamed and the current Prime Minister, Datuk Seri Mohd. Najib Tun Abdul Razak, who was then the Defence Minister, met with several Swedish business owners during a trip to Stockholm, Sweden in September 2003. Among the Swedish business owners was the previous President of BAE Systems Bofors AB, Mr. Magnus Ingesson. During the meeting Mr. Magnus Ingesson raised the issue of the difficulty faced by BAE Systems Bofors AB in conducting business in Malaysia. Then Tun Dr. Mahathir Mohamed suggested to Mr. Magnus Ingesson to partner with local Malaysian company to setup a joint venture company in Malaysia to provide through life support services for Bofors guns in Malaysia and Asia Pacific region, and to manufacture Bofors guns parts and components in Malaysia.

Mr. Magnus Ingesson accepted the suggestion from Dr. Mahathir Mohamed. Subsequently after the meeting, BAE Systems Bofors AB had several meetings with several companies in Malaysia before deciding to partner with Boustead Heavy Industries Corporation Bhd. The main reason why Boustead Heavy Industries Corporation Bhd was selected was due to the fact that the company was the only company in Malaysia that has a well-equipped weapon workshop. Soon after the selection of a local Malaysian partner, BAE Systems Bofors AB had several rounds of negotiation with Boustead Heavy Industries Corporation Bhd on the terms and conditions of Shareholders Agreement. Upon conclusion of the negotiations, BAE Systems Bofors AB signed a Shareholder Agreement with Boustead Heavy Industries Corporation Bhd on 14th April 2004. The Shareholders Agreement enabled a joint venture company BAE Systems Bofors AB and Boustead Heavy Industries Corporation Bhd to be established. BHIC Bofors Asia Sdn Bhd was established on 28th May 2004 with paid up capital of RM 1,000,000 and commenced operation 1st October 2004 with corporate office in Kuala Lumpur and operation offices or workshops in Lumut, Perak and Kota Kinabalu, Sabah. BHIC Bofors Asia Sdn Bhd was established to provide through life support services for Bofors guns in Malaysia and Asia Pacific region, and to manufacture Bofors guns parts and components in Malaysia.

BHIC Bofors Asia Sdn Bhd is jointly owned by BHIC Defence Technologies Sdn Bhd and BAE Systems Bofors Holdings Sdn Bhd. BHIC Defence Technologies Sdn Bhd owned fifty one percent (51%) of BHIC Bofors Asia Sdn Bhd. While the remaining forty nine percent (49%) of BHIC Bofors Asia Sdn Bhd is owned BAE Systems Bofors Holdings Sdn Bhd. BHIC Defence Technology Sdn Bhd is a holding company involved in defense industry. BHIC Defence Technologies is one hundred percent (100%) owned by Boustead Heavy Industries Corporation Bhd. Boustead Heavy Industries Corporation Bhd is a heavy industries corporation that is involved in defense maintenance, repair and overhaul; oil and gas structure fabrication, and shipbuilding and ship repair. Boustead Heavy Industries Corporation Bhd was the shipbuilder for Next Generation Patrol Vessels and Littoral Combat Ships for the Royal Malaysian Navy. Boustead Heavy Industries Corporation Bhd is listed in the Kuala Lumpur Stock Exchange. Boustead Heavy Industries Corporation Bhd is seventy percent (70%) owned by Boustead Holdings Bhd. Boustead Holdings Bhd is also a listed in the Kuala Lumpur Stock Exchange. Boustead Holdings Bhd is one the biggest conglomerate in Malaysia with businesses in finance and investment; heavy industries; manufacturing; pharmaceutical; plantation; properties, and trading. Boustead Holdings Bhd is seventy percent (70%) owned by Lembaga Tabung Angkatan Tentera. Lembaga Tabung Angkatan Tentera is the Armed Forces providence fund.

BAE Systems Bofors Holdings Sdn Bhd is one hundred percent (100%) owned by BAE Systems Bofors AB, Sweden. BAE Systems Bofors AB is the second biggest barrel weapon systems developer and manufacturer in Europe. BAE Systems Bofors AB is one hundred percent (100%) owned by BAE Systems Inc., USA. BAE Systems Inc. is the biggest land and naval weapon systems developer and manufacturer in the USA. BAE Systems Inc. is one hundred (100%) owned by BAE Systems Plc., UK. BAE Systems Plc. is the sixth biggest defence conglomerate in the world. The revenue for BAE Systems Plc. in 2014 was GBP 1.637 Billion while their operating profit was GBP 1.3 Billion. Figure 2.2 below illustrates the ownership of BHIC Bofors Asia Sdn Bhd.

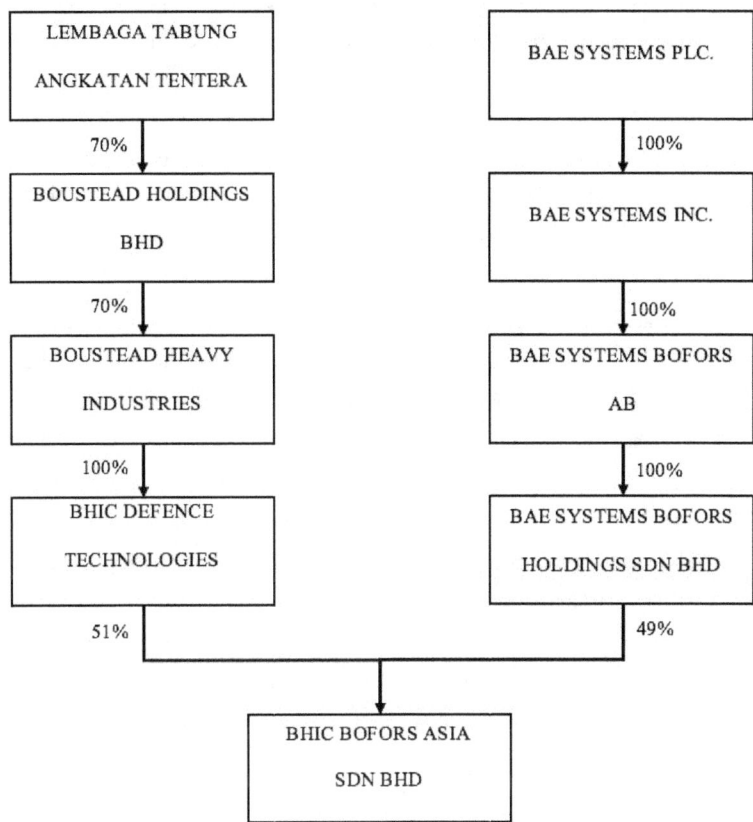

Figure 2: The Ownership of BHIC Bofors Asia Sdn Bhd

Nature of Business

The main nature of business of BHIC Bofors Asia Sdn Bhd as mandated in the Shareholders Agreement signed between the shareholders of BHIC Bofors Asia Sdn Bhd is through life support of Bofors guns in Malaysia and Asia Pacific region. Through life support services of Bofors guns provided by BHIC Bofors Asia Sdn Bhd includes but not limited to spare parts supply and delivery; maintenance, repair and overhaul; trainings for operators, maintainers and instructors, and obsolescence management services. BHIC Bofors Asia Sdn Bhd is a joint venture company between BHIC Defence Technologies Sdn Bhd and BAE Systems Bofors Holdings Sdn Bhd. BHIC Defence Technologies Sdn Bhd owns fifty one percent (51%) of BHIC Bofors Asia Sdn Bhd while BAE Systems Bofors Holdings Sdn Bhd owns forty nine percent (49%) of BHIC Bofors Asia Sdn Bhd. Both companies signed the Shareholders Agreement on 14th April 2004 to enable the setup of the joint venture company and to provide legal framework for the implementation and operation of the joint venture company. The Shareholders Agreement defines:

(a) The authority to appoint key personnel of BHIC Bofors Asia Sdn Bhd. BHIC Defence Technologies Sdn Bhd has the right to appoint the Chief Executive Officer and Business Development Manager. While BAE Systems Holdings Sdn Bhd has the authority to appoint the Deputy Chief Executive Officer, Finance Manager, Commercial Manager, ILS Manager and Quality Manager. The reason for BAE Systems Bofors Holdings Sdn Bhd has the right to appoint the Deputy Chief Executive Officer, Finance Manager, Commercial Manager, ILS Manager and Quality Manager is to ensure that BHIC Bofors Asia Sdn Bhd follows the processes and procedures of BAE Systems Bofors AB and the products and services provided by BHIC Bofors Asia Sdn Bhd met the quality standard of BAE Systems Bofors AB.

(b) The business scope of BHIC Bofors Asia Sdn Bhd, which is through life support of Bofors guns, which includes but not limited to Bofors guns spare parts supply and delivery; maintenance, repair and overhaul; trainings for operators, maintainers and instructors, and obsolescence management. The Shareholders Agreement defined the business scope of BHIC Bofors Asia Sdn Bhd in order to ensure that the company fulfilled the purpose the setup of the joint venture company.

(c) The market for BHIC Bofors Asia Sdn Bhd, which is Malaysia and Asia Pacific region. The Shareholders Agreement defined the market for BHIC Bofors Asia Sdn Bhd in order to ensure that the company does not encroached into the market for BAE Systems Bofors AB.

Mission

The mission of BHIC Bofors Asia Sdn Bhd is "BHIC Bofors Asia aspires to become the preferred partner and the centre excellence for weapon systems through life support in Malaysia and Asia Pacific region by supplying and delivery weapon systems and associated services that meet customers, statutory and regulatory requirements at competitive price and within specific time frame. We will provide healthy financial rewards for our shareholders, empowerment for our employees, values for our customers and improvement to the communities in which we operate. We will do this through our values of belonging, honour, integrity and commitment."

The mission statement of BHIC Bofors Asia Sdn Bhd consists all the nine essential components of mission statement which are customers; product or services; markets; technology; concern for survival, growth and profitability; philosophy; self-concept; concern for public image, and concerns for employees. (David, 2013). Therefore the mission statement of BHIC Bofors Asia Sdn Bhd is complete and comprehensive since the mission statement of the company consists all the nine essential components of mission statement.

Objective

The ultimate goal of BHIC Bofors Asia Sdn Bhd is to become the preferred partner and the centre of excellence for weapon systems through life support in Malaysia and Asia Pacific region. The goals for BHIC Bofors Asia Sdn Bhd are divided into short term and long term goals. Short term goals of BHIC Bofors Asia Sdn Bhd are:

(a) To increase the local content of spare parts supplied to the Government of Malaysia to seventy percent (70%) by the year 2016. The actions that have been taken to achieve this goal are identifying Bofors guns spare parts that can be sourced and produced locally; identifying local vendors that can source or produce Bofors guns spare parts locally, and cooperating with the original equipment manufacturer of Bofors guns, BAE Systems Bofors AB and local vendors to produce Bofors guns spare parts.

(b) To prime new weapon systems contract for smaller calibre weapon systems in Malaysia by 2016. The actions that have been taken to achieve this goal are identifying the manufacturers of the smaller calibre weapon systems; partnering with these manufacturers to supply the smaller calibre weapon systems to the Government of Malaysia; obtaining pricing for smaller calibre weapon systems from the manufacturers, and submitting proposals to the Government of Malaysia for the supply of smaller calibre weapon systems.

(c) To venture into Brunei, Indonesia and Thailand market by 2016. The actions that have been taken to achieve this goal are giving product and services presentation to the relevant officers in these countries; participating in the defence exhibitions in these countries; advertising in defence publications in these countries; meetings and communicating with the relevant officers in these countries, and sponsoring relevant events in these countries.

While the long terms goals of BHIC Bofors Asia Sdn Bhd are:

(a) To perform final assembly, test and commissioning of new Bofors guns supplied to the Government of Malaysia by 2020. The actions that planned or taken to achieve this goal are upgrading Lumut workshop to meet world class weapon workshop standard; purchasing of the required special tools, test equipment, jigs and fixtures, and production personnel trainings in original equipment manufacturer, BAE Systems Bofors AB factory in Karlskoga, Sweden.

(b) To manufacture parts and components for new Bofors guns supplied to the Government of Malaysia by 2020. The actions that are planned or have been taken to achieve this goal are identifying Bofors guns parts and components that can be sourced and produced locally; identifying local vendors that can source or produce Bofors guns parts and components locally, and cooperating with the original equipment manufacturer of

Bofors guns, BAE Systems Bofors AB and local vendors to produce Bofors guns parts and components.

(c) To setup a new world class weapon workshop in the new Boustead Heavy Industries Corporation Bhd integrated MRO complex in Kota Kinabalu by 2020. The actions that are planned or have been taken to achieve this goal are determining the requirements for the new Kota Kinabalu workshops, and submitting the requirements to Boustead Heavy Industries Corporation Bhd. Figure 2.3 shows the artist impression of the new Boustead Heavy Industries Corporation Bhd integrated MRO complex.

Business Model Canvas

Business canvas model is a strategic management, business and entrepreneurial tool for start-up, new, small, medium and big companies to quickly generate business model visually and to analyze the viability of the generated business model. Business canvas model enables the users to invent, illustrate, challenge and modify the business model accordingly. Business canvas model consists of customer segments, value propositions, channels, customer relationships, revenue streams, key resources, key activities, key partnerships and cost structure.

Customer Segments

The customer segment for BHIC Bofors Asia Sdn Bhd is divided according to the existing and potential market in Malaysia and other countries in South East Asia. The customers of BHIC Bofors Asia Sdn Bhd in Malaysia and other countries in South East Asia are:

(a) Brunei: Navy
(b) Indonesia: Army and Navy
(c) Malaysia: Army, Navy and Coast Guard
(d) Thailand: Army and Navy

Value Propositions

BHIC Bofors Asia Sdn Bhd provides unique selling propositions to the customers. These unique selling propositions give added value to the customers and provide competitive advantage to BHIC Bofors Asia Sdn Bhd. The unique selling propositions of BHIC Bofors Asia Sdn Bhd are:

(a) BHIC Bofors Asia Sdn Bh is a joint venture company between Boustead Heavy Industries Corporation Bhd and the original equipment manufacturer, BAE Systems Bofors AB, Sweden.

(b) The products and services provided by BHIC Bofors Asia Sdn Bhd are met the quality standards of BAE Systems Bofors AB but at local competitive price.

(c) Technical specialist from BAE Systems Bofors AB is hired by and available in BHIC Bofors Asia Sdn Bhd.

(d) BHIC Bofors Asia Sdn Bhd has signed a "Trademark License, Technical Assistance and Know How" Agreement with BAE Systems Bofors AB. This agreement enabled BHIC Bofors Asia Sdn Bhd the access to the Bofors guns technical information.

(e) BHIC Bofors Asia Sdn Bhd is capable of conducting total maintenance and total training for Bofors guns in Malaysia and other countries in South East Asia.

(f) Majority of spare parts supplied BHIC Bofors Asia Sdn Bhd to the Government of Malaysia are locally sourced and produced.

(g) BHIC Bofors Asia Sdn Bhd workshops are located within close proximity to the locations of the customers.

(h) BHIC Bofors Asia Sdn Bhd has a world class weapon workshop (operation office) located inside Lumut Naval Base, Perak.

(i) BHIC Bofors Asia Sdn Bhd provides employment for ex-servicemen who are competence in Bofors guns maintenance, repair and overhaul.

(j) BHIC Bofors Asia Sdn Bhd provides industrial placement positions for interested college and university students in the field of automation, electronic, electrical, instrumentation, mechanical and mechatronic eningeering.

Channels

Channels are the methods used by companies to deliver their value propositions to their customers. The type of channels that is being used by BHIC Bofors Asia Sdn Bhd to deliver its value propositions is direct channel since there is no intermediary in between the company and its customers in the delivery of its value propositions. Quite a number of communication channels has been available in the age of information technology. The channels that are being used by BHIC Bofors Asia Sdn Bhd in delivering its value propositions are:

(a) Membership in Malaysian Industry in Defence, Enforcement and Security association. Malaysian Industry in Defence, Enforcement and Security association provides the platform for the companies involved in defence industries to raise any issues concerning Malaysia defence industry and to provide suggestions for the improvement of the Malaysian defence industry.

(b) Participation in defence exhibitions in Malaysia and other countries in South East Asia. Participation in defence exhibitions provides the opportunity for BHIC Bofors Asia Sdn Bhd to meet up with customers from all level from all customers segments in one avenue. BHIC Bofors Asia Sdn Bhd has to date participated in defence exhibitions in Malaysia (Defence Services Asia, and Langkawi International Maritime and Aerospace), Brunei (Brunei International Defence Exhibition) and Indonesia (Indonesian Defence).

(c) Advertisement in defence publications in Malaysia and other countries in South East Asia. Advertisement in defence publications provides mass customers awareness towards BHIC Bofors Asia Sdn Bhd, and towards products and services provided by the company.

(d) Products and services presentations to the customers in Malaysia and other countries in South East Asia. Products and services presentations provides targeted audiences awareness towards BHIC Bofors Asia Sdn Bhd, and towards products and services provided by the company.

(e) Meetings with customers in Malaysia and other countries in South East Asia. Meeting with customers provides direct interactions with customers. BHIC Bofors Asia Sdn Bhd could respond to the requirements of the customers accordingly promptly.

(f) Email and telephone communications with customers in Malaysia and other countries in South East Asia. Email and telephone communications provide another form direct communication with the customers. BHIC Bofors Asia Sdn Bhd could also respond to the requirements of the customers accordingly promptly

(g) Sponsorship of events in Malaysia and other countries in South East Asia. Sponsorship of events provides advertisement for BHIC Bofors Asia Sdn Bhd and improves the public image of the company.

Customer Relationships

BHIC Bofors Asia Sdn Bhd strives to achieve and maintain excellent relationship with the customers by ensuring utmost satisfaction of the customers to the products and services provided by the company and by ensuring excellent experience of the customers when dealing with the company. BHIC Bofors Asia Sdn Bhd ensures utmost satisfaction of the customers to products and services provided by the company by meeting and exceeding quality requirements of the customers. BHIC Bofors Asia ensures excellent experience for customers by providing prompt response to requirements. BHIC Bofors Asia Sdn Bhd has set target date line for each personnel to respond to each customers requirements.

Revenue Streams

The revenue for BHIC Bofors Asia Sdn Bhd are generated from the following business activities of the company:

(a) Bofors guns spare parts supply and delivery
(b) Bofors guns maintenance, repair and overhaul
(c) Bofors guns trainings for operators, maintainers and instructors
(d) Bofors guns obsolescence management

Key Resources

The key resources of BHIC Bofors Asia Sdn Bhd are:

(a) Highly competent, knowledgeable, skilled and experienced personnel. Ten out of eighteen production personnel are ex-servicemen who were previously trained in their respective service to perform maintenance, repair and overhaul on Bofors guns. While the remaining eight of the production personnel started as apprentices for the company.

(b) Fully equipped weapon workshop within close proximity to the location of the main customers. Lumut workshop is located inside Royal Malaysian Navy Base in Lumut, Perak. While Kota Kinabalu workshop is located Kota Kinabalu Industrial Park, Sabah, which is near the Royal Malaysian Navy Base in Kota Kinabalu, Sabah. Lumut workshop has been renovated to world class weapon workshop.

(c) Technical support from BAE System Bofors. BHIC Bofors Asia Sdn Bhd has signed a "Trademark License, Technical Assistance and Know How" Agreement with BAE Systems Bofors AB. This agreement ensures technical support from BAE Systems Bofors AB to BHIC Bofors Asia Sdn.

(d) Established local vendors supplying full range of Bofors guns parts and components. Local vendors have certified and qualified by BAE Systems Bofors AB to produce Bofors guns parts and components since 2004. Local production of Bofors guns parts and components by local vendors has commenced since 2005.

(e) Fully stocked warehouse with Bofors guns spare parts. BHIC Bofors Asia Sdn Bhd has a fully stocked warehouse with Bofors guns spare parts worth approximately RM 4 Million in Lumut workshop. The warehouse was previously owned by BAE Systems Bofors AB. However the ownership of the warehouse was transferred to BHIC Bofors Asia Sdn Bhd on 2013 in order to help BHIC Bofors Asia Sdn Bhd to generate additional revenue.

(f) Fixed deposit with local banks. BHIC Bofors Asia Sdn Bhd has several fixed deposit accounts with few local banks. The total amount of the fixed deposit is RM 10 Million. The fixed deposit is allocated for capital asset investment and emergency fund.

Key Activities

The main activity of BHIC Bofors Asia Sdn Bhd is through life support of Bofors guns in Malaysia and Asia Pacific region. Through life support services of Bofors guns provided by BHIC Bofors Asia Sdn Bhd includes but not limited to the following key activities:

(a) Supply and delivery of Bofors guns spare parts

(b) Maintenance, repair and overhaul of Bofors guns

(c) Training of Bofors guns for instructors, maintainers and instructors

(d) Obsolescence management of Bofors guns

Key Partnerships

The key partnership of BHIC Bofors Asia Sdn Bhd are:

(a) Boustead Naval Shipyard Sdn Bhd provides a secured workshop space, amenities and support facilities for Lumut workshop at very competitive price. Boustead Naval Shipyard Sdn Bhd is strategically located inside Royal Malaysian Navy Base, Lumut, Perak.

(b) BAE Systems Bofors AB provides technical support for Bofors guns maintenance, repair and overhaul, and technical data packages for Bofors guns parts and components production by local vendors.

(c) Royal Malaysian Navy provides highly competence, knowledgeable, skilled and experienced workforce pool in the maintenance, repair and overhaul of Bofors guns to fulfil technical personnel vacancy in BHIC Bofors Asia Sdn Bhd.

Cost Structure

The cost structure of BHIC Bofors Asia Sdn Bhd is divided into cost of sales and overhead cost. Cost of sales is the cost associated with each sale that was made by BHIC Bofors Asia Sdn Bhd. The sales made BHIC Bofors Asia Sdn Bhd are derived from the key activities of the company. Therefore, the cost of sales are only available for Bofors guns spare parts supply and delivery; Bofors guns maintenance, repair and overhaul; Bofors guns training, and Bofors guns obsolescence management. The cost of sales Bofors guns spare parts supply and delivery only consists of cost of spare parts purchased from local vendors. The cost of sales for Bofors guns spare parts supply and delivery is approximately seventy percent (70%) of the sales.

The cost of sales for Bofors guns maintenance, repair and overhaul is only consists of labor cost or man-hours cost. The cost of sales for Bofors guns maintenance, repair and overhaul is approximately fifty five percent (55%) of the sales.

The cost of sales for Bofors guns training is consists of labour cost or man-hours cost and training material. The cost of sales for the labour or man-hours for Bofors guns training is approximately fifty five percent (55%) of the sales of labour and man-hours for Bofors guns training. While the cost of sales for training material for Bofors guns training is one hundred percent (100%) of the sales of the training material.

The cost of sales for Bofors guns obsolescence management is consists of labour cost or man-hours cost and cost of spare parts purchased from local vendors. The cost of sales for the labour or man-hours for Bofors guns obsolescence management is approximately fifty five percent (55%) of the sales of labour and man-hours for Bofors obsolescence management. While the cost of sales for spare parts purchased from local vendors for Bofors obsolescence management is seventy percent (70%) of the sales of the spare parts for Bofors guns obsolescence management.

The overhead cost of BHIC Bofors Asia Sdn Bhd are divided into variable cost and fixed cost. Variable cost are the costs associated with the cost of the personnel and directors of BHIC Bofors Asia Sdn Bhd travelling locally and abroad for official duties, and the costs associated with guns transportation from locations of the customers to the workshop of the company and vice versa. The costs that are associated with the personnel and directors of BHIC Bofors Asia Sdn Bhd travelling locally and abroad for official duties are flight tickets, taxi fares, mileage for personal vehicle, petrol for official company vehicle, hotels, lodging allowance and daily allowance. While the costs that are associated with guns transportation from the locations of the customers to the workshop of BHIC Bofors Asia Sdn Bhd and vice versa are low loader, crane and insurance for the transportation of the guns.

Products & Services

The main product and services of BHIC Bofors Asia Sdn Bhd is Bofors guns through life support services. BHIC Bofors Asia Sdn Bhd provides through life support services for Bofors guns in Malaysia and other countries in South East Asia. The through life support services for Bofors guns provided by BHIC Bofors Asia Sdn Bhd is for all types of Bofors guns in service in Malaysia and other countries in South East. The types of Bofors guns that are through life supported BHIC Bofors Asia Sdn Bhd are Bofors 40mm/L70 (Manual), 40mm/L70 (Power), 57mm/L70 Mk1, 57mm/L70 Mk2 and 57mm/L70 Mk3 guns. The through life support services for

Bofors consists of but not limited to Bofors guns spare parts supply and delivery; Bofors guns maintenance, repair and overhaul; Bofors guns training for operators, maintainers and instructors, and Bofors guns obsolescence management.

The types of Bofors guns spare parts supplied and delivered by BHIC Bofors Asia Sdn Bhd could be categorized into proprietary and non-proprietary spare parts. Proprietary spare parts are spare parts that the intellectual property belongs to BAE Systems Bofors AB, Sweden. While non-proprietary spare parts are generic spare parts that the intellectual property does not belong to BAE Systems Bofors AB, Sweden. The types of Bofors guns proprietary and non-proprietary spare parts supplied and delivered by BHIC Bofors Asia Sdn Bhd could be further categorized into electrical, electronic, hydraulic and mechanical spare parts. Figures 8.1 below shows the sample of Bofors guns electrical spare parts. Figure 8.2 below show the sample of Bofors guns hydraulic spare parts. Figure 8.3 below shows the sample of Bofors guns mechanical spare parts.

Bofors Guns Maintenance, Repair and Overhaul Services

Bofors guns maintenance, repair and overhaul services provided by BHIC Bofors Asia Sdn Bhd consist of emergency repair, defect rectification, Onboard Level Maintenance, Intermediate Level Maintenance, Depot Level Maintenance, modification and upgrade. Bofors guns Depot Level Maintenance is also known as Bofors guns overhaul. Currently, BHIC Bofors Asia Sdn Bhd only provides Bofors guns maintenance, repair and overhaul services to domestic customers, which are the Royal Malaysian Navy and Malaysian Maritime Enforcement Agency. However as part of the market development strategy, BHIC Bofors Asia Sdn Bhd will provide Bofors guns maintenance, repair and overhaul services to other countries in South East Asia such as but not limited to Brunei, Indonesia and Thailand.

Industry Analysis

Defence industry is the most lucrative industry since the dawn of civilization because mankind has been engaged in warfare since the dawn of civilization. Mankind uses weapons to protect themselves or to inflict harm on each other. Mankind has invented weapons even before mankind discovered fire even though the weapons was initially for hunting purposes but they were later used for protection or inflict harm. Countries invest in defence as a matter of insurance to ensure their safety and sovereignty.

Countries that heavily invest in their defence and have strong military postures can deter any potential external and internal act of aggression towards their countries. Defence industry is a lucrative business during period of conflicts where the demands for defence products and services are high. Countries allocate huge amount of monies for defence expenditures during conflicts. Defence industry has been a growing industry until the collapse of the United States of Soviet Russia. The countries in the world was divided into three groups of countries before to the collapse of the United States of Soviet Russia. The first group of countries is the Western Bloc countries embracing democracy and free economy, and led by United States of America. The second group of countries is the Eastern Bloc countries embracing communist socialist community and is led by United States of Soviet Russia. The group of countries is the Non-Aligned Movement countries which is also known as neutral countries and is led by several countries depending on the time period.

The existence of Western and Eastern Bloc countries has made the world was bi-polar with each side of the poles opposing each other. The world became uni-polar after the collapse of the United States of Soviet Russia. The United States of America became the only remaining super power after the collapse of the United States of Soviet Russia and there is no other countries that can oppose the United States of America. There was no longer a threat or bogey man for most countries in the world to justify their defense expenditures after the collapse of the United States of Soviet Russia. Therefore most of the countries in world has reduced their defense budget after the collapse of the United States of Soviet Russia. Figure 4.1 below shows the global defense expenditures from the year 2010 until the year 2014. Figure 4.1 illustrates the declining global defense expenditures or the negative trend of global defense expenditures.

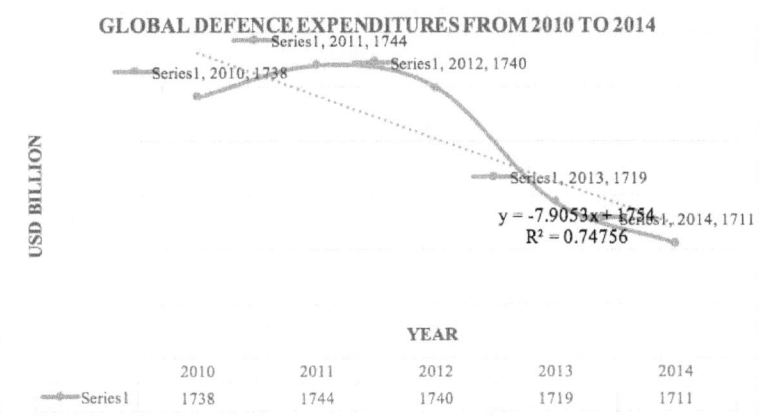

Figure 3: Global Defense Expenditures from 2010 to 2014
Source: http://www.sipri.org

The Malaysian defense industry was established in late 1960's with the establishment of the first defense company in Malaysia, Syarikat Malaysia Explosive on 12 November 1969. The company was established through joint equal equity ownership by two foreign partners namely Dynamit Nobel of Germany, Oerlikon Machine Tools of Switzerland and two local partners namely Syarikat Permodalan Kebangsaan and Syarikat Jaya Raya Sdn Bhd. Since then there have been a significant number of defense companies established in Malaysia with capabilities ranging from supply of finished military hardware, raw material and other services, maintenance and training of military hardware, production of finished military hardware or military hardware components, and research and development of indigenous military hardware. The defense industry has been identified by the Government of Malaysia as a strategic industry that is important to the sovereignty of Malaysia as a country. This is because defense industry contributes towards the self-reliance, self-sufficiency and sustainability in the defense of Malaysia by reducing the dependency towards foreign countries for military hardware and software. Defense industry has been used by the source countries of the military hardware and software to subject the importing countries to the foreign policies of the source countries. Therefore it is important for any countries to have their own defense industry in order to maintain their sovereignty. An example of an importing country that has been subjected to the foreign policies of a source country is Malaysia. During the confrontation between Malaysia and Indonesia from 1963 to 1966, Malaysia had requested to the company Bofors for replenishment of ammunition for the Carl Gustav recoilless rifles. However, Bofors was unable to fulfil the request as Swedish law prohibited any Swedish companies to export weaponries to countries that are having conflicts. Bofors inability to replenish the ammunition for these rifles that were intensively used by the Malaysian army has rendered these rifles useless. Figure 4.2 below shows the increasing Malaysian defense expenditures from the year 2010 until the year 2014.

Industry Analysis

Defence industry is the most lucrative industry since the dawn of civilization because mankind has been engaged in warfare since the dawn of civilization. Mankind uses weapons to protect themselves or to inflict harm on each other. Mankind has invented weapons even before mankind discovered fire even though the weapons was initially for hunting purposes but they were later used for protection or inflict harm. Countries invest in defense as a matter of insurance to ensure their safety and sovereignty. Countries that heavily invest in their defense and have strong military postures can deter any potential external and internal act of aggression towards their countries.

Defense industry is a lucrative business during period of conflicts where the demands for defense products and services are high. Countries allocate huge amount of monies for defense expenditures during conflicts. Defense industry has been a growing industry until the collapse of the United States of Soviet Russia. Countries in the world were divided into three groups of countries before to the collapse of the United States of Soviet Russia. The first group of countries is the Western Bloc countries embracing democracy and free economy, and led by United States of America. The second group of countries is the Eastern Bloc countries embracing communist socialist community and is led by United States of Soviet Russia. The group of countries is the Non-Aligned Movement countries, which is also known as neutral countries and is led by several countries depending on the time period.

The existence of Western and Eastern Bloc countries has made the world was bi-polar with each side of the poles opposing each other. The world became uni-polar after the collapse of the United States of Soviet Russia. The United States of America became the only remaining super power after the collapse of the United States of Soviet

Russia and there is no other countries that can oppose the United States of America. There was no longer a threat or bogey man for most countries in the world to justify their defense expenditures after the collapse of the United States of Soviet Russia. Therefore most of the countries in world has reduced their defense budget after the collapse of the United States of Soviet Russia. Figure 4.1 below shows the global defense expenditures from the year 2010 until the year 2014. Figure 4.1 illustrates the declining global defense expenditures or the negative trend of global defense expenditures.

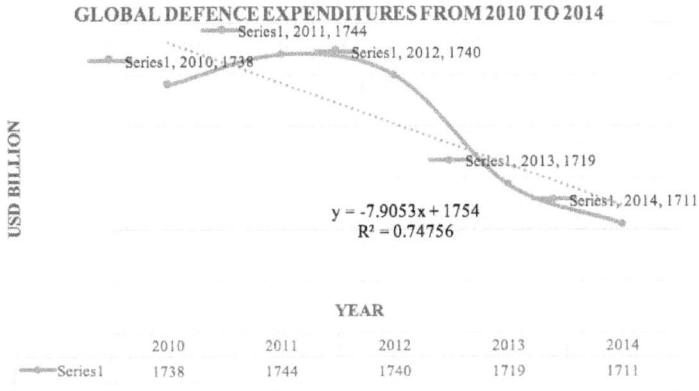

Figure 4: Global Defense Expenditures from 2010 to 2014
Source: http://www.sipri.org

The Malaysian defense industry was established in late 1960's with the establishment of the first defense company in Malaysia, Syarikat Malaysia Explosive on 12 November 1969. The company was established through joint equal equity ownership by two foreign partners namely Dynamit Nobel of Germany, Oerlikon Machine Tools of Switzerland and two local partners namely Syarikat Permodalan Kebangsaan and Syarikat Jaya Raya Sdn Bhd. Since then there have been a significant number of defense companies established in Malaysia with capabilities ranging from supply of finished military hardware, raw material and other services, maintenance and training of military hardware, production of finished military hardware or military hardware components, and research and development of indigenous military hardware. The defense industry has been identified by the Government of Malaysia as a strategic industry that is important to the sovereignty of Malaysia as a country. This is because defense industry contributes towards the self-reliance, self-sufficiency and sustainability in the defense of Malaysia by reducing the dependency towards foreign countries for military hardware and software.

Defense industry has been used by the source countries of the military hardware and software to subject the importing countries to the foreign policies of the source countries. Therefore it is important for any countries to have their own defence industry in order to maintain their sovereignty. An example of an importing country that has been subjected to the foreign policies of a source country is Malaysia. During the confrontation between Malaysia and Indonesia from 1963 to 1966, Malaysia had requested to the company Bofors for replenishment of ammunition for the Carl Gustav recoilless rifles. However, Bofors was unable to fulfil the request as Swedish law prohibited any Swedish companies to export weaponries to countries that are having conflicts. Bofors inability to replenish the ammunition for these rifles that were intensively used by the Malaysian army has rendered these rifles useless. Figure 4.2 below shows the increasing Malaysian defence expenditures from the year 2010 until the year 2014.

Opportunities

Opportunities for BHIC Bofors Asia Sdn Bhd is one of the two external factors of the company. Opportunities for BHIC Bofors Asia Sdn Bhd are the external factors that are in favour of the company. The opportunities for BHIC Bofors Asia Sdn Bhd are:

(a) High number of Bofors guns in the inventory of Malaysia and South East Asia countries. There are 315 Bofors guns in Malaysia and South East Asia countries combined. The Government of Malaysia has the highest number of Bofors guns in the inventory with 117 Bofors guns.

(b) The customers have a preference for spare parts that met the quality standard of the original equipment manufacturer, BAE Systems Bofors AB.

(c) BHIC Bofors Asia Sdn Bhd has signed the "Trademark License, Technical Assistance and Know How Agreement" with the original equipment manufacturer, BAE Systems Bofors AB. This agreement enables BHIC Bofors Asia Sdn Bhd to access technical information to perform maintenance, repair and overhaul of Bofors guns, and technical data package to produce Bofors guns spare parts. Both of the technical information and technical data package reside with the original equipment manufacturer, BAE Systems Bofors AB.

(d) The "Trademark License, Technical Assistance and Know How Agreement" that BHIC Bofors Asia Sdn Bhd signed with the original equipment manufacturer, BAE Systems Bofors AB also provides BHIC Bofors Asia Sdn Bhd with technical support from BAE Systems Bofors AB.

(e) Bofors guns technical specialist from original equipment manufacturer, BAE Systems Bofors AB specialist is available in BHIC Bofors Asia Sdn Bhd. The technical specialist provides consultation on Bofors guns maintenance, repair and overhaul services, and Bofors guns training to the production personnel of BHIC Bofors Asia Sdn Bhd and to the customers.

(f) BHIC Bofors Asia Sdn Bhd workshops are located within close proximity to the locations of the customers. This has enables BHIC Bofors Asia Sdn Bhd to provide prompt respond to the urgent requirements of the customers, and reduces the travelling cost to the locations of the customers from the locations of the company and vice versa.

(a) BHIC Bofors Asia Sdn Bhd provides employment opportunities for ex-servicemen who are highly competence, experienced, knowledgeable and skilled in Bofors guns maintenance, repair and overhaul. These ex-servicemen were highly in the maintenance, repair and overhaul of Bofors guns in their respective service.

(b) BHIC Bofors Asia Sdn Bhd provides industrial placement opportunities for students from the universities and colleges in the field of automation, electrical, electronic, instrumentation, mechanical and mechatronic engineering.

Threats

Threats for BHIC Bofors Asia Sdn Bhd is other external factors of the company. Threats for BHIC Bofors Asia Sdn Bhd are the external factors that are against the company. The threats for BHIC Bofors Asia Sdn Bhd are:

(a) Depleting market in Malaysia due to RMN is decommissioning old ships and is not replacing the decommissioned ships on one-to-one basis, and MMEA is replacing their Bofors 40mm guns with 30mm guns from another supplier as the standard gun onboard their ships.

(b) The emergence of new competitor in supplying and delivering non-genuine Bofors guns spare parts. The price of non-genuine Bofors guns spare parts supplied and delivered by these new emerged competitors are fairly low since these spare parts do not meet the quality standard of the original equipment manufacturer, BAE Systems Bofors AB and does not have warranty.

Strategic Group Map

Strategic group map is a strategic management tools that is used to map the positioning of companies that have similar business model within an industry. The number of companies in the strategic group map depended on the criteria used to group these companies together. The criteria used in the strategic group map for this business plan is Bofors guns through life support services. There is no competition for Bofors maintenance, repair and overhaul, and Bofors guns training for operators, maintainers and instructors services. The competition only exists for Bofors guns spare parts supply and delivery services.

Therefore there are only two bubbles representing two companies in the strategic group map since there is only one competitor for BHIC Bofors Asia Sdn Bhd. The first bubble is for BHIC Bofors Asia Sdn Bhd. While the second bubble is for the competitor, which is Waris Bumi Gajah Sdn Bhd. Two elements used in determining the positioning the bubbles are market share and price of Bofors guns spare parts supplied and delivered to the Government of Malaysia. Figure 4.4 below illustrates the strategic group map for BHIC Bofors Asia Sdn Bhd.

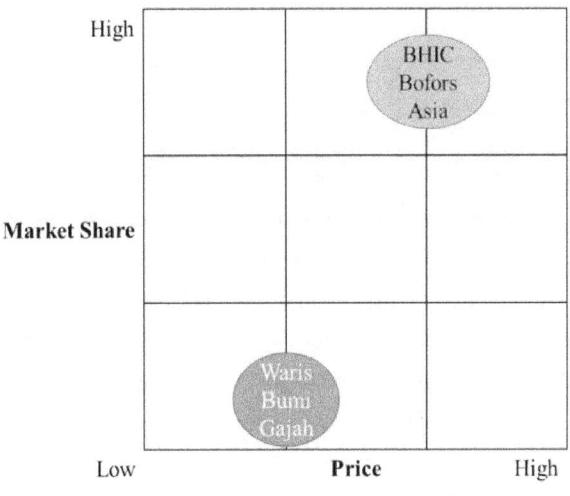

Strategic Group Map

Market analysis

There are approximately 314 Bofors guns in Malaysia and South East Asia countries consisting mostly legacy Bofors guns such as 40mm Bofi, 40mm/L70 (Manual), 40mm/L70 (Power), 57mm Mk1 and 57mm Mk 2 guns. Table 5.1 below shows the Bofors guns users and population in Malaysia and South East Asia countries.

Entity	Number of Guns					
	40mm Bofi	40mm (Manual)	40mm (Power)	57mm Mk1	57mm Mk2	57mm Mk3
Malaysian Army	23					
Malaysian Coast Guard		20	8	2		
Malaysian Navy		24	16	22	2	
Brunei Navy						4
Indonesian Army	30					
Indonesian Navy		15	30	5	8	
Thai Army	86					
Thai Navy			17	3		

Bofors Guns Users and Population in Malaysia and South East Asia Countries

The market for Bofors guns is growing. Brunei has already three Bofors 57mm Mk3 guns and has ordered another 57mm Mk3 gun for spare. Malaysia has ordered six 57mm Mk 3 guns for the LCS project. Indonesia has ordered three 57mm Mk 3 guns for their KCR 60 FAC project. Since Bofors 57mm Mk3 gun has been selected as the standard medium calibre gun for the United States Navy and the United States Coast Guard therefore most probably United States of America closest allies in South East Asia such as Singapore and Philippine will follow suit by selecting Bofors 57mm Mk3 gun as their standard medium calibre gun for their ships.

Most of the operators of the Bofors guns are now focusing their limited resources on their core business which are combat and law enforcement role. Most of these operators does not retain their competency in maintenance, repair and overhaul of Bofors guns anymore. They have opted to privatize the maintenance, repair and overhaul of their Bofors guns. This trend has created opportunities for Bofors guns maintenance, repair and overhaul services in Malaysia and Asia Pacific region.

Market Segmentation

The market segmentation for Bofors guns through life support in Malaysia and South East Asia could be segmented according to the countries: The market segmentation for Bofors guns through life support in Malaysia and South East Asia are:

(a) Malaysia: Malaysian Army, Malaysian Maritime Enforcement Agency and Royal Malaysian Navy
(b) Brunei: Royal Bruneian Navy
(c) Indonesia: Indonesian Army and Indonesian Navy
(d) Thailand: Thai Army and Royal Thai Navy

Target Market Segment Strategy

Target market segment strategy are the strategies used to penetrate the target market segment. The strategies that are used to penetrate the target market segments are:

(a) Participation in defence exhibition in target market countries. Participation in defence exhibitions provides the opportunity for BHIC Bofors Asia Sdn Bhd to meet up with customers from all level in the target market country in one avenue. BHIC Bofors Asia Sdn Bhd has to date participated in defence exhibitions in Malaysia (Defence Services Asia and LIMA), Brunei (Brunei International Defence Exhibition) and Indonesia (Indonesian Defence).

(b) Products and services presentations to the respective customers from the target market countries. Products and services presentations provide targeted audiences awareness towards BHIC Bofors Asia Sdn Bhd, and towards products and services provided by the company.

(c) Advertisement in defence publications in target market countries. Advertisement in defence publications provides mass customers awareness towards BHIC Bofors Asia Sdn Bhd, and towards products and services provided by the company.

(d) Meetings with customers from the target market countries. Meeting with customers provides direct interactions with customers. BHIC Bofors Asia Sdn Bhd could respond requirements of the customers accordingly promptly.

(e) Continuous communications through email and telephone with customers from the target market countries. Continuous communications through email and telephone communications provide another form direct communication with the customers. BHIC Bofors Asia Sdn Bhd could also respond to the requirements of the customers accordingly promptly.

(f) Sponsorship of events in the target market countries. Sponsorship of events provide advertisement for BHIC Bofors Asia Sdn Bhd and improves the public image of the company.

Market Needs

Market needs are the expectations for the products and the services from the market segments. The market needs for Bofors guns through life support are driven by the following factors:

(a) Bofors gun spare parts that are competitively price. The market expects the Bofors guns spare parts to be affordable to them.

(b) Bofors guns spare parts that met the quality standards of the original equipment manufacturer, BAE Systems Bofors AB. The market expects the Bofors guns spare parts that are sourced or produced locally to meet the quality standards of BAE Systems Bofors AB.

(c) Genuine Bofors guns spare parts. The market expects the Bofors guns spare parts to come from the original equipment manufacturer, BAE systems Bofors AB or from local vendors that are certified, qualified and appointed by BAE Systems Bofors AB.

(d) Bofors guns maintenance, repair and overhaul services that meet the quality standard of the original equipment manufacturer, BAE Systems Bofors AB.

(e) Prompt response to inquiries and requests by the customers. The market expects prompt response to each and every of their inquiries and requests.

(f) Good value proposition. The market expects the company that provides Bofors guns through life support to provide good value proposition to them.

Competitive Analysis

The original equipment manufacturer, BAE Systems Bofors AB has only one joint venture company in Malaysia and South East Asia countries, which BHIC Bofors Asia Sdn Bhd. BHIC Bofors Asia Sdn Bhd provides Bofors guns spare parts supply and delivery; Bofors guns maintenance, repair and overhaul; Bofors guns trainings to operators, maintainers and instructors and Bofors guns obsolescence management services that meet the quality standards of the original equipment manufacturer, BAE Systems Bofors AB. There is no other company in Malaysia and other countries in South East Asia that could provide Bofors guns spare parts supply and delivery; Bofors guns maintenance, repair and overhaul, and Bofors guns trainings to operators, maintainers and instructors services that meet the quality standards of BAE Systems Bofors AB.

However there is one competitor for Bofors guns spare parts supply and delivery even though there is no company in Malaysia and other countries in South East Asia that could provide Bofors guns spare parts supply and delivery services that meet the quality standards of BAE Systems Bofors AB. The sole competitor for Bofors guns spare parts supply and delivery services is Waris Bumi Gajah Sdn Bhd. The quality of Bofors guns spare parts supplied and delivered by Waris Bumi Gajah Sdn Bhd does not meet the quality standard of BAE Systems Bofors AB.

Competitive Edge

Competitive edge is the key advantages that a company has over the competitor. BHIC Bofors Asia Sdn Bhd has a competitive edge over the Waris Bumi Gajah Sdn Bhd. The competitive edge that BHIC Bofors Asia has over Waris Bumi Sdn Bhd are:

(a) BHIC Bofors Asia Sdn Bhd is a joint venture company between Boustead Heavy Industries Corporation Bhd and the original equipment manufacturer, BAE Systems Bofors AB, Sweden. Boustead Heavy Industries Corporation Bhd is a heavy industries corporation that is involved in defence maintenance, repair and overhaul; oil and gas structure fabrication, and shipbuilding and ship repair. Boustead Heavy Industries Corporation is the ship builder of the Next Generation Patrol Vessels and Littoral Combat Ships for the Royal Malaysian Navy. BAE Systems Bofors AB is the second biggest barrel weapon systems developer and manufacturer in Europe.

(b) BHIC Bofors Asia Sdn Bhd has signed the "Trademark License, Technical Assistance and Know How Agreement" with the original equipment manufacturer, BAE Systems Bofors AB. This agreement enables BHIC Bofors Asia Sdn Bhd to access technical information to perform maintenance, repair and overhaul of Bofors guns, and technical data package to produce Bofors guns spare parts. Both of the technical information and technical data package reside with the original equipment manufacturer, BAE Systems Bofors AB.

(c) The "Trademark License, Technical Assistance and Know How Agreement" that BHIC Bofors Asia Sdn Bhd signed with the original equipment manufacturer, BAE Systems Bofors AB also provides BHIC Bofors Asia Sdn Bhd with technical support from BAE Systems Bofors AB.

(d) Bofors guns technical specialist from original equipment manufacturer, BAE Systems Bofors AB specialist is available in BHIC Bofors Asia Sdn Bhd. The technical specialist provides consultation on Bofors guns maintenance, repair and overhaul, and Bofors guns training to the production personnel of BHIC Bofors Asia Sdn Bhd and to the customers.

(e) The production personnel in BHIC Bofors Asia Sdn Bhd are highly competence knowledgeable, skilled and experienced in the maintenance, repair and overhaul of Bofors guns. Fifty five percent (55%) the production personnel are ex-servicemen who were previously trained in their respective services on the maintenance, repair and overhaul of Bofors guns.

(f) BHIC Bofors Asia Sdn Bhd has a world class weapon workshop (operation office) located in Lumut, Perak. The Lumut workshop has been renovated in 2014 to become a world class weapon workshop. Lumut workshop is fully equipped to perform maintenance, repair and overhaul services for all types of Bofors guns.

(g) BHIC Bofors Asia Sdn Bhd is capable of conducting total maintenance and total training services for Bofors guns in Malaysia and other countries in South East Asia since the company has the resources and the manpower to provide total maintenance and total training for Malaysia and other countries in South East Asia.

(h) Bofors guns spare parts supplied and delivered by BHIC Bofors Asia Sdn Bhd met the quality standard of the original equipment manufacturer, BAE Systems Bofors AB. The quality of the Bofors guns spare parts supplied and delivered by BHIC Bofors Asia Sdn Bhd have been certified by BAE Systems Bofors AB.

(i) The customers demand genuine Bofors guns spare parts since genuine Bofors guns spare parts are reliable, guarantee the operations of Bofors guns and come with warranty.

(j) The customers also demand locally sourced and produced Bofors guns spare parts that meet the quality standard of the original equipment manufacturer, BAE Systems Bofors AB since the locally sourced and produced Bofors guns spare parts that meet the quality standard of BAE Systems Bofors AB are also reliable, guarantee the operations of

Bofors guns and come with warranty but cheaper than genuine Bofors guns spare parts from BAE Systems Bofors AB.

Market Share

The market for Bofors guns through life support in Malaysia has been monopolized by BHIC Bofors Asia Sdn Bhd since there is no other company that could provide Bofors spare parts supply and delivery; Bofors guns maintenance, repair and overhaul, and Bofors guns training for operators, maintainers and instructors services that meet the quality standard of the original equipment manufacturer, BAE Systems Bofors AB Sdn Bhd. BHIC Bofors Asia Sdn Bhd has been awarded contract by the Government of Malaysia to provide Bofors guns spare parts supply and delivery; Bofors guns maintenance, repair and overhaul, and Bofors guns training for operators, maintainers and instructors services for the Royal Malaysian Navy. BHIC Bofors Asia Sdn Bhd has also been awarded jobs to provide Bofors guns spare parts supply and delivery, and Bofors guns maintenance, repair and overhaul services for the Malaysian Maritime Enforcement Agency as and when required by the Malaysian Maritime Enforcement Agency.

The market for Bofors guns through life support services in other countries in South East Asia has not been penetrated by BHIC Bofors Asia Sdn Bhd yet. The market for Bofors guns spare parts supply and delivery, and Bofors guns trainings for operators, maintainers and instructors services in other countries in South East Asia is being monopolized by the original equipment manufacturer, BAE Systems Bofors AB.

Marketing Plan

The marketing plan for Bofors guns through life support services are divided into three phases, which are creating customers awareness on the products and services of BHIC Bofors Asia Sdn; developing customers base for BHIC Bofors Asia Sdn Bhd, and building customers loyalty for products and services of BHIC Bofors Asia Sdn Bhd. The marketing plans for Malaysia and other countries in South East Asia are slightly different. The marketing plan for Malaysia only involved the final phase, which is building customers loyalty. While the marketing plan for other countries in South East Asia involved all the three phases, which are creating customers awareness for products and services of BHIC Bofors Asia Sdn Bhd; developing the customers base for the company, and building customers loyalty for products and services of the company.

Sales Strategy

Sales strategies are the strategies that used by companies to sell their products and services to their target market. The sales strategies for BHIC Bofors Asia Sdn Bhd to sell its products and services to its target market in Malaysia and other countries in South East Asia are:

(a) Participation in defence exhibition in target market countries. Participation in defence exhibitions provides the opportunity for BHIC Bofors Asia Sdn Bhd to meet up with customers from all level in the target market country in one avenue. BHIC Bofors Asia Sdn Bhd has to date participated in defence exhibitions in Malaysia (Defence Services Asia and LIMA), Brunei (Brunei International Defence Exhibition) and Indonesia (Indonesian Defence).

(b) Products and services presentations to the respective customers from the target market countries. Products and services presentations provide targeted audiences awareness towards BHIC Bofors Asia Sdn Bhd, and towards products and services provided by the company.

(c) Advertisement in defence publications in target market countries. Advertisement in defence publications provides mass customers awareness towards BHIC Bofors Asia Sdn Bhd, and towards products and services provided by the company.

(d) Meetings with customers from the target market countries. Meeting with customers provides direct interactions with customers. BHIC Bofors Asia Sdn Bhd could respond requirements of the customers accordingly promptly.

(e) Continuous communications through email and telephone with customers from the target market countries. Continuous communications through email and telephone communications provide another form direct communication with the customers. BHIC Bofors Asia Sdn Bhd could also respond to the requirements of the customers accordingly promptly.

(f) Sponsorship of events in the target market countries. Sponsorship of events provide advertisement for BHIC Bofors Asia Sdn Bhd and improves the public image of the company

Sales Forecast

The sales forecast is based on provision of the Bofors guns spare parts supply and delivery; Bofors guns maintenance, repair and overhaul, and Bofors guns trainings for operators, maintainers and instructors services to Malaysia and other countries in South East Asia. The sales to other countries in South East Asia are expected to commence from the year 2016. The table below show the sales forecast for BHIC Bofors Asia Sdn Bhd. The sales forecast for Bofors guns spare parts supply and delivery services is higher than the sales forecast for Bofors guns maintenance, repair and overhaul services since Bofors guns spare parts supply and delivery services cost more than Bofors guns maintenance, repair and overhaul services. The sales is forecasted to reach the peak in the year 2020 with sales reaching RM 24 Million compared to the sales captured for year 2014 at RM 14 Million.

Customer /Project	Products and Services	Year				
		2016	2017	2018	2019	2020
Malaysian Army	Maintenance					
	Spares					
Malaysian Coast Guard	Maintenance	500,000.00	500,000.00	500,000.00		
	Spares					
Malaysian Navy	Maintenance	4,837,936.20	2,876,727.20	3,186,385.20	3,912,587.20	3,608,940.20
	Spares	8,449,000.00	7,249,000.00	8,332,000.00	8,466,000.00	7,483,000.00
Littoral Combat Ship	Maintenance		1,015,520.00	607,200.00	853,560.00	626,560.00
	Spares					
Brunei Navy	Maintenance					
	Spares	0.00	100,000.00	200,000.00	400,000.00	500,000.00
Indonesian	Maintenance					

Army	Spares	240,000.00	480,000.00	960,000.00	1,920,000.00	2,400,000.00
Indonesian Navy	Maintenance	176,000.00	264,000.00	264,000.00		
	Spares	500,000.00	750,000.00	750,000.00	500,000.00	500,000.00
Thai Army	Maintenance					
	Spares	720,000.00	1,360,000.00	2,720,000.00	5,440,000.00	6,800,000.00
Thai Navy	Maintenance					
	Spares	360,000.00	720,000.00	1,160,000.00	1,680,000.00	2,100,000.00
Total	Maintenance	5,337,936.20	4,392,247.20	4,293,585.20	4,766,147.20	4,235,500.20
	Spares	10,489,000.00	11,349,000.00	16,252,000.00	23,266,000.00	25,983,000.00
Grand Total		15,782,936.20	15,315,247.20	18,679,585.20	23,172,147.20	24,018,500.20

Table 7: The Sales Forecast for BHIC Bofors Asia Sdn Bhd

The Sales Forecast for BHIC Bofors Asia Sdn Bhd

Marketing Strategy

Marketing strategy are the strategies used by companies to market their products and services to their target market. The marketing strategy of BHIC Bofors Asia Sdn Bhd to market its products and services to its target market in Malaysia will focus on market development since the company has already monopolized the market in Malaysia. While the marketing strategy for BHIC Bofors Asia Sdn Bhd to market its products to other countries in South East Asia will focus market penetration since the company has not yet penetrated the market in other countries in South East Asia. The marketing strategy of BHIC Bofors Asia Sdn Bhd to market its products and services to its target market in Malaysia and other countries in South East Asia are:

(a) Participation in defence exhibition in target market countries. Participation in defence exhibitions provides the opportunity for BHIC Bofors Asia Sdn Bhd to meet up with customers from all level in the target market country in one avenue. BHIC Bofors Asia Sdn Bhd has to date participated in defence exhibitions in Malaysia (Defence Services Asia and LIMA), Brunei (Brunei International Defence Exhibition) and Indonesia (Indonesian Defence).

(b) Products and services presentations to the respective customers from the target market countries. Products and services presentations provide targeted audiences awareness towards BHIC Bofors Asia Sdn Bhd, and towards products and services provided by the company.

(c) Advertisement in defence publications in target market countries. Advertisement in defence publications provides mass customers awareness towards BHIC Bofors Asia Sdn Bhd, and towards products and services provided by the company.

(d) Meetings with customers from the target market countries. Meeting with customers provides direct interactions with customers. BHIC Bofors Asia Sdn Bhd could respond requirements of the customers accordingly promptly.

(e) Continuous communications through email and telephone with customers from the target market countries. Continuous communications through email and telephone communications provide another form direct communication with the customers. BHIC Bofors Asia Sdn Bhd could also respond to the requirements of the customers accordingly promptly.

(f) Sponsorship of events in the target market countries. Sponsorship of events provide advertisement for BHIC Bofors Asia Sdn Bhd and improves the public image of the company.

Marketing Mix
Products and Services
The main products and services for BHIC Bofors Asia Sdn Bhd is Bofors guns through life support services which consist of but not limited to:

(a) Bofors guns spare parts supply and delivery services
(b) Bofors guns maintenance, repair and overhaul services
(c) Bofors guns trainings for operators, maintainers and instructors services
(d) Bofors guns obsolescence management services

Price
The price structure for Bofors guns through life support services is different according to the services.

(a) Bofors Guns Spare Parts Price

The prices of Bofors guns spare parts supplied to the customers are marked up by not less than thirty percent (30%) from the cost price to ensure minimum thirty percent (30%) gross profit margin from Bofors guns spare parts sales.

(b) Bofors Guns Maintenance, Repair and Overhaul Services Price

The prices of Bofors guns maintenance and overhaul services offered to the customers are packaged prices which are inclusive food, travel and lodging. The packages prices are based on the man-hour rate RM 180 per hour times the total number of man-hours to perform each maintenance, and overhaul jobs plus food, travelling and lodging expenses for different locations in Malaysia. The man-hour rate RM

180 per hour is calculated on the basis of the overhead cost including forty five percent (45%) profit margin.

While the prices of Bofors guns repair offered to the customers are based on the man-hour rate RM 180 per hour times the total number of man-hours to perform each repair. The man-hour rate RM 180 per hour is calculated on the basis of the overhead cost including forty five percent (40%) profit margin.

(c)   Bofors Guns Trainings Services

The prices of Bofors guns trainings for operators, maintainers and instructors' services offered to the customers are packaged prices which are inclusive food, travel, lodging and training material for the trainees. The packages prices are based on the man-hour rate RM 180 per hour times the total number of man-hours to perform each training plus food, travelling and lodging expenses for different locations in Malaysia, and training material for the trainees. The man-hour rate RM 180 per hour is calculated on the basis of the overhead cost including forty five percent (45%) profit margin. The price for the training material for Bofors guns trainings is one hundred percent (100%) of the cost price of the training material. BHIC Bofors Asia Sdn Bhd does not make profit from training material.

(d)   Bofors Guns Obsolescence Management Services

The prices of Bofors guns obsolescence management services offered to the customers are packaged prices which are inclusive of food, travel, lodging and Bofors guns spare parts. The packages prices are based on the man-hour rate RM 180 per hour times the total number of man-hours to perform each obsolescence management services plus food, travelling and lodging expenses for different locations in Malaysia, and Bofors guns spare parts. The man-hour rate RM 180 per hour is calculated on the basis of the overhead cost including forty five percent (45%) profit margin. The prices of Bofors guns spare parts are marked up by not less than thirty percent (30%) from the cost price to ensure minimum thirty percent (30%) gross profit margin from Bofors guns spare parts.

Promotion

Promotion for products and services at BHIC Bofors Asia Sdn Bhd is done by the company through:

(a) Participation in defense exhibition in target market countries. Participation in defense exhibitions provides the opportunity for BHIC Bofors Asia Sdn Bhd to meet up with customers from all level in the target market country in one avenue. BHIC Bofors Asia Sdn Bhd has to date participated in defense exhibitions in Malaysia (Defense Services Asia and LIMA), Brunei (Brunei International Defence Exhibition) and Indonesia (Indonesian Defence).

(b) Products and services presentations to the respective customers from the target market countries. Products and services presentations provide targeted audiences awareness towards BHIC Bofors Asia Sdn Bhd, and towards products and services provided by the company.

(c) Advertisement in defence publications in target market countries. Advertisement in defence publications provides mass customers awareness towards BHIC Bofors Asia Sdn Bhd, and towards products and services provided by the company.

(d) Meetings with customers from the target market countries. Meeting with customers provides direct interactions with customers. BHIC Bofors Asia Sdn Bhd could respond requirements of the customers accordingly promptly.

(e) Continuous communications through email and telephone with customers from the target market countries. Continuous communications through email and telephone communications provide another form direct communication with the customers. BHIC Bofors Asia Sdn Bhd could also respond to the requirements of the customers accordingly promptly.

(f) Sponsorship of events in the target market countries. Sponsorship of events provide advertisement for BHIC Bofors Asia Sdn Bhd and improves the public image of the company.

Place

BHIC Bofors Asia Sdn Bhd is located in close proximity to the location of the customers. The corporate office is located in Kuala Lumpur which is in close proximity to Ministry of Defense and Royal Malaysian Navy headquarter in Kuala Lumpur and to Prime Ministers Department and Malaysian Maritime Enforcement Agency headquarter in Putrajaya. The operation office in Lumut is located inside the Royal Malaysian Navy Base in Lumut within close proximity to Malaysian Maritime Enforcement Agency base in Lumut. While the operation office in Kota Kinabalu is in close proximity to Royal Malaysian Navy Base in Kota Kinabalu and to Malaysian Maritime Enforcement Agency in Kota Kinabalu.

Financial analysis
Balance Sheet

	2016	2017	2018	2019	2020
Assets					
Fixed Assets					
Office Equipment	354,907	354,907	354,907	354,907	354,907
Office Equip- Accum Depr	(326,445)	(342,502)	(354,440)	(354,906)	(354,906)
Total Office Equipment	28,462	12,405	467	1	1
Machine & Special Tools	1,312,781	1,312,781	1,312,781	1,312,781	1,312,781
Machine & Special Tools Depr.	(1,206,035)	(1,226,422)	(1,246,810)	(1,266,838)	(1,286,170)
Total Machine & Special Tools	106,746	86,359	65,971	45,943	26,611

Computers & Software	271,344	271,344	271,344	271,344	271,344
Computers & Softw - Accum Depr	(235,635)	(259,160)	(270,998)	(271,343)	(271,343)
Total Computers & Software	35,709	12,184	346	1	1
Motor Vehicles	542,576	542,576	542,576	542,576	542,576
Motor Vehicles - Accum Depr	(446,920)	(525,424)	(542,293)	(542,575)	(542,575)
Total Motor Vehicles	95,656	17,152	283	1	1
Total Fixed Assets	266,573	128,100	67,067	45,946	26,614
Current Assets					
Cash & Bank	10,455,173	13,210,595	15,065,146	17,965,793	20,791,377
Receivables	4,336,548	184,500	184,500	184,500	184,500
Amt Due From Customer on Contract	3,269,209	3,269,209	3,269,209	3,269,209	3,269,209
Taxation Recoverable	451,920	492,519	665,660	1,004,030	980,891
Other Assets					
Deposits Paid	68,633	68,633	68,633	68,633	68,633
Advance to Staff	9,395	9,395	9,395	9,395	9,395
Advance to Director	12,000	12,000	12,000	12,000	12,000
Prepayments and Advance	400	400	400	400	400
Amount Due from BNS	112,233	112,233	112,233	112,233	112,233
Amt Due from BAE Sys. Bofors	77,044	77,044	77,044	77,044	77,044
Amount due from BPSSB	26,213	26,213	26,213	26,213	26,213
Retention Sum for BG-BNS	147,135	147,135	147,135	147,135	147,135
Amt Due from Staff - Rishi	28,701	28,701	28,701	28,701	28,701
Total Other Assets	481,754	481,754	481,754	481,754	481,754
Total Current Assets	18,994,604	17,638,576	19,666,269	22,905,286	25,707,731
Total Assets	19,261,178	17,766,676	19,733,336	22,951,232	25,734,345
Liabilities					
Long-Term Liabilities					
H/P Creditor-M/Benz WYH2272	34,737	8,888	-	-	-
H/P Creditor - Hilux AJF4907	18,760	2,708	-	-	-
H/P Creditor - Hilux SAB5646M	20,272	2,908	-	-	-

Total Long-Term Liabilities	73,768	14,504	-	-	-
Current Liabilities Hire Purcase Creditors					
H/P Creditor-M/Benz WYH2272	(0)	0	-	-	-
H/P Creditor - Hilux AJF4907	0	(0)	-	-	-
H/P Creditor - Hilux SAB5646M	(0)	0	-	-	-
Total Hire Purcase Creditors	(0)	0	-	-	-
Payables	2,976,122	240,546	240,547	240,547	240,547
Provision for Taxation	357,214	397,813	570,954	909,324	886,185
Provision for Director Fee		-	-	-	-
Provision for Bonus	23,336	23,336	23,336	23,336	23,336
Accruals & Other Payable	31,212	31,212	31,212	31,212	31,212
Accrual - Cost of Sales	750,000	750,000	750,000	750,000	750,000
Amt. Due to BPng.Shipyard	2,958	2,958	2,958	2,958	2,958
Total Current Liabilities	4,140,842	1,445,865	1,619,007	1,957,377	1,934,238
Total Liabilities	4,214,610	1,460,369	1,619,007	1,957,377	1,934,238
Net Assets	15,046,567	16,306,307	18,114,329	20,993,855	23,800,107
Equity					
Paid-Up Capital	1,000,000	1,000,000	1,000,000	1,000,000	1,000,000
Retained Earnings	12,915,390	14,046,567	15,306,307	17,114,329	19,993,856
Current Year Earnings	1,131,177	1,259,740	1,808,022	2,879,526	2,806,252
Total Equity	15,046,567	16,306,307	18,114,329	20,993,856	23,800,107

Balance Sheet of BHIC Bofors Asia Sdn Bhd

Ratio Analysis

Ratio analysis is an analysis of the information in the financial statements. Ratio analysis provides an insight into the financial health and business performance of a company. Table 8.5 below shows the ratio analysis of BHIC Bofors Asia Sdn Bhd forecasted from the year 2016 until the year 2020.

	2016	2017	2018	2019	2020
Balance Sheet					

Assets					
Fixed Assets:					
Office Equipment	28,462	12,405	467	1	1
Machine & Special Tools	106,746	86,359	65,971	45,943	26,611
Computers & Software	35,709	12,184	346	1	1
Motor Vehicles	95,656	17,152	283	1	1
Total Fixed Assets	266,573	128,100	67,067	45,946	26,614
Current Assets:					
Cash & Bank	10,455,173	13,210,595	15,065,146	17,965,793	20,791,377
Receivables	4,336,548	184,500	184,500	184,500	184,500
Other Assets	481,754	481,754	481,754	481,754	481,754
Amt Due From Customer on Contract	3,269,209	3,269,209	3,269,209	3,269,209	3,269,209
Taxation Recoverable	451,920	492,519	665,660	1,004,030	980,891
Total Current Assets	18,994,604	17,638,576	19,666,269	22,905,286	25,707,731
Total Assets	**19,261,178**	**17,766,676**	**19,733,336**	**22,951,232**	**25,734,345**
Liabilities					
Long-Term Liabilities	73,768	14,504	-	(0)	-
Current Liabilities:					
Hire Purcase Creditors	(0)	0	-	(0)	-
Payables	2,976,122	240,546	240,547	240,547	240,547
Provision for Taxation	357,214	397,813	570,954	909,324	886,185
Provision for Bonus	23,336	23,336	23,336	23,336	23,336
Accruals & Other Payable	31,212	31,212	31,212	31,212	31,212
Accrual - Cost of Sales	750,000	750,000	750,000	750,000	750,000
Amt. Due to BPng.Shipyard	2,958	2,958	2,958	2,958	2,958
Total Current Liabilities	4,140,842	1,445,865	1,619,007	1,957,377	1,934,238
Total Liabilities	**4,214,610**	**1,460,369**	**1,619,007**	**1,957,377**	**1,934,238**
Net Assets	**15,046,567**	**16,306,307**	**18,114,329**	**20,993,856**	**23,800,107**
Equity					

Paid-Up Capital	1,000,000	1,000,000	1,000,000	1,000,000	1,000,000
Retained Earnings	12,915,390	14,046,567	15,306,307	17,114,329	19,993,856
Current Year Earnings	1,131,177	1,259,740	1,808,022	2,879,526	2,806,252
Total Equity	**15,046,567**	**16,306,307**	**18,114,329**	**20,993,856**	**23,800,107**
Income Statement					
Revenue	15,782,936	15,315,247	18,679,585	23,172,147	24,018,500
Cost of Sales	10,263,165	9,507,124	12,102,838	15,082,191	15,880,467
Gross Profit	5,519,771	5,808,123	6,576,747	8,089,956	8,138,033
Total Operating Expenses	4,260,362	4,379,552	4,426,752	4,530,087	4,650,578
Operating Profit	1,259,410	1,428,571	2,149,994	3,559,869	3,487,455
Total Other Income	228,982	228,982	228,982	228,982	204,982
Profit Before Tax	**1,488,391**	**1,657,553**	**2,378,976**	**3,788,850**	**3,692,437**
Total Corporate Tax	357,214	397,813	570,954	909,324	886,185
Net Profit / (Loss) After Tax	**1,131,177**	**1,259,740**	**1,808,022**	**2,879,526**	**2,806,252**
Liquidity Ratio					
Current Ratio	4.59	12.20	12.15	11.70	13.29
Cash Ratio	2.52	9.14	9.31	9.18	10.75
Operating Efficiency Ratio					
Operating income return on investment					
Total asset turnover	0.82	0.86	0.95	1.01	0.93
Fixed Assets turnover	59.21	119.56	278.52	504.33	902.46
Leverage Ratio					
Debt to assets ratio	0.22	0.08	0.08	0.09	0.08
Debt-equity ratio	0.28	0.09	0.09	0.09	0.08
Equity multiper	1.28	1.09	1.09	1.09	1.08
Profitability Ratio					
Operating profit margin	0.08	0.09	0.12	0.15	0.15
Profit margin	0.35	0.38	0.35	0.35	0.34
Return on assets	0.06	0.07	0.09	0.13	0.11
Return in equity	0.08	0.08	0.10	0.14	0.12

Table 10: Ratio Analysis of BHIC Bofors Asia Sdn Bhd

Ratio Summary

a) Liquidity ratio

Current ratio also known as working capital ratio which measures the ability of a company to pay its current obligations using current assets or ability of a company to meet its short term debt obligations. From the above table, it shows that the current ratio of our company is increasing from 2016 until 2018 and decreasing in 2019 and increasing again in 2020 which are 4.59, 12.20, 12.15, 11.70 and 13.29 each year.

Cash ratio is a liquidity ratio that measures a company ability to pay off its current liabilities with only cash and cash equivalents. The cash ratio is more restrictive than current ratio because no other assets can be used to pay off current debt. From the above table, it shows that the cash ratio is increasing from 2016 until 2018 and decreasing in 2019 and increasing again in 2020 which are 2.52, 9.14, 9.31, 9.18 and 10.75. A higher cash ratio means that the company is more liquid and can more easily fund its debt.

b) Operating efficiency ratio

Total assets turnover ratio is used to measure how efficiency of the company in using their assets to generate sales. From the above table, it shows that the total assets turnover ratio is increasing from 2016 until 2019 and decreasing in 2020 which are 0.82, 0.86, 0.95, 1.01 and 0.93. The higher the ratio, the better it is as it implies the company able to generate more revenues from assets.

c) Leverage ratio

The debt to assets ratio is used to measure the extent of the company's leverage. It also used to measure the percentage of debt used to finance assets. The higher of this ratio, the more leveraged the company and the greater its financial risk. From the above table, it shows that the debt to assets ratio of our company is decreasing from 2016 until 2018 and increase in 2019 and decrease back in 2020, which are 0.22, 0.08, 0.08, 0.09 and 0.08.

Debt to equity ratio is used to measure the company's financial leverage calculated by dividing its total liabilities by stockholders' equity. The company used this ratio to indicate what proportion of equity and debt being used to finance their assets. From the above table, it shows that the debt to equity ratio of our company is decreasing from 2016 until 2018 and increase in 2019 and decrease back in 2020, which are 0.28, 0.08, 0.08, 0.09 and 0.08.

d) Profitability ratio

Operating profit margin ratio used to measure the efficiency of the company in controlling the costs and expenses with company operations. The higher the ratio, the efficiency it is to control its costs and expenses. From the above table, it shows that our operating profit margin is increasing from 2016 until 2020 which are 0.08, 0.09, 0.12, 0.15 and 0.15. Thus, it means that our company is efficiency to control our costs and expenses to generate profit.

Profit margin ratio is used to measure how much of sales actually keep in earnings. A higher profit margin indicates a more profitable company that has better control over it costs.

Return on assets ratio is used to measure how profitable a company is relative to its total assets. It gives an idea to how efficient management is at using its assets to generate earnings. Therefore, the higher of the ratio, the efficiency it is to generate the income. From the above table, it shows that our return on assets is increasing from 2016 until 2019 and decreasing in 2020, which are 0.06, 0.07, 0.09, 0.13 and 0.11.

Return in equity ratio is used to measure a company's profitability by revealing how much profit a company generates with the money shareholders has invested. This measure is very important to shareholder, which they will know how much they are able to earn in the company. From the above table, it shows that our return in equity ratio is increasing from 2016 until 2019 and decreasing in 2020, which are 0.08, 0.08, 0.10, 0.14 and 0.12.

APM Automotive Holdings

Company Background

APM Automotive Holdings Berhad is one of the largest auto parts manufacturing company in Malaysia. Its main business operation involves in manufactures and sales of automotive parts and accessories. The manufacturing history begins in 1970 with the anticipation of rapid industrialization in Malaysia particular in the automotive industry with the advent of the national car project. Its first manufacturing facility was built in Pandamaran Industrial Estate, to produce leaf spring parts. After a successful venture, the company had started to produce other automotive parts such as shock absorbers, seats, air conditions and many more.

Currently its manufacturing facility operates from number of location and under four divisions. Four Division as below namely i) Suspension Division for leaf springs, parabolic springs, coil springs, shock absorbers and metal parts; ii) Interior & Plastics Division for plastics parts, interiors, seating for motor vehicles, buses, auditoriums and cinemas; iii) Electrical & Heat Exchange Division for air-conditioning systems, radiators, starter motors and other electrical parts; and Marketing Division for export parts. All this four division manufacturing facility is located in Port Klang, Bukit Beruntung and Tg Malim.

Business model

The manufacturing facilities of this division are concentrated mainly in Bukit Beruntung area of Selangor, closely located nearby to its main OEM customers. Auto Parts Manufacturers Co Sdn Bhd main core business model is to produce and supply original component and complete car seat to OEM customers. Commencing in 1985 in Port Klang before shifting-up to Bukit Beruntung in 2006 as part of its strategic plan to further expand on its customer portfolio. Paid up capital reported is RM60 million and with a built up area of 30,00m2. Current production capacity is 18,000 vehicle seats per month with its total employee of 450pax.

Product Offering

Seats act as one of the most important parts of a vehicle. A car seating system provides postural support for people when driving. In APM, they produces the full line of components that go into automotive seats. A complete automotive car seat basically consists of few main parts, namely

- Complete Front Seat Driver Side
- Complete Front Seat Passenger Side
- Complete Rear Seat Cushion
- Complete Rear Seat Back

Moreover, APM also produces sub-parts as per the chart below. Parts were either proceed for final assembly internally or delivered to its supplier for next assembly process.

- Mechanism Parts- Seat Recliner
- Trim Cover
- Seat Frame

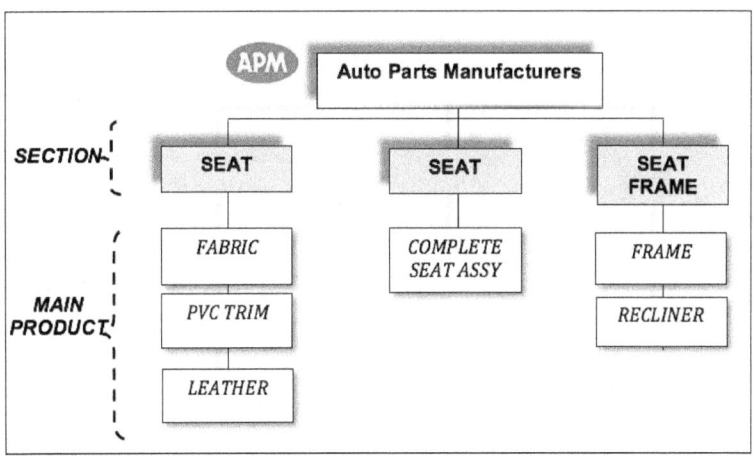

APM Seat Division Products

Business Partner

175

Automotive parts are known as either Original Equipment (OE), or aftermarket parts. Original equipment parts are used in the assembly of a new automotive automobile, light truck, or truck. Parts that are purchased by the manufacturer for its service network and defined as Original Equipment Service (OES) parts. Aftermarket parts are divided into two categories: replacement parts and accessories. Replacement parts are automotive parts was need remanufactured to replace OE parts as they become worn or damaged.

Suppliers of OE parts are broken into three levels.

TIER	DESCRIPTION
TIER 1	Suppliers who sell finished components directly to the vehicle manufacturer.
TIER 2	Suppliers who sell parts and materials for the finished components to the Tier 1 suppliers.
TIER 3	Suppliers who supply raw materials to any of the above suppliers or directly to vehicle assemblers.

Category of Supplier Level

APM as tier 1 and tier 2 supplier, 80% of its parts cater for OEM customer while the balance 10% caters to its aftermarket sales.

TIER	CUSTOMER	Model	PRODUCT
TIER 1	Tan Chong Motor Assembly	Nissan Teana Various Pick UP Truck	Complete Seat Assembly
	Perusahaan Otomobil Nasional Berhad - PROTON	Proton Iriz	Complete Seat Assembly
	TC Subaru	Subaru XV	Complete Seat Assembly
	Isuzu Hicom	Truck 729	Complete Seat Assembly
	Mazda Malaysia	Mazda 3 Mazda CX5	Complete Seat Assembly

	Inokom Corporation	Hyundai Elantra Hyundai Santafe	Complete Seat Assembly
TIER 2	Fuji Seat Malaysia Sdn Bhd	Perodua Myvi Perodua Alza	Complete Trim Cover Complete Mechanism Slide
	APM Tachi S Seating System Sdn Bhd	Nissan Almera Nissan Livina	Complete Trim Cover
	APM Seating Sdn Bhd	Isuzu Vietnam Corp	Complete Trim Cover Complete Mechanism Slide

APM Seat Division customer and its model supply

The Making Process of Complete Car Seats at APM

A good automotive seating system plays an important role not only in providing comfort and convenience to passengers, but also concern on its safety fixtures. Throughout the years, one can actually notice how innovation had influenced the selection of material type to produce and fix a complete seat seating system. More functional and comfortable design has phase in using more convenient and environment friendly material to produce mechanism and structure that can be fix into a vehicle seating system. In order to produce parts to assemble complete seats for both front and rear side, a bill of material of at least 50 parts required. Parts are either manufactured or source from local or overseas suppliers depend on customers model base. In APM, parts are produced at different section before all the required parts will be send for final seat assembly process.

A car seat main components part can be listed into 5 types main categories.

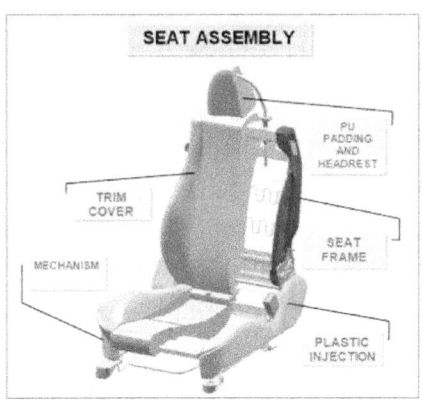

Front Seat Main Component Structure

Competitive Environment

It's important to address the internal and external strategic factors related to business operation, as identified in SWOT analysis. As one of the largest auto part manufacturing company in Malaysia, APM effectively addresses such factors. SWOT analysis provides insights into possible influencing factors and solutions to its current business operation.

Strenghts
Financial Background

APM Holdings have a strong financial performance. Its business continues to growth both in revenue and profitability. As per reported in 2014 Annual Report, the group had recorded revenue of RM1228 million pre tax, for the financial year ended 31 December 2014. Profit were reported at RM111 million slight lesser than year 2013 at RM141 million. Basic earnings per share at 0.53 sent, was reported in the same period. As part of major OEM automotive parts supplier, a strong financial is essential to the company itself. New products are normally developed alongside with OEM customer at the R&D stage and this will need to spend a lot of money and time.

Production Concept-Full Product Range

APM is taking an important role in its manufacturing process of automotive seat to provide maximum level of comfort to passengers. The company prides itself on its ability to have full range of parts production start from raw material till the end result of a complete automotive car seat. With its combining advanced engineering and manufacturing expertise, it aims to offer vehicle manufacturers seating components of high level quality and value. A wide range capability of parts produced by APM as its offered its OEM customer a one stop centre of parts sourcing and with a better quality control. In APM, a segmentation production process was implemented. Each production section was been assigned to produced different type of product before all complete parts will be delivered to end process which all the parts will be assemble into a complete car seats. Below figure explain four main sections and its core main core product. Sub assemblies parts like frame, recliner, trim cover, padding will be send to seat assembly area whereas final process of seat assembly begin.

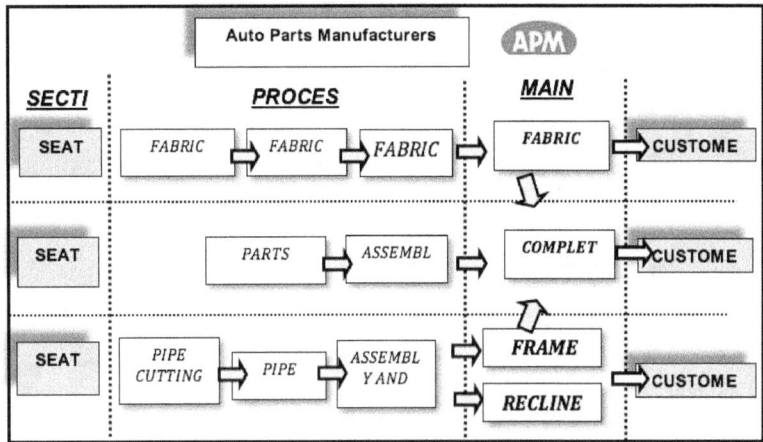

APM Seats Division Process Flow

Distribution Network
As been widely practiced in Malaysia car automotive industry, they required their part supplier to supply parts by using Just In Time (JIT) Supply System. In this system, carmakers only accept inventory as needed. In APM's case, a seat must be delivered as per variant sequencing and has to arrive to customer at the right station and at the right time. Being close to customers is one of the benefit for APM to implement a JIT supply system. The manufacturing plant will build according to base on JIT sequencing and ship out to end user without delays. Realizing such benefit, in 2010 APM Automotive started its plan to relocate its manufacturing facility close to main suppliers. Approximately RM80m on capital expenditure had been spent on this plan. Among those moved are the seat and plastic division facilities which have been shifted up to Bukit Beruntung area, from the port city of Port Klang as part of centralization process of parts supply close to OEM customer such as Perodua, Tan Chong Motor Assemblies and Proton Tg Malim. Moreover, a new facility of seat assembly-line was setup in Tg Malim area as part of seat assembly expansion project. This is possible because APM had secured a new contract to supply seats for Proton's

new model "Iriz". Hence, relocation to Tg Malim area was essential in cost cutting, speed of delivery and operational control.

Quality as Highest Priority

In order to remain competitive in the automotive parts supply market, APM treat quality as priority. APM is certified under International Quality Management System ISO TS16949. Its quality management system provides for continual improvement, emphasizing defect prevention and the reduction of variation and waste in the supply chain. A set of procedure has been set as guidelines for internal processes and product quality control. External and internal audit has been carried out regularly to ensure all procedures comply with quality requirements. Additionally, APM had invested in testing equipment and facility to ensure its product meet standard requirement criteria set by its OEM customer. Among testing available are:

- Hip-point Measurement,
- Seat and Seat Belt Anchorage Test
- Seat Back Reclining Endurance
- Cushion Endurance Machine

With a good quality reputation and control, APM has the opportunity venture out into larger markets in attempt to gain foot hold and play a role in the wider global automotive industry.

Strong Focus on Design and Research Development

APM seats are designed to incorporate and integrate the complex areas of concentration: safety, comfort, ergonomics and styling. Based on years of experience, APM management realized that design, research and development plays an important role in developing new products. Moving in that direction, a restructuring had been carried out for research and design teams at APM. Hence, APM Engineering and Research Sdn Bhd had been established few years ago. Located close by, the facility provides various R&D services and testing programs to APM Holdings for four main divisions. The latest completed research and design by APMER team is the model Proton "Iriz", which is currently in mass production phase and under supply to main carmaker in Malaysia, Proton. Stages of comprehensive work and strong effort focus on designing seats that comply with automotive Asean NCAP standards and safety features.

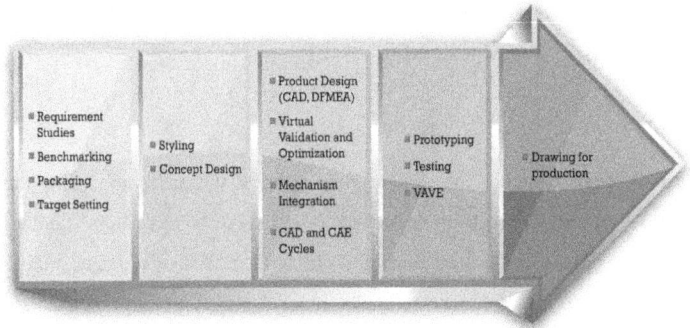

Engineering and Research Facility

Weakness
APM Sales Depend on Domestic Automotive Industry Trend

APM known as first tier and second tier supplier of OEM with estimated 85% of automotive parts sales cater for Original Equipments (OE) products and the remaining 15% is for repair and modification (aftermarket). As an OEM manufacturer, supply depends on market trends, car sales volume, and sales performance. Sales performance depends on domestic automotive industry trend. When vehicle production goes down, automotive parts production and sales follow as well. Based on the APM Group 2014 Annual Report, the Interior and Plastic Division remained the largest divisions, contributing 53% of the Group's total gross revenue and 62% of Group profit before tax in 2014. The Division posted RM848.6 million in revenue from RM988.1 million a year ago. Profit before tax fell 30% from RM128.9 million to RM89.8 million.

A drop in sales performance may be attributed to the automotive market sector trends and overall performance. In early 2013, APM had secured a contract from Proton to supply Proton Iriz model car seats. Budget infrastructure plan had been schedule in and supply expects to commence by January 2014. Marketing department had eventually budgeted in sales volume to start by early 2014 based on initial Proton launching plan. However, Proton itself had delayed its production plans, which eventually sees the model kicking off in the 3rd quarter of 2014. Approximate delay of 6 months from the initial target. Other event also caused APM sales performance to drop, reflecting automotive market performance. For instance, MAA 2014 report shows that Nissan sales were badly affected and this subsequently affected APM as Tan Chong constitutes 40% APM total sales.

Limited Pricing Power

At today business environment, suppliers for various OEM industries are facing the same challenges. Suppliers have been pressured to follow OEM customers standard parts selling pricing strategy. Suppliers unable to utilize the power of efficient pricing mechanisms to optimize their returns. Details breakdown of pricing mechanism required to be approved by customer. All Tier 3 suppliers had been also appointed by customer itself whereas pricing already determined. Tier 1 supplier like APM eventfully no any bargain powers and pricing opportunity.

Due to competitive market itself, domestic automotive customer are reducing price to attract customer to boost up their sales. This eventually makes automakers put pressure on seeking price concessions and tasking their suppliers to take on more research, design and manufacturing responsibilities, and by absorbing the higher costs for their inputs

Opportunities

Collaboration with Joint Ventures and Technical Partners

APM has the advantages to venture into foreign model assembly locally based on technical partner credibility. Such collaboration will act as a platform to supply into OEM customer especially technical partners supply base connection in their home country. APM Joint-Ventures profile PT Armada Johnson Controls and PT APM Armada Auto parts in Indonesia as well as IAC APM Automotive Systems Limited of Thailand. Their major products include Automotive Seats, Interior Automotive Components, Consoles, Door Trims, Instrument Panels, IP Pads and Soft Trims. In APM- Seat Division an agreement has been signed with an foreign technical partners A strong and good relationship with foreign technical partners will enable both parties to leverage on each other's knowledge and collective experiences to harness their know-how in design, development, manufacture and assembly of car seat.

Growth opportunity due to its facility expansion

APM had a strong position to supply parts and component to overseas market due to its various operation setup in outside Malaysia. It will bring more chances for APM to expand its customer base. As per reported in APM Annual Report 2014, currently they have manufacturing capabilities in 3 countries namely, Vietnam, Indonesia and Australia and have established good working relationship with local OEM customers and to a wider suppliers' network. Besides that, manufacturing facilities are currently being built in Thailand while the manufacturing plant in Indonesia will be operational by end 2015. APM Financial Report 2014 highlight, APM operations outside Malaysia contribute RM74.5 million an increase of 89% from RM39.5 million recorded in 2013. Revenue and profitability continue grow and it shows that acceptance of our products by the overseas market. These activities are in line with the strategic transformation and growth process of the Group in its progress to be a regional automotive manufacturer

Threats
Intense Competition:

Malaysian automotive industry is full of challenges. As an OEM automotive part supplier, they face numerous challenges not only locally, but global challenges as well. As a car seat maker, APM is facing challenges to secure new and innovative model project. The latest model Proton Iriz, is the only new model awarded by OEM carmaker Proton to APM after more than 8 years of waiting. In Malaysia alone there is quite number of international locally base assemblers that has the capability to assemble car seats. There are too many players in the marketplace aiming for the small pie. Once a particular assembler is being selected, there is unlikely any changes for supply till the end of model lifetime. This means that every assembler should grab the next business opportunity once a new car model is announced.

APM further faces challenges from competing international seat makers. Although they assemble locally, foreign car manufacturers like Toyota, Honda, Nissan and Subaru, have a large number of suppliers to choose from. Parts are similar due to its global design base. Selection choice is subject to product quality, features, the amount of time required for innovation and development, pricing, reliability, safety, and other financing terms. Increased competition may lead to pressure of price downwards for automotive parts market. A company might eventually face financial and operational problems as a result of price driven competition, caused by the desire to secure new contract.

A New Product Line Introduction

Leather Trim Cover Strategy

In the dynamic automotive business environment, changes are occurring with a faster pace than ever; creating both opportunities and challenges for manufacturers. APM realize that in order to remain competitive, they must be flexible to change and offer a wider range of product to its OEM customer. As part of internal expansion plan program, APM Seat Division in 2015 has introduced a new product line to their existing product range.

The leather seat project was drafted and kicked off by the end of 2014. A team of process development engineer lead by the senior manager was tasked to plan out the development of new product line. A details schedule with new line setup targeted completion within ten months and pin pointing the right plant layout, machinery purchase, manpower, training, raw material sourcing, and various processes. The main advantage to APM to venture into the new product line is their long experiences in the sewing line. Hence, setting up a leather line is complementary and familiar territory. Their production capacity is thirty car sets daily. Internal marketing team aggressively promoted the new product line to OEM customer. During the annual ALAMI Proton Open Day carnival, APM took the opportunity to invite Proton and other suppliers to exhibit their new leather seat product line. This event was an ideal platform to show case new capabilities to various OEM manufacturers.

A new and dedicated sewing line was setup to sew and produce leather trim cover to fulfill the high market demand for leather type car seat by OEM customer. There was a growing concern by APM when initially decided to expand into trim cover product line, largely because of the slowdown in automotive sales worldwide during the end of 2015 and 2016. A new expansion means that a high capital investment must be allocated to resources in facilities, equipments and labor forces requirements.

However, the primary motive for the new line expansion was to fulfill the increasing demand for leather seat type by OEM car manufacturers. Car manufacturers product marketing strategy in part was to offer wider range of choices to its customers to improve sales and increase available options. The change in consumer preferences for leather type seats is evolutionary in nature, as consumers tend to demand more variety of options and higher luxury car interior. Owning a full leather car seat was associated to luxury and improving brand image. Historically, APM seat trim division only produced fabric type trim covers. However, market sales of leather type seats are only about 20% year on year. During this period, leather trim covers were outsourced from other suppliers and later assembled with APM's own components. Latest trends shows that only about 60% of APM seat orders by OEM customers are leather type and while 40% are fabric type car seats. APM currently supplies models such as "TC Subaru MF1" model, which is full leather type seat variant and TCMA model for Nissan "Teana" leather type seat, which collectively mounts to 80% of total orders. With the new sewing leather trim line under their belt, it is expected that the new line is capable of meeting current demand for leather type trim cover. APM will no be longer required to outsource leather jobs from other supplier, and this in turn will eventually reduce handling cost and improve quality control. As of today, the leather seat product line is running at full capacity.

Conclusion

Automotive operations of OEM's is becoming increasingly complex. APM is continually attempting to strengthen their position in the global automotive marketplace, capitalizing on their competitive advantages. A gradual transformation of operations and improving product design through R&D will pay off in the long run. Expanding into countries will also help during economic downturns. More effort is needed by APM to establish brand excellence to be broadly acknowledged as a leader in their market. APM also need to meet customer's expectation and mediate future challenges as far as innovation and product development, while intensifying training and skill upgrading programs.

VADS

Company background

VADS Berhad was incorporated on 29 November 1990 as a joint venture between IBM Global Network Services and Telekom Malaysia Berhad (TM) which earlier managed network services, contact centre services and system integration services as main core business, providing new value-added product for the development of ICT and telecommunication industry in Malaysia. The company started its fully operation by following next year. Other than TM Berhad and IBM, this company was received investment from Permodalan Nasional Berhad (PNB) on 1993 and The Employees Provident Funds on 1995.

On 22nd September 2008, TM Berhad had decided with makes VADS Berhad become wholly TM's subsidiary as long period plan for enhance position and profit. Thus, TM Berhad could maintain as top leading in telecommunication and ICT sector. It was because VADS Berhad could provide a verity of services in telecommunication and ICT value- added business as new alternative income source for TM group. Besides that, TM officially has withdrawn from cellular telecommunication market after its subsidiaries; Celcom and TM International Berhad had been demerger and combined as new business entity known as Axiata Group. By that, TM Berhad could stay focused his core business in fixed line and internet broadband provider but own a subsidiary which could provide the value-added product for their customer covered all clients such as government, multi national companies (MNC), government agencies, government linked companies (GLC) and Small Medium Enterprise (SME). VADS Berhad brings together people, technologies and methods to enable more effective and dynamic use of information technology and communication. Team personal comes from diverse backgrounds and cultures, collaboratively presenting the right mix of skills and experience to drive VADS' operations from research to architecture development, solutions and project management. The team is committed to empowering businesses by offering its expertise to deliver value-based innovative solutions and services, enabling customers to focus on their core business.

VADS Berhad was the only and first TM subsidiary that listed on the Second Board of Kuala Lumpur Stock Exchange (KLSE) on 7th August 2007 and transferred to the main board of Bursa Securities on 10 March 2005. Although VADS Berhad focused on local market, they enters Indonesia market hen establish PT VADS with core services lie in Contact Centre Solutions, Customer Service Learning Centre, Human Capital Management and Data Centre Co-location. Two operations centers opens, namely Puri VADS, Jakarta and Puri VADS, Yogyakarta. PT VADS is constantly looking at ways to grow via sustained performance and excellent service delivery. Both together, VADS and PT VADS are expanding their reach across the region by providing services across the borders where they can lend their expertise to new emerging markets.

After more than twenty years, VADS Berhad is now in track as the Malaysia's leading Integrated Managed Information and Communications Technology (ICT)/Business Process Outsourcing (BPO) service provider in local market with over 7,000 employees, manage around 80 million customer interactions and revenue in year 2012 was total USD 262 Million (RM805 million).
VADS Berhad announced financial statement for year 2014 totaled RM 921.9 million in revenue, with BPO contributing RM327.8 million, ICT bringing in RM364.9 million, PT VADS contributing RM64.1 million and RM165.0 million coming from Managed GSP and others.

For the year 2015, they obtained multi awards from various organization such as Top 100 Global Outsourcing Service Provider from International Association of Outsourcing Professionals® (IAOP®), Data Centre Service Provider of the Year 2015, from Frost & Sullivan Malaysia and Contact Centre World Awards, APAC Region from Contact Centre World. Currently, VADS Berhad has two main core businesses; integrated IT services and Integrated BPO services.

Integrated ICT Services provides quite diverse technologies that can be offers where their commitment to accurately assess clients real business needs with focus on 'efficient' as a culture and 'effective' as a result. Data Centre & Cloud Services are the services where VADS is the largest data centre provider in the region with the capabilities to meet the most demanding business operations. VADS DC was backed by a robust network infrastructure with unlimited data transfer. Thus offer unparalleled availability and redundancy at the highest level of security. They have eleven data centers including two international data center located near Kowloon, Hong Kong and Los Angeles, U.S.A. VADS cloud services offers the full suite of Public, Private and Hybrid Cloud services, which are specially designed to manages for businesses of all sizes, across all sectors, be it large enterprises, government or SMEs. The managed could services offerings that include Infrastructure as a Service (IaaS), Platform as a Service (PaaS) and Software as a Service (SaaS).

Communication and Collaboration has several services such as VADS Managed TelePresence Services (MTP) is a power tool comes from combination of collaboration and communication. This technology in High Definition video conferencing enables face-to-face collaboration in real-time, accurate image size and spatial audio effects over a TPX Access. VADS MTP provides new real virtual presence on accurate time, client can conduct the meeting around the world without leaving office, saving time and travelling costs but able empowering the business with accelerate decision making and strengthen rapport with your business stakeholders. Furthermore, VADS-TPX is a new way of service for client conduct business interactions whether it's a private intra-company discussion or a global inter-company conference. VADS-TPX is the first TelePresence exchange in Malaysia, and is connected to other TelePresence exchanges worldwide. It is a national hub that provides a borderless reach enabling you to have powerful communications and collaborations in a highly secured environment.

VADS Managed Unified Communications Services (MUC) is a comprehensive and scalable IP communications system with integrates voice, video, data, and mobility to form as effective collaboration tool for client to effectively communicate within the organization, with business partners and customers. VADS Managed Unified Communications services give the power to choose the best communications solution for your business needs such as IP Telephony, Integrated Conferencing Services (Audio, Video, Web Conferencing), Mobility and Collaborative Business Solutions (Contact Centre Solutions, Enterprise Social Network Solutions, Digital Media Solution). All service offerings includes benefits such as improvement in business dealings, increase in efficiency and convenient, minimize travel costs, investment and go green technology. Managed Security Services (MSS) offers four different services such as; VADS Cloud Based Web Security, which is an advanced protection from malicious attacks and emerging threats. It provides organizations with the most advanced Internet protection such as URL filtering, Anti-Virus & Anti-Spyware scanning for HTTP traffic, and it's solely hosted in the cloud.

VADS Managed Unified Threat Management (MUTM) functions as networks protection and remove all types of security threats such as viruses, hackers, spyware, Trojan horses, worms and blended attacks. VADS Managed SecureWAN secured client HQ and branches against all types of security threats such as viruses, hackers, spyware, Trojan horses, worms and blended attacks up to your branch level. On the other hand, VADS Managed Web Application Firewall (MWAF) protects websites and web applications from attackers leveraging on protocol or application vulnerabilities such as SQL injection, cross-site scripting, cookie tampering and directory traversal attacks, that potential instigate data theft, denial of service, or defacement of an organization's web site. All services are 24 hours 7 days a week for dedicated security monitoring centre at VADS Security Operation Centre (VSOC) and achieved United Kingdom Accreditation Service (UKAS) for ISO/IEC27001: 2005. End User Computing Services Offering called VADS Managed Desktop and Managed Service Desk (MSD). VADS Managed Desktop offers a comprehensive solution for desktops, printers, and office-software applications; with complete support operations for ensure fulfillment of any desktop lifecycle needs. Managed Service Desk (MSD) is basically the enterprise IT service management solution. Its integrated applications are designed for hosted implementation, with best practice workflows that help organizations support their infrastructure, drive competitive advantage in their core businesses, which cover ITSM processes in compliance with industry best practices.

The newly appointed CEO, Massimo Migliuolo was on quest to determine VADS Berhad business value. Since he holds more than 20 years field experience in technology, such as telecommunications and ICT, and over the years he cultivated a deep interest in mobility and more recently on Internet of Things. VADS Berhad is similar to other companies, such as; Cisco, AT&T and Lucent Technologies. At Cisco, Massimo decided to make his primary goal to accelerate revenue growth through transformational and sustainable business models focusing on the needs of vertical market and industries including smart cities when he was appointed as vice president of the Go to Market (GTM) strategy and segments group for the emerging markets theater. He also designed AT&T business model, through better understanding of market and technology trends, and how to create and deliver valuable services to end users. Given his previous work experience with VADS Berhad and TM Berhad, Massimo knew his company's core technological competency, which can take development and business activities into new stage. However, situation in the Malaysia market is different from other countries. Malaysia is a middle-high income country but not developed enough to produce its own technology. It depends highly on technology transfer from other high-income countries. The Malaysia economy traditionally focuses on material imports to fulfill local industrial demand. That is partially why Malaysia is unable to develop its own technology. Furthermore, Malaysia lacks behind its neighboring country Singapore, in terms of product base technology.

This complicates the situation to VADS Berhad and its CEO. VADS Berhad offers various technologies to assist entities or businesses to achieving their goals. The problem stems from clients. Some of the clients are comfortable using the old or existing technologies such as physical storage, emails, single phone calls and documentation management in paper method then storing them manually into computer. Small Medium Enterprise (SME) sector clients are reluctant to use new technology, even if it has been proven to increase business efficiency flow. Additionally, the service sector such as Oil and Gas, financial, heath care, and others, were found not to be interested in new ICT technology investments. This is either because of budgeter constrains or dissatisfaction with constant changes in the world of ICT. Massimo and management attempting to use same business model as that of Cisco, but need more research and new business outlook to fit it into the Malaysia market. Massimo is well aware that technology adoption is highly governed in Malaysia by the business culture of Malaysian, which is not fast on adopting new methods. Hence, persuading Malaysian market of new approach is time consuming and frustrating not only to Massimo, but also to many global companies doing business in Malaysia.

VADS has innovative products and new market segments to serve, however, they need to develop and manage ICT and BPO services by positioning themselves as a partner. VADS is confident to provide solutions that bring growth to clients. Additionally, they can increase business efficiency with minimum operational cost.

VADS management came to the realization that Malaysians are not ready and unable to adopt quickly to new Information Communication Technology (ICT) and business process development. At this point, they are revising their business model just to keeps the firm afloat in local market. Although VADS was industry pioneer in Business Processing Outsource (BPO) twenty years ago till today, yet like all evolving industries, changes, expansion and new local and foreign companies participates and competing in the market for the same clients. The company is highly affected by the realities of the Malaysian culture and business environment, which is influenced by connections and slow adaptation.

Business Processing Outsource And ICT Shared Management in Malaysia

According to Performance Management And Delivery Unit (Pemandu, 2014 report) BPO and ICT service management sector is a business service element, which falls under the Business Services Team NKEA (National Key Economics Area). The government is targeting Gross Net Income for business processing outsourcing industry about RM 6,863.8 millions and to provide 43,330 jobs by 2020. The Malaysian government has introduced new sub-business sector called Knowledge Processing Outsourcing (KPO) to make services more diversifies and attractive to foreign investor. Revenues in 2014 were RM 2.02 Billion and surpassed the expectation value of RM1.83 Billions. The high revenues of 2014 were attributed to higher exports of value-added services, joint ventures and partnerships with international outsourcing players in attempt to take Malaysia to the next phase.

Moreover, the positive impact on Malaysia's BPO industry was the creation of 13,953 jobs, compared with targeted 13,836 jobs. Despite that achievement, the government has assigned two entities; Multimedia Development Company (MDeC) and Outsourcing Malaysia (OM) for reviewing EPP in BPO industry sectors to find alternatives to maintain the strength of industry's competitive advantage. This achievement, caused industry players to agreed on few initiatives such as focusing on transformational programs aimed increasing scale, improving business value, enhancing SSO ecosystems and strengthening market access for targeted sectors (NKEA Business Services Report 2014).

Data Centre Service In Malaysia

Data Centre (DC) services in Malaysia have shown significant increase in recorded revenues of 2014 and 2015. Local DC service in Malaysia achieved revenues of RM795 million (NKEA analysis). This represents a growth of near 101 per cent more than the targeted KPI. Malaysian DC industry has continued to experience 40% growth for the past three years, which is 16% growth ahead of the rest of Asia Pacific regions. Such results, makes Malaysia the preferred destination for DC investments and increase the supply of internationally certified DC space. To continue such momentum in DC markets, Malaysian Data Centre Alliance (MDCA) was established as a professional body to sustain alliance, provides a collective voice for the industry, ensures all member abide by the set regulation and reduce risks poised to the industry. MDCA also serve as a platform for members and to ensure best practices, training, industry trends and technical changes, and acts as the Malaysian voice in the forward development of data centers. MDCA is a special unit under Outsourcing Malaysia (OM), which is a chapter of PIKOM.

MDCA facilitates many Business-to-Business relationship and industry development workshops. In 2014, MDCA successful hosted the South-East Asia Data Centre and Cloud Congress in Iskandar region of Southern Malaysia. In November of the same year, MDCA held its inaugural Data Centre Conference as well. Both events were essential for providing industry insight, networking opportunities and platforms for greater national and regional exposure. MDCA also attempts to standardize service delivery by signing a memorandum of understanding for exchange of industry practices, and organizing joint marketing promotion events with Japan Data Centre Council. Additionally, Data Centre Organizational Certification (DCOC) agreed to recognize six data centers to receive international certifications in energy management, data security and service management to enhance local DCs competitiveness. Programs are in place to offer international certifications include the Uptime Institute Tier III Design Certification, LEED certification and ISO 27001: Information security management system.

MDEC still involved in the development in network infrastructures by launching Inter Data Centre Network (IDCN), which was operational since 2015. The idea for MDeC is to serve as project manager by leasing dark fiber to participating DCs in Cyberjaya area in the suburbs of Kuala Lumpur, to improve connectivity and resilience. Plans also involves the expansion of international submarine cable systems network to improve on design capacity, increase speed by 141 terabytes per second, which is expected to finish by 2016. This project will cater to Malaysia's rapidly increasing bandwidth demands, especially demand by the commercial sector.

The Malaysia DC market experienced more competition after numerous countries started to participate by partnering and investing with local industries. For example, Senior International Representative (SIR) program under MDeC, tends to attracts Japanese firms to Malaysia partly because of the special attention given to the Japanese market. This have resulted in Malaysian–Japanese acquisitions and joint ventures. The "Freenet Business Solutions" and "Powerware Systems" by Hitachi Sunway is an example of that cooperation.

Integrated Business Process Outsourcing
The following services are examples of integrated business process outsourcing. Customer Experience Management (CEM) helps businesses deliver value through interactions and better communication to attract and engage users and clients in meaningful and effective customer service, technical support, helpdesk and CC Lite. Revenue generation services on the other hand provides clients with an extended virtual sales team with business clients by allowing clients to immediately connect customers interests in a higher level by engagement with targeted products and services. Such services include telemarketing, telesales, inbound sales and virtual account management. Business Analytics & Insights (BAI) services assists businesses to predict, manage and reduce risk in a cost-effective and customer-centric approach. Services include business insights, dashboard reporting and social media analytics. Contact Centre Facilities (CCF) offers facility management service and disaster recovery contact centre enabling businesses facing challenges in contact centers, by providing world-class facilities and state-of-the-art technologies. Business excellence consultancy and training functions are designed to assist organization clients to

develop their workforce by delivering training modules, training services, and talent development programs based on a Lean Six Sigma approach.

VADS Business Values

VADS Berhad has five core business values in place to reflect their relevance to the marketplace. The core values are also designed to maintain customer loyalty and trust regarding provided service. These are:
- Customer focus (dedicated to your business).
- Innovation (reach out to the future).
- Professionalism (world of experience).
- Friendliness (help is always at hand).
- Reliablity (peace of mind).

New Product & Service

VADS CC Lite, is designed specifically to fulfill the needs of small and medium companies that are facing resource challenges. Quality customer service is not exclusive to large enterprises. All businesses, need to have that competitive edge and this can be gained through quality customer service. For instance, clients are able to call VADS customer service directly to discuss any issue they face.

Nusa Jaya Data Centre Project

VADS Bhd. is investing RM130 million to build its a multi-phased, purpose-build data centre in Nusajaya Tech Park, as part of VADS strategy to fulfill the growing demand for business data services in the region. Located near the southern state of Johor Bahru, a new gateway for VADS to expand capability in southern Malaysia Peninsula, and attempting to expand service to clients in neighboring Singapore. VADS can compete with Singaporeans on cost bases. The first phase of the data centre would comprise of a built-up area of 30,000 square feet on a 3.213-acres piece of land. The second phase will be based on market requirements. The first phase is expected to be completed by 2017. VADS Data Centre, which is a carrier neutral data centre, will additionally house Telekom Malaysia (TM) *Iskandar international gateway*, which is to serve as a regional hub in providing end-to-end managed Information Communication Technology (ICT) services. The plan is to provide cloud-services via digital marketplace and high-speed broadband connectivity to its Malaysian and ASEAN customers.

Competitors: Symphony (MSC) Berhad

Symphony Group is one of the main competitor to VADS, especially in business processing outsources industry. The company was recognized as one of Asia's leading business process outsourcing (BPO) market leaders, and is considered as the partner of choice for more than 3,000 organizations and firms ranging from government agencies to private and public-listed companies. Most clients are recognized or listed in Fortune 500, Global 500 and large conglomerates across the Asia Pacific region. Symphony (MSC) Berhad is among Malaysia's 100 Global Off-shore Companies. A status awarded only to Symphony for three consecutive years in the Global Services 100 list (an annual study recognizing excellence among global service providers published by Global Services/neoIT). Symphony (MSC) Berhad is a subsidiary of Symphony House Berhad, The mother company was successfully listed on the MESDAQ Market of Bursa Securities Exchange (then known as the Kuala Lumpur Stock Exchange) in 2003. Two years later, Symphony House was ranked the 5th in the Corporate Governance Survey (2007) carried out by the Minority Shareholder Watchdog Group (MSWG) in collaboration with Nottingham University Business School. Other branches of symphony operate in foreign markets like Osaka, Japan and Bangalore. India's Symphony core business is in BPO sector delivering contact management, human resource, financial, corporate secretarial, share issuance registration and cheque processing solutions. Symphony House Bhd was acquired by Aegis, one of the world's largest business services providers, for an estimated US$6.6 million. This was the largest BPO MOU deal ever reported in Malaysia.

Scicom Sdn. Bhd

Scicom is a global CRM consulting, technology services, education and outsourcing company. With domain experience, and comprehensive capabilities across most industries and business functions. Scicom partners with clients to help them focus on customers to optimize businesses performance, both in the public and private sectors. They operate out of 3 sites around the world, namely Kuala Lumpur, Tampa and Bangalore, India. Scicom CRM and consulting is built on the principle of understanding customers and proactively addressing each of customer's individual requirements. They create in-house applications as well as exclusively licensed products to deliver mass customization. This is the ideal model for Scicom to offer clients superior customer service and maintain competitiveness. Customer data is modulated into intelligence. And that intelligence can be leveraged to increase market base, retain existing customers, improve customer experience and grow the business value of each customer. Scicom CRM and consulting services is built around three main service offerings; business analytics, loyalty programs, and E-commerce. Services offered are aligned with their capacity and business objectives. They no longer outsource only processes. The development and improvement in their talent pool has become a critical factor in meeting regional and global consumer needs. The Technology Solutions Division has fixed Scicom's core business in Business Process Outsourcing. This division focuses on three key areas, namely technology consulting, technology systems & solutions, and infrastructure.

Industry Outlook

The Malaysian business process outsourcing and IT shared management sector needs to adopt to the rising challenges. Adaptability will lead to enhancing their competitive advantages and staying relevant to global competitors. Most local Malaysian companies still offering technologically outdated services. This in turn, makes offered products and services to be less appealing and relevant to customers need. Malaysia is in need to offer high-value services if they plan to remain in business and ultimately compete in the global marketplace. An example of high-value services offering is moving from basic call-centre functions to analytics. Malaysian companies are also encouraged to be on alert and ready for changing nature of competitive landscape in the future in the eve of the Transatlantic Trade and Investment Partnership (TTIP). Being involved in a number of areas in the global outsourcing business, Malaysia needs to adapt to become more specialized, by identifying strong niches and subsectors to serve of the global market. Malaysian industries are also obliged to invest in enhancing existing human capital. HCD for instance does not see such investments as a priority because of the associated costs, which prevent them from reaping future benefits. The data centre industry in Malaysia faces growing competition in the DC space. Firms are struggling to maintain regional competitiveness. The federal government heavily subsidizes numerous Malaysian firms with links to the government, and that's how they manage to support operational costs and remain in business. Dealing with alternative broadband and power issues is essential. Raising powers tariffs is no longer a viable strategy and threatens service prices for Malaysians, where dedicated server hosting bandwidth can be as much as 57 times more expensive than Singapore. That is one reason why current charges were offered at commercial rates, which is way higher than industrial rates given to manufacturing companies.

Formation of Data Centre Task Force comprising MIDA, MDeC and PEMANDU has increase inter-agency collaboration which is critical because of failure of large-scale investments where potential investors requires wide range of inputs and expertise from multiple owners and stakeholders as part of their site selection process. Such failures could lead to loss of badly needed future investments. Attract more international cloud players into Malaysia, is needed to fill the gap in the country's digital content and services ecosystem. To be able to attract more Internet hosting and cloud content, bandwidth and capacity has to dramatically increase. This will require far greater and urgently needed. Only then Malaysia will be able to increase its attractiveness for regional traffic and achieve economies of scale in international connectivity.

Conclusion

VADS Berhad need to reassess their market position and expand their market based on core competencies rather than generic products. As existing local clients are not ready to switch to newer technology, which is an Asian phenomenon in general because of cost preferences. VADS needs to educate the local market and persuade switching to their products based on cost benefit analysis. When users can see and feel the benefits, they are more likely to make the shift. Additionally, Malaysia's BPO and ICT *Shared Service Management* is still in the expansion phase. Given that VADS has a variety of innovative product, the pressure on them is higher to gain market share and bring new customers onboard. Malaysian corporate and individual consumers are risk avers by nature, and not willing to charter in an unfamiliar territories. This is reflective in the level of technological advancement and innovation. VADS is a very representative case study that illustrates some of the issues an average Malaysian company face and the way they react to existing technological and market forces.

Question
1. What's is the nature of the problems facing VADS?
2. Describe your understand of VADS operations, and how they can progress from their current position?
3. How can BPO services help the SME sector to improve their revenue streams?

Asia Assistance Network

Introduction

This case deals with the implementations of *Wellness Program* by Asia Assistance Network (AA). The four client involved in this case are classified as; Employer A, Employer B, Employer C and Employer D for client privacy protection. Third-party health insurance basically consists of usual health insurance policies that cover the owner and employees of small-business. Third-party health insurance is what an insurance company pays the actual provider of healthcare services for services rendered to employees. This is commonly known as third-party health insurance. There is an alternative way where third-party insurance is self-funded, whereby a given company covers employees' medical cost directly with the help of an administrator. Third-party insurance is widely known for its versatility and comprehensiveness and as a viable option of health insurance.

Types of Third-Party Health Insurance

Third-party health insurance offers public and private health insurance programs that includes managed care and preferred provider networks. Looking at the Malaysian public health insurance programs, one quickly realizes that it is open only to the disadvantaged, aged, and government workers. Third party insurance however, covers private health care insurers, benefiting ultimately all policy holders. Private healthcare providers agree to participate with the managed care and preferred provider networks by getting into an agreement where they would be paid for the services rendered. Healthcare coverage issued by such networks is typically cheaper than regular private third-party health insurance.

However in Malaysia, the aged and disadvantaged has the privilege to receive medical treatment for as low as RM1 (about 25 cents US) in government hospitals. Basically it is companies or agencies that often provide the privilege of receiving treatments in the private sector based on purchased policies by the insurer as in the example of Allianz Life Insurance, Great Eastern Insurance, Takaful Insurance and so on. The leading substitute to third-party health insurance is direct health care coverage or self-insurance. This is where the employer undertakes to pay healthcare providers directly for any expenses incurred without involving any party. This tends not to be convenient for most small businesses. However, for larger companies with large staff and employee base, where employers provide direct coverage, prices are usually negotiated to be reduced based on large number of patients. Self-funded employers usually find it to be more feasible to set aside trust with funds allocated to cover employees medical expenses.

Advantages of Third-Party Health Insurance

In most cases, third party health insurance shifts the burden of payment to the insurance company. Certain policyholders however are required to pay a co-payment, while others are required to pay a certain portion of the bills. Others may choose to bear some routine healthcare services such as drug prescription or second opinion visits. Some policyholders that have to pay their own cost until yearly deductible amounts are met. Based on the type of policy insurance companies might have to pay in order to cover up to the balance limit.

Obtaining Third-Party Health Insurance

The standard procedure for small-business owners who wish to obtain third-party health insurance is to get it directly from insurance companies, or by joining purchasing groups. Purchasing groups regularly offer participating employer or partner to choose between a numbers of insurance policies with variable benefits. Small businesses are typically able to enter into an agreement with only one insurance provider where employers may pay the entire premium for their employees or partially move the burden to the health insurer.

Medical Card Third Party Liability & Coordination of Benefits

It is very common for a given medical card to have one or more additional healthcare coverage for services under different policies. Third Party Liability (TPL) refers to the legal commitment by third parties (e.g. certain individuals, entities, insurers or programs) to pay partially if not the entire expenditure of medical assistance furnished under a medical card. Lawfully, all other available third-party entities must meet their legal obligation by pay claims before the medical card programs pays for care received by an individual, based on member's eligibility.

Coordination of Benefits

Coordination of benefits is actually classified as the activities involved in deciding benefits to be received by card holder, where the enrolee is covered through an individual, insurance, entity or program that is entitled to pay for health care services. Individuals who are entitled for medical card, may enjoy the benefits with payment being made by third party to medical agencies. Examples of third parties which may be subjected to be paid for its services are;

- Group health plans
- Self-insured plans
- Managed care organizations
- Pharmacy benefit managers
- Medicare
- Court-ordered health coverage
- Settlements from a liability insurer
- Workers' compensation
- Long-term care insurance
- Other state or Federal coverage programs (unless specifically excluded by law)

Introduction to Asia Assistance Network

Asia Assistance Network Sdn. Bhd (Asia Assistance) is located at Petaling Jaya business hub of Malaysia. Incorporated in 1998, Asia Assistance rose as Malaysia's leading assistance service provider/third party administrator. In 2005, Asia Assistance stretched its operating services regionally with the incorporation of AA International Inc. At the moment, they have 10 branches located throughout Asia-Pacific Region and Europe; with local offices and 24/7 call centers in Malaysia, Thailand, Indonesia, Philippines, Singapore, Hong Kong, Korea, Taiwan, Australia & Germany.

For the past few years, Asia Assistance (i.e. AA International Inc. collectively known as "AA") has gained a global reputation for excellence in delivering optimum combination of cost control and quality service. The company provides a 24 hours in house call services to a large array of companies and organizations from nationally prominent to internationally renowned brand names. AA covers insurance, financial services, automotive, pharmaceutical, health providers, government and public sectors, aviation, schools and higher education. Each of AA's offices runs its own 24 hours call centre with local language support. AA's team of professionals are trained to handle medical, logistical and technical aspects of minor and major emergencies with the efficiency and compassion that such events require. AA stood out amongst the rest as Asia's most diversified assistance company with diversified services catering to the needs of varying clients.

AA's which was attached to International Assistance Group (IAG) has a global presence. AA is the sole partner and shareholder of IAG. Currently, IAG is known as a global network of independent assistance companies specialising in facilitating worldwide assistance services. IAG was formed in 1992, has gathered independent yet like-minded companies whose rationale is to grow global, strategic assistance solution. The group consists of 61 member companies throughout the world, merging shared global values with a comprehensive knowledge of local cultures. The company maximizes its benefits of flexibility and responsiveness with other strength such as sharing agent networks, negotiating purchasing power, exchanging knowledge and expertise and setting global best practice. Asia Assistance has several other services in addition to providing medical healthcare insurance services.

Air Ambulance

AA operates three of its own fleet of air ambulances under the brand name *AeroMed Asia*, with a Hawker 400 and Hawker 800 based in Kaohsiun, Taiwan and a Hawker 400 based in Singapore. The air ambulance offers 24 hours both emergency and non-emergency medical transport services in all region of Asia. The clients and customers receive utmost care and precise services combining the aptitude, medical air crews and ground management team. They are committed in providing cost effective service and solutions for their clients. The air ambulance is constantly evolving around the safety and stability of the customer's medical condition at all times prior to any arrangement of air transportation from one destination to another.

Car Assistance

With AA, the company offers 24 hours assistance to customers whenever they endure vehicle breakdown. The company provide outstanding case management service and an assurance that drivers are taken from initial call receiving to return of vehicle. Below is list of services provided by this division:

- Towing Assistance

- Referral to service centers

- Minor Roadside Repair

- Referral to panel workshop

- Car rental referral

- Hotel referral

- Emergency message relay

- Legal referral

Customer Care

The 21st century contact centre usually fully integrates the online and land line communications. The call centre offers services which consist of managing and monitoring emails, voice, real-time chat, fax, website orders or queries, IVR (interactive voice response) menus, mobile SMS, call routing, multimedia queuing, automated call-backs and more. The call centre delivers a range of multi-lingual services, from managing marketing campaigns and promotions to giving advice and information on medical and lifestyle services.

Digital Brand Services

Asia Assistance explored the new the Digital Brand solutions services in July of 2013, which is associated with Corporation Service® (CSC) a leader in business, financial and legal services worldwide. CSC was established in 1899 and its headquarter in Wilmington, Delaware USA. As partner of CSC Asia, Asia Assistance is offering digital brand services to protect its brand.

Asia Assistance has gained popularity for its range of brand protection services, strongly based on technological superiority and ranked top quality service provider by World Trademark Review, which has channelled more than half of the Best Global Brands (Interbrand ®) to associate with CSC with more companies seeking aid from Asia Assistance. CSC on the other hand is a leading name management and brand protection company, ranking top in customer approval for domain name and online services, based on World Trademark Review survey.

Emergency Medical Assistance

Another services being provided by Asia Assistance is the routine medical check-ups to sudden illness and injury where representatives are highly knowledgeable in local healthcare systems and resources are available to provide medical assistance around the world. Monitoring and control of standards and cost are the main focus in delivering the highest quality services for the company's clients. From first call made to the final provision of service, the company customizes each step that is best suited for the client and their customer's needs. The "Emergency Medical Assistance" service includes:

- Medical Evacuation and/ or Repatriation
- Repatriation of Mortal Remain
- Medical Monitoring
- Arrangement of Hospital Guarantee
- Medical Referral and Advice
- Emergency Message Transmission
- Return of Dependent Children
- Dispatch of Essential Medication not Available Locally
- Compassionate Visit

Expert Medical Opinion

When facing a serious illness, patients and their treating doctors want to be certain of every option available before making critical decisions regarding the treatment of particular illness. Through the company's "Expert Medical Opinion" program, the diagnoses and treatment plans are made available for evaluation by disease-specific specialists across the world. With access to a team of highly specialized physicians, the "Expert Medical Opinion" program provide customers with comprehensive information in which experts' advice would help them make important future health decisions.

Home Assistance

With one phone call, customers will be referred to the nearest preferred providers as needed. The home assistance service includes:

- Plumbing Repairs
- Locksmith Services
- Air Conditioning Maintenance & Repairs
- General Home Repairs
- Pest Control Assistance

MediCheck

MediCheck services aim to provide convenience to policyholders, customers or employees. This service is essential since people tend to be preoccupied with their daily schedules, and too busy to allocate time for pre-requisite check-ups. The MediCheck team comprises of mobile paramedics equipped to conduct check-ups at member's convenience either in their office or at home. Supported by the company's vast panel of providers, check-ups at clinics, and hospitals, screening centres are possible as well. MediCheck is designed to serve insurance companies, banks and corporate entities. The MediCheck service consists of:

- Mobile Health Check-ups
- Arrangement of Appointments
- Issuance of Guarantee Letters
- Pick up and Delivery of Reports

MediClinic (Outpatient Management) Services

Designed for outpatient care, MediClinic is created to provide hassle-free services for clients and their employees while seeking treatment at local panel clinics and/or specialist clinics. As part of value added service, the cost containment measures including visitation reports and analysis to provide convenience and care to employees. The MediClinic service consists of:

- Administration support for Human Resource Department
- 24-hours call centre
- Issuance of Membership Cards
- Wide choice of participating clinics, specialists and hospitals
- Issuance of Guarantee letters
- Cost Containment
- Health campaigns

Security & Risk Management Services

Securing one's business from operational risks is a first priority for any organisation. Losses of life, intellectual property, physical assets and reputation can have a devastating and lasting impact on a business. AA provides in depth risk management services, meaning that for every solution AA would provide the client at least a second and third tier of solutions. AA is well equipped to help its clients identify, evaluate and mitigate operational risks. Additionally, should an incident occur, AA is recognised as a leading provider of crisis response and assistance services.

- Risk assessment of any work activity
- Controlling, monitoring and mitigating such risks
- Communicating these risks to all persons involved

Security Assistance Services

Business travelers often have to work and travel to destinations that can be hostile, sensitive or even unfamiliar, putting travelers, expatriates and business units at risk. Through the brand name of Global Secure, AA International's security experts with over 19 years of experience are able to provide emergency security assistance along with travel risk management and protection services for corporates, expatriates and travelers worldwide.

Intelligence is available to the clients through the combination of state of the art technology and risk intelligence information, AA travel risk management experience and expertise along with 24/7 crisis response management centres provides the client with an immediate response and if required immediate escalation. AA looks at crisis and emergency planning as an essential element in any companies' emergency response procedures.

Third Party Administration

With AA team of highly-trained professionals, they attempt to provide value added services to clients with the aim of ensuring higher efficiency, standardization of charges, greater awareness and penetration of health insurance to a larger segment of people. Whenever policyholders obtain treatment at panel hospitals, AA ensures that the patient receive hassle-free facilities and settlement of hospital bills will be organized and guaranteed in accordance with each individual's policy's terms and conditions. The Third Party Administration service consists of;

- Issuance of Guarantee Letters
- Issuance of Medical Cards
- Claims Management

Travel Assistance

With Travel Assistance program, clients will have access to travel assistance services when faced with an emergency while traveling abroad. With one phone call, clients will be connected to 24 Hours hotline and the call center personnel will assist and support clients wherever they are. The Travel Assistance service consists of:

- Inoculation & Visa Information
- Flights Information
- Loss Passport Assistance
- Legal Firm Referral
- Loss Luggage Assistance
- Interpreter Referral
- Weather Information
- Contact Details of Consulate and Embassy
- Foreign Exchange Information
- Emergency Cash Advance

Knowing the Market

The main competitors were identified and categorized into insurer and third-party administration. Third-party administration is the main competitor because they provide similar services. AA compete to secure clients to use AA services. As for the insurer, some of them outsource portions of their services to Asia Assistance Network. Hence, in a way the insurer is also an AA client. In Malaysia, there are not many third-party administration providers. However, Micare (formerly known as Metronic iCare), Mediexpress and PM Care are the main competitors of AA. Below is the table for the services provided by the company generally:

Type of BPO products	Targeted customers	Key features of the services
Third party administration ("TPA")	Self-insured customers and/or insurance companies	Actual medical expenses are borne directly by corporate clients.
Fully insured programme	Insured customers	Medical expenses are fully insured by an appointed licensed insurer.
Combination of TPA	Combination of self-	TPA services in relation to

and insured programmes	insured and insured customers	outpatient services and insured programme for inpatient services.
Consultancy	Corporate clients	Advisory work in areas related to Human Resource and Employee Benefits

Introduction to Wellness Program

Rising healthcare expenses can be reduced by getting employees to change unhealthy habits such as smoking, inactive lifestyle and stress reduction. These elements significantly contribute to absenteeism, increased claims, turnover and, most importantly, chronic and costly disease. However, getting the employees to actually change their lifestyle can be perplexing. It is essential to have a well thought-out plan with built-in basics that capitalize on participation and triggers long-lasting changes.

Employers have recently became more absorbed in workplace wellness programs to improve worker's health. An example of such involvement is wellness screenings, onsite clinics, healthier foods options in cafeterias and vending machines, and greater opportunities for physical activity (Spezzano, Michael J. 2015). To better comprehend how workplace wellness programs are executed and to understand participating employees perception of such programs; a study has been conducted on four companies, a clients of Asia Assistance Network. These case studies are part of a larger project planned and executed by Asia Assistance Network.

Asia Assistance facilitates the medical check-up process under both Medicheck and Mediclinic department. Some policy holders are insured for free medical screening while others are limited to certain preventive tests, depending on client's policy. While some companies are covered for preventive screening through insured policy, others are covered directly by their own companies. Even so, some companies do not see the importance of engaging their employees in such tests.

In conjunction with the rise in awareness among the policy holders, Asia Assistance came up with a new proposal to establish a new division called "Wellness Care" to focus on improving and promoting health and fitness offered through work place (although insurance plans can offer them directly to enrolees). This division is mandated to educate client's employees and by offers the benefits of healthy living through better lifestyle. The primary objective is to be proactive as a preventative measure of future health problems. Asia Assistance *Wellness Care* division offers clients discounts on their health insurance premiums with terms and conditions applied depending on insurers and client's premiums.

The *Wellness Care* works on annual basis. The portfolio which only covers participating clients with preventive screening to detect the health issues. Based on initial research findings, AA then construct a series of programs and method designed to reduce the risk factors associated with each employee. There is also cash rewards and discounts being offered such as free gym memberships for participants. Depending on the nature of health problem faced by individual employees, AA work hand-in-hand with clients to provide suitable programs that improves the quality of lifestyle for employee.

Case Selection

There has been too many studies written about wellness programs implemented by large companies, but little known about the smaller ones. Hence, the focus in this case is on smaller clients with 100 workers but not more than 10,000. They have come up with a site selection protocol that could aid in reaching the maximum level of informational generation. They also have planned to accept sites that vary along the following measures:
- Company size
- Type of client based on their industry for example heavy industry, retail, services and   government)
- Region
- Program origin (self-funded vs insured)
- Employer willingness to support in promoting wellness program; AA looks for at least one firm that provides rewards to achievement health-related standards that are close to the allowed limit.

Due to lack of databases availability of employer wellness programs, case study candidates were selected based on published information such as companies listed in the *Partnership for Prevention "Leading by Example"* publications, featured in newspaper articles and managers of wellness program vendors and their own physician. Based on the wide range of sources of information concerning workplace wellness programs, AA is able to recognize which programs are unpopular and that has not been publicised or received attention, as well as those who have potential to offer substantial financial incentives to promote wellness participation and changes in lifestyle. AA managed to secure a list of 35 candidates of employers to participate in the Wellness program, from which participants are randomly selected to achieve balanced representation of AA's selection criteria. Their primary target was contacted to secure participation. If they refused however, a replacement of another client in the same field would be made.

The case study method
Method of Data Collection
Interviews were conducted with wellness program coordinators, wellness program staff, human resource department, worker representatives, senior executives and team leaders. Additional data was gathered from focus groups, published material about wellness programs such as brochures, internal documentation on the effectiveness of programs and nutrition guides. Specialized teams directly collect information from their own domains, office's cafeteria and access to available informational materials. To select the focus group participants, human resource department for each client was communicated with via email to identify eligible candidates based on their willingness to participate in wellness activities. The time and date of each visit to the clients is determined based on the convenience of participants. AA sent dedicated team for two days at each client's locations for data collection purposes.

Background of Participating Companies
Employer A
Employer A is a local university located in western Malaysia, where employees enjoy various benefit plans including medical, dental and optical. The University has an overall benefit structure for employee and students, whereby they offer their own wellness program. However, they chose to assign Asia Assistance to administer the program. The wellness program offered services to all staff, students, and faculty members. In addition to the willingness of the university to fund the wellness program, the medical insurer of the University policy also has offered to cover medical check-up. Based on the gathered information, it was determined that

significant number university staff and students suffer from hypertension, paediatric asthma and diabetes. Malaysia according to the World Health Organisation is Asia's largest in per capita diabetic disease.

Employer B
Employer B is a state government agency in charge for ensuring safety, health and well-being of citizens as well as other human services for the community in that state. Employer B is one of the largest government agencies employing about 19,000 employees working in several locations. Many employees work in the capital Kuala Lumpur, while others spread across the state. The majority of about 73% consist of female with an average of 45 years old. 42% of the employees had suffered chronic conditions such as hypertension (37.4%), diabetes (12.0%) and mental illness (8.0%).

Employer C
Employer C is a global financial firm with primary products consisting of life insurance, mutual funds, long-term care insurance and annuities. Employer C, is the largest insurance company employs approximately 4,894 employees in Asia-Pacific region alone, where the majority of them are based in Kuala Lumpur. Other employees work across other states. Almost 50% of employee are women with average age of 42 years old and had worked for the firm for over 10 years. About 26% of employee are aged 18-29 while the majority are aged between 30-45 (37%) or 45-64(36%) and one per cent are over 65 or older.

Unlike employer A & B, employer C health plans depend on geography because of those employees working in urban and remote areas. Results of data collection shows that employees suffer from lifestyle related conditions such as obesity, hypertension and stress. Chronic diseases such as diabetes and cancer are also part of employees' medical history. The company's wellness activities are focused then on healthcare cost reduction and behavioural change towards a healthier life.

Employer D
Employer D is a large manufacturer with RM1 billions in annual sales, employing 9,000 individuals working in both manufacturing and service centres across Malaysia and South-East Asia. About 57% of worker are male with an average of 43 years old.

The average service period for each employee is 8 years. The managing components of the firm believes tobacco use and lifestyle-driven conditions such as obesity, high cholesterol and hypertension are considered common among their workers. Company D has purchased a policy from a major insurer that covers health, optical and dental benefits. Policy holder enjoys the benefits of preventive care, which includes medical check-ups, mammograms, pap's smear and colonoscopies and immunisation.

Organizational Strategy: Making the shift from Low to High Employee Engagement
Employer A
As for employer A, there were two independent events which alerted the management team of employer A to be involved in the wellness program. In 2013, the university recognized smoking was a major health concern. The second event was the dismissal of university employees' accessibility to the campus health clinic due to restriction in 2014 budget. Because of that, management were able to gather the nursing and nutrition department to provide sessions tasked with the creating cross campus awareness. This seemed realistic and reachable at that time. Consequently upon Asia Assistance's proposal to work with the university, they have widened the task force to identify major health and wellness-related areas of concern. The task force concentrated on stress and work-life issues while trying to influence people to change their habits and life-style. In 2015, human resources department officially initiated the wellness program.

Program Development and Implementation
Employer A requested a program specially designed to provide additional benefits to help faculty, staff and students cope with busy lifestyle. Saving in health cost was not part of the initial plan to join this program since their main goal was to raise health and wellness awareness in alignment with the overall mission of the university. The wellness program is being run by a department within human resource itself under the "*Employee Assistance Program*". Before the initiation of the program, hypertension, pediatric asthma and diabetes were considered the highest risks for health. However, once data was collected, it became apparent that the university was facing weight and blood pressures problems. To cut cost, the university collaborated with different academic departments such as *School of Nursing & Health*, The *College of Business*, *School of Social Work*, *Recreational Services* and *student health office*. These

graduates and students helped wellness services providers while faculty were able to give free lectures on health related topics.

Because of program's gained popularity, management decided to increase the budget for wellness programs. Events and activities organised by the program included lectures on health and wellness topics and personalized health coaching while providing access to wellness-related information. Given the commited university resources, employer A organized activities such as yoga, meditation and massage therapy to reduce the stress levels which included twelve ongoing wellness programs, events, and activities on campus, most offered at no cost to students. These activities are administered by health plan, Asia Assistance and university management itself.

Programs administered by health plans

Beginning with online questionnaire and upon completion of screening, individualized recommendations were suggested thereafter. Alternative treatments were being brought into recommendations during the wellness program such as chiropractors, acupuncturists, massage therapist and dieticians. There was an on campus hotline provided and administered by registered nurses to guide and support those in need. The insurer has also cooperated to offer a patient-centred model of total health programs where the disease management programs concentrated on chronic medical conditions and provided evidence-based guidelines for treatment and screening, broad and targeted outreach and reminders to members, self-management tools and resources and speciality services (e.g. diabetic nurse educators and Clinical Pharmacy Services to improvise cholesterol control).

Program administered by Asia Assistance Network

- Yoga Classes: Classes held 3 times per week with a minimum cost RM20 (about $5 USD) per class or a monthly payment of RM150 (about $30 USD) in advance has a lot students enrolling in it.
- Guided meditation: Only held on Fridays based on appointments, the instructor offers personal training for those interested.
- Massage Service: A licenced masseus comes upon appointments.
- Weight Manager: Inspired by the TV show 'The Biggest Loser', a similar format was followed but on lower altitude based on the budget allocated. Meetings were held on weekly basis.

- Fresh and Healthy Meal Services: With the guidelines from the dietician, there are some volunteer who mainly comes from Asia Assistance client who is not participating in this wellness program, preparing meals cost between RM10-RM15 a day and does food deliveries three times a day for the university staff and students.

Program administered by Employer A
- Wellness Wednesday: This weekly event is held to provide the best practices in health and wellness with few ways. Experts are either invited to give talks or each class there will be 10 minutes video recordings shown before classes for the students to see. There was also a webinar format used to reduce the cost of inviting external speakers.
- Smoking Cessation: Recently started, a four-phase program designed by the Health Ministry and administered every Wednesday by the Department of Respiratory Therapy. The main aim is to provide important information to help participants quit smoking.

Communication/Marketing Strategy

The wellness program for this company had multiple approaches that targeted faculty, staff and students. Collaboration with its campus partners and co-sponsoring different programs, they managed to draw people's attention and help them remember activities held on campus. Besides investing in printing high-quality color flyers, passed around the campus, and posted online, the wellness program hired an intern from the Business School to open, manage and publicise wellness events in Facebook, Twitter and YouTube that highlights different wellness programs events and activities. Highlighting events and activities taking place in "Wellness Wednesday" as well as yoga and meditation activities are posted to draw more attentions to include the general public. Within six months, the numbers of enrollment in yoga and meditation classes doubled from 10 students to more than 30. Next, the word of mouth was used to hire undergraduates and graduate students to encourage their peers to work on projects that are wellness based. Students functioned as promoters indirectly spreading the word on activities.

Employer B

The wellness program was launched early 2010 in collaboration with the state's public health department to launch a model of a worksite wellness program and contain healthcare cost by creating awareness and reducing the risk factors. Initially the program has two main levels; the department level, to provide overall direction; and the facility level to shape the wellness activities on the ground. At the department level, the wellness director is responsible to coordinate the program during her contract. Upon the termination of that position in 2011, automatically the oversight, coordination and council meetings no longer is carried out.

At the facility level, the wellness committee acts as a representative and was elected to focus on the relevant health risks and organise their own events. The de-centralized structure allows for customization and personalization for the particular members to organise events based on their convenience.

Table 2: Organizational Structure of Employer B's Wellness Program

Position	Roles
Department Level	
Wellness Director (this position was eliminated in September 2011)	<ul><li>Coordinates across agencies</li><li>Chairs the wellness council</li><li>Represent department on various health and wellness initiatives</li></ul>
Wellness council	<ul><li>Wellness representatives from each facility</li><li>Advices on wellness policy and program needs</li></ul>
Facility Level	
Wellness representatives	<ul><li>Provide leadership to the facility committee</li><li>Report wellness activities to their agency director and the Wellness Director</li><li>Make up the wellness council</li></ul>
Wellness committees	<ul><li>Provide wellness programs and</li></ul>

	activities in each facility.

In early 2015, Employer B has assimilated their wellness program with Asia Assistance Network as proposed. Working together, the objective is to focus on changing both formal and informal organizational policies and working place to increase support for the wellness and on-going evaluation. Asia Assistance has suggested a wellness policy where Employer B is to authorize 4 hours per person per month of work time for wellness committee work and 6 hours per month for representing at each facility. This allows the flexible working hours schedules to allow participation of the members.

The wellness policy has been reconstructed with the guidance of Asia Assistance Network's. Part of the policies includes maintaining agency wellness committees, department wellness council and a wellness director to plan and carry out wellness program among the department. The next stage in policy, is to raise awareness among the workers with the information and resources on the changes that reduces their risk factor towards chronic illness. The body will also provide programs and activities at the work which offers workers opportunities to be more physically active, eat healthier food and stop using tobacco while managing stress. The workers may also elicit on-going feedback to plan and carry out the programs that meet the needs and interest of all.

Program Development and Implementation

The program and activities at Employer B are organised based on state employee health plan and Employer B together with Asia Assistance Network.

Programs administered by the state employee health plan

- Wellness Services and Case Management: They offer numerous prevention and case management services; smoking cessation program, weight management program done online, health assessment and psychiatrist services for those in stress and has mental disorders. For smoking cessation, there is one-on-one online chat support and also personal counselling for severe cases.

Programs administered by Employer B & Asia Assistance Network

- Education Activities: Posters, seminars and bulletin boards are posted in the workplace and held on monthly basis. External experts are called in to talk about 30 minutes during lunchtime per month.
- Wellness Fair: Asia Assistance holds annual wellness fairs to teach and organise screening as well. The fair includes games and activities. One of it is where workers are encouraged to donate fruits and vegetable.
- Walking/Running Events: It has been a trend for the past few decades to hold such events. Walking in groups to reach a certain goals. Encouraging all employees to join VITAGEN Healthy Digestion Walk.
- Individualized Walking Program: They developed a few walking trails near the working site where those who are interested may use the trail to walk together with colleagues. The walks range from 1KM to 2KMs which includes a local university campus.
- Fruit and Vegetable 30-days Challenges: Each employees will receive weekly emails on the recipes which they are to follow during the 30 days. They will also keep a log of their meals and those who manage to complete the challenge wins prizes including a two days hotel stay in Melaka.

Impact of Wellness Program

Since Employer B has initiated the wellness program in 2010, they managed to get some data for their own analysis. The program impact at the employee level was evaluated using surveys. From 2010 up to 2014, the portion of employees who seem to have a positive behavior change (except for smokers) was higher amongst active employees involved in the program. Figures 1 and 2 as reported by the human resource department.

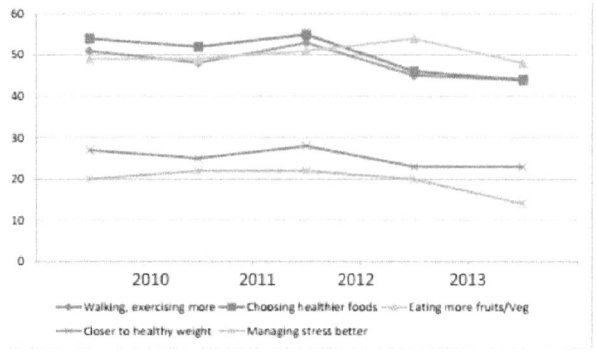

Figure 1: Percent of Department Employees Annually Reporting Positive Health lifestyle Changes in Year (2010-2013)

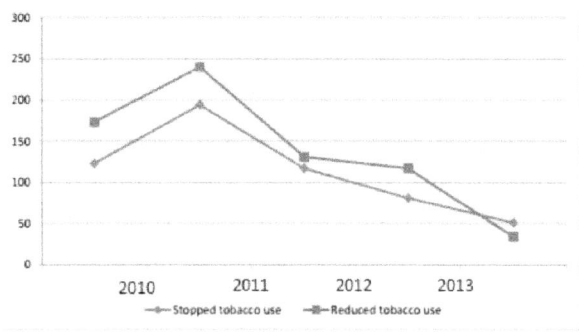

Figure 2: Number of Department Employees Reporting Quitting or Reducing Tobacco Use in 12 Months (2010-2013)

Employer C

Employer C was completely unaware of any wellness program until they were approached by Asia Assistance Network. The primary motivation for Employer C to go with Asia Assistance Network proposition was primarily driven by corporate responsibility for the staff, which in a way saves healthcare cost, and increase in employees morale and health, which ultimately reflects on employees performance. As upper management become more worried of the rising health cost, human resource department was enthusiastic about the prospect of being ahead, by preventing health cost from causing a hole in the company's revenue. The focus was then is to pay better attention to employee well-being. An HR manager shared the following comments *"We have always had a real focus of looking at the workplace as more than just a place of work. We have a method that goes far beyond 'what do you pay.' We have a good name in helping employees become engaged in their own health and feel better about life and work"* The expanding of wellness programs was considered as in sync with their "vibrant" work culture.

Program Development and Implementation

For a beginner in the wellness program, Asia Assistance Network worked together with employer C to examine claims data to verify the cost drivers and to conduct instantaneous changes towards developing wellness initiatives that allow employees to take charge of their own health. Human resource department create a small wellness team charged with creating a dialogue by discussing ideas and carve out collaborative programs with Asia Assistance Network team. This was mutually agreed upon as a first step. Online questionnaire, disease management programs and reimbursements for joining gym and health clubs were part of this initials step. Soon after, a quarterly biometrics screening and health coach training was introduced. Employer C allocated 100,000 RM for the wellness program.

Implementation of Wellness Programs and Events

Programs administered by Insurers

- Biometric Screening: The primary insurer provides metrics such as blood pressure, cholesterol, body mass index, weight and height to be examined.
- Health Risk Questionnaire: Insurer offers online health questions to be answered for record purpose. Upon completion, a report was prepared for each individual to see their health status.
- Reimbursement programs: Participant are given RM400 to be used at selected gym. There are also rewards for those attending smoking cessation programs, weight management meetings and nutritional programs.

Programs administered by Asia Assistance

- Healthy eating program: Participant is provided with an access to variety interactive tools to communicate with health specialist on proper eating and recipes and any other wellness-related issues.
- Nurse Hotline: A 24/7 hotline services is provided for the workers to receive confidential health information and advice.
- Weight Management: meeting once bi-weekly during lunch hour onsite to discuss ways to manage weight also encourage each other to manage weight issues.
- Cafeteria Calorie Labelling: Calories are clearly labelled each menu sold at employer-C cafeteria.

Communication/Marketing Strategy

Employer C uses multiple online channels to get their employees to embark on practicing in healthy habits and to serve as information decimation channel of all available wellness opportunities. The programs are updated through online bulletin, all cafeteria outlets and company's intranet. The company also emphasised awareness creation as an effective tool of improving employee engagement. A campaign was organised to deliver multidimensional, focused health awareness program through variety of communication channels including newsletters, call-out and emails.

Employer D

Organizational leadership at employer D became increasingly concerned of the rising cost of healthcare. In responding to such rising concern, employer D rushed to get policies with their existing insurance company to provide voluntary onsite preventive screenings with the aims of early diseases detection to reduce disease escalation, and as a measure of sustaining employee wellness. For a self-funded company, they typically engaged in their own early detections guidelines. However employees participation rate was low. The following comment was shared by an employee *"I was requested to participate in medical check-ups but because they were not compulsory, many of us decide not to join."* At the same time, those who participated were already considered healthy and highly motivated, and therefore their effort had no effect on improving overall health or controlling costs.

When their effort failed to generate tangible results, employer D began offering educational seminars based on Asia Assistance Network suggestions. Employer D managers got assistance from local resources such as programs and materials offered by local hospitals, however participation remained disappointingly low. Hence, Asia *Assistance Wellness Care* was put to trial with six months period of program design evaluation and to get employees' attention. Upper management was determined to limit spiralling healthcare costs and to reach out to health professionals. Once became aware of the fact that lifestyle-related diseases constitute a high percentage of corporate expenditure on Malaysian health, a top management personal made the following comment *"I can't help existing victim but I can help somebody who's pre-diabetic from becoming diabetic by creating awareness of the risk."*. In 2011, employer D, which previously handled wellness programs as something voluntary to and outcome-based incentive program with built-in premium differentials based on the number of risk factors.

Program Development and Implementation
Wellness activities generally falls into two categories, which is data collection (e.g. biometric screenings) and interventions (e.g. fitness competitions). Asia Assistance Network is in-charge of administering the company's onsite annual health screening. The results of the biometric screening, which consist of measures such as blood pressure, cholesterol, body mass index (BMI) and tobacco/nicotine consumption was used in providing feedback reports and findings at a companywide level. Results are shared via email with each individual, where they may also have access to online health risk assessment, educational materials and nurse hotlines for riskier employees. The screening data would be used to set individuals premium rates. Wellness budget at employer D is estimated at RM165,000 per year. RM100,000 was allocated for third-party (Asia Assistance Network) for fee related with services administered including coordinating screenings, employee outreach, data collection, reporting medical issues, and arranging reasonable alternatives for those who are unable to reach biometric benchmarks. The remaining RM65,000 is reserved for other expenditures and incentive rewards for participant wining at various competition.

Employer D was then offered a wellness initiatives consisting of weight-loss programs and fitness classes. The aim of such programs is to boost healthy diet consumption and lifestyle, and smoking prevention mechanism. A one year post-implementation period was allocated to evaluate results.

Communication/Marketing Strategy

Employer D uses various communication channels to inform employees of wellness activities. Multiple outreach programs designed with diverse employee population in mind that consist of sales representatives, corporate leaders, and manufacturing workers disbursed at various locations. On line systems were used as wellness portals via company's intranet. Weekly newsletters decimating healthy tips, future competitions and notices of annual onsite screenings were posted in the pantry, office and dropped in employee's mailboxes. Line managers were in-charge of communicating wellness messages, and encouraged to do so during team meetings. To further improve the effectiveness of the wellness messaging system, a team was elected to develop a recognizable brand and logo for the program, which later was applied to both online and printed communications.

Future Directions

In light of employers concern of improving the general health, all four Employers will recognize achieved goals with tangible health improvements by rewarding achievers with monetary compensation. This movement is designed to make the programs more effective, increase engagement and participation and to measure and reward achievements made. Plans were suggested for wellness committees to work with each other to co-sponsor wellness events and share knowledge to leverage available resources and improve effectiveness. The degree of partnering, however, is largely based on the degree of commitment and willingness to achieve set objectives. Plans are also in place to expand programs to include family members in weekly activities and programs that involve children and the elderly.

Conclusion

The four companies worked with Asia Assistance Network, begun with small-scale preventive program while others totally ignoring employee health and well-being. Overtime, when proposals of health and well-being improvement programs were introduced, results were outstanding and activities were expanded to include comprehensive wellness program. Such programs involves multiple channels of wellness activities ranging from biometric screening to marathon training to nutrition consultations. Wellness teams begin the process by collecting data through screening and health questionnaires before designing an intervention program. Some companies build partnerships with their primary health insurer to achieve set goals.

Interviews conducted showed that the average participation of the four companies involved in the wellness activity is approximately 41% and only one-third of employees come forward to joined the biometric screening program. Attendance and participation in the programs still is still below the desired level, both management and front-line team leaders need to multiply their effort in increasing participation. Obstacles detected that reduced participation included privacy concerns, time constraints, negative influence by co-workers and lack of adequate dissemination of wellness information employees. Upper management bares the bulk of the responsibility for the lack of effectiveness and deficiency of participation.

The four companies described in this case have renewed their contracts with Asia Assistance Network for 2016-2017 to continue the wellness programs. However, more activities featuring organizational commitment are proposed to create awareness and an atmosphere that provides employees with the opportunity and social support needed that rewards improvements to individual's health.

D'YANA

Introduction

Founded in 2009, D'yana is a homegrown fashion boutique centered towards Muslim women. It is owned by Jubah Emas Global Sdn. Bhd. and is headquartered in Kuala Lumpur, Malaysia. The impetus for the company occurred while its founders, a married couple, were supplying Muslim women apparels to other retailers as a business. Due to high demand, the first official D'yana boutique was introduced in 2013. The boutique received high traction by the local market, prompting the opportunity to open more boutiques.

The company launched a licensing program for D'yana label in 2014 to expand its presence in various states. With the introduction of licensing program, pricing would also be standard for every boutique. This is contrast to when D'yana operated as a wholesale business, where retailers were able to set prices freely. The inconsistency in pricing resulted in confusion and dissatisfaction among consumers.

Jubas Emas Sdn. Bhd. is involved in the manufacturing, exporting, distributing, retailing, and licensing of D'yana label for the domestic Malaysian market as well as for international buyers (e.g. from Singapore and Brunei). The company has engaged a range of marketing strategies for the label via commercials, social media, celebrities as product ambassadors, and more. To date, six D'yana boutiques are operating around the country (three boutiques are managed by its licensees) to provide an array of fashion choices for Muslim women, which include Wangsa Melawati (headquarters), Shah Alam, Bangi, Seremban 2, Alor Setar and Sungai Petani. Two more boutiques will commence operations in December 2015 after the company had signed the agreement with two new licensees.

Following an interview in October 2 with the Managing Director, Mr. Syafie, there was continued focus in the expansion of new licensees and boutiques, as well as the development and launching of new designs to diversify the products available to the market.

History of Muslim Women Apparel in Malaysia

Muslim women apparel is based on catering to the religious practices and needs of Muslim women. Their choice of apparel is a sensitive matter as it is pursued to respect their sense of religious and cultural identity. The Quran, in particular, advises Muslim women to dress modestly. However, legislations that govern the specifics of what is considered modest can vary among Muslim countries. Not all countries make it mandatory for Muslim women to cover almost every part of their body as it is commonly observed in countries in Middle East. In Malaysia, Muslim women are not obliged to cover their face and are given the freedom to choose for themselves.

There are numerous type of Muslim women apparel available in the market. Among the famous choices are headscarf (hijab), jubah, baju kurung, baju kebaya, dress and blouses. Historically, Muslim women apparel has only been popular among its designated consumers. Nevertheless, innovation and creativity in clothing design over the years has increased its appeal to a much larger population. The Muslim clothing market has evolved and gained more attention among non-Muslim women. There has also been a shift in understanding the products among this segment of the population. Non-Muslims are no longer labelling Muslim women apparel strictly as religious wear but at part with being its own fashion line instead.

Considering the developments, the market of Muslim women fashion label is no longer limited to only Muslim women, but to all races in Malaysia. There is ongoing demand and trends for Muslim women apparels for a variety of situations and events beyond religious circumstances (e.g., work, sports, and casual outing). Furthermore, there is huge potential in the industry as younger generations are keen in purchasing and wearing Muslim women apparels that are constantly updated and at par to current standards in the world of fashion.

Problem Identification

D'yana has shown tremendous promise since its launch. The company has an advantage in terms of the unique clothing designs it has to offer, which distinguishes them from other competitors. However, it appears that the trend is experiencing a slowdown due to the stagnation in demand, especially during the non-festive seasons. Furthermore, the company struggled to achieve its sales target of RM6, 000,000 in the year 2015 from all the retail boutiques and online market. There are multiple issues to consider in relation to sales, product differentiation and product accessibility to explain the challenge. More importantly, these issues have become a major barriers to the company's growth at present and in the future.

Given the context, the following questions should be raised to the management for attention and deliberation:

i) How can sales be increased during the slower seasons?
ii) How can D'yana's unique design to be protected from being duplicated by competitors?
iii) To what extent is it necessary for consumers to visit a physical boutique in order to purchase D'yana's products? How well are its online services doing in catering the needs of non-physical visitors?
iv) Should D'yana join ventures with online market retailers such as Groupon, Zalora, Lazada or Lelong to widen its marketing strategies?
v) What is the target number of new D'yana boutiques in 2016? Will the management leverage or form a partnership with existing funders such as Tekun or Perbadanan Nasional Berhad (PNS) to create and provide opportunities to young entrepreneurs, which could in turn widen the company's business?

Industry Analysis: Competitiveness
Business view and current trend

According to Thomson Reuters and Dinar Standard report (2015), globally, Muslim consumers spent $266 billion on clothing in 2013. It is expected that the spending will rise up to $484 billion by 2019. In addition, Pew Research Centre (2015) projected that the Muslim population will grow faster than any other religion, from 1.6 billion in 2010 to 2.76 billion by 2050. Global Islamic apparel market is expected to be driven by huge Muslim population growth. Romanna Bint-Abubake, chief executive officer of fashion website Haute Arabia, described the Muslim fashion market is an extremely exciting and profitable market, following e-mail interview with Bloomberg in April 7. She added that the demand will be fostered by "a generation of young, confident and tech-savvy Muslims who are comfortable and proud of their faith". Being considered as a segment that is yet to be fully developed for capital interest, huge brands and designers are eyeing on this booming Muslim fashion market.

Overall, the Muslim women apparel industry in Malaysia has been growing steadily, driven mainly by strong domestic demand. However, considering the challenging global economy condition and market instability, consumer spending would be a major concern to the industry. As a result, there is an expectation for the increasing cost of living to negatively impact household spending power on apparel and lifestyle products.

At the same time, export orders of Muslim women apparel and accessories have shifted to ASEAN countries with cheaper production cost and higher labor supply. A more attractive foreign currency exchange rate for investors following the weakening Malaysian Right has realized opportunities for the industry to expand in manufacturing and export. Furthermore, government-implemented initiatives and measurements in the midst of a tough market environment have ensured support for the industry to become a major contributor to the nation's growth. For instance, Islamic Fashion Festival that features international brands from all around the world will be held annually in Malaysia to promote Islamic fashion.

There is intense competition in the Muslim women fashion apparel industry due to low barriers to entry. The number of competitors is ever-growing and new products enter the market at a rapid pace. As a result, D'yana consistently faces the pressure of competition from both local and international companies in this lucrative industry. Procuring and applying resources, unique designs, cheaper pricing, or a combination of these in a strategic manner is critical to remain at the top of the competition.

SWOT Analysis and Future Outlook

The managing director of the company, Mr. Syafie, recently commented on the decline in sales from a year-to-year basis (e.g., comparing Oct 2015 to Oct 2014) during a quarterly review meeting. Consistent with current trends in the economy, he attributed lowered sales to weakening spending power owing to global economy instability. It was reported however, that the decrease in sales did not occur in every boutique. At least two performed well, which begs the question as to the other factors that may be in play in relations to the performances of the boutiques beside the immediate concern over spending power.

Following this, several discussions were reportedly held by the management team, which also sought input and feedback from every licensee and boutique supervisor. The following SWOT analysis was derived from the different perspective acquired and given the company's strong profile, the opportunities to grow remain intact and positive. The company will leverage on the rise of technology by expanding its venture into social media and online sales presence as their customers are undoubtedly using new technology such as smartphones increasingly.

SWOT ANALYSIS

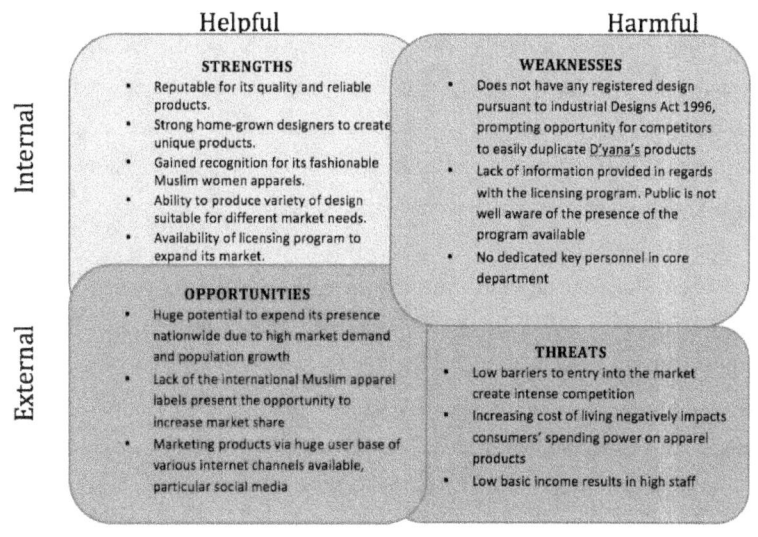

Conceptual framework

A number of factors affected sales performance were developed from the research:

a. Staff Competency

Staff turnover rate in the industry is relatively high. Recent graduates frequently enlist to work temporarily in the company as a safety net while aiming to secure jobs with better pay and that are more relevant to their studies. The continuity in building human capital in the long-term is often disrupted as staff members may not work as soon as their alternative motif is realized, which can be as short as six months in the industry. Unfortunately, it is time consuming to train new staff to make sure that they are familiar with the products and compatible with the daily operation tasks. There is furthermore a correlation between staff competency and boutique's performance. A boutique with staff who do not have the intention to work in the long-term and grow with the company tends to have lower sales than those without such issues.

b. Products Suitability

A product that is selling well in the Kuala Lumpur region may not perform as well in other regions. This is mainly due to the difference in perception across regions. Consumers in Kedah, for example, are known to prefer traditional Muslim women apparel design, whereas consumers in Kuala Lumpur are open and keener towards trendy and creative design. Consumers who stay in capital cites tend to have higher acceptance level in trying out new designs.

c. Marketing Channel

With the progress of changing technology, Syafie admitted that marketing through conventional methods such as television commercials and magazines were no longer effective channels. Consumers are constantly shifting their approaches in searching products via the various internet channels. Shifting trend towards online shopping will open new opportunities. It was therefore crucial that D'yana allocated an increased budget in broadcasting its label by seizing the opportunity of the internet channels available, particularly social media (e.g., Facebook and Instagram). The number of users of social media applications are numerous, with more than a million accounted for each. As such, the management team were in the consensus that ongoing efforts ought to be focused on capturing market shares by marketing, promoting, and sharing information regarding the label through social media applications. It was also to ensure that D'yana remains competitive in the industry.

d. Industrial Design

A major issue in the industry is product shelf life in terms of new design. It is common within the industry that competitors attempt to duplicate and sell newly launched designs at a lower price than the original product. D'yana is not an exception with regards to the challenge. As a label that took pride and strived on its unique designs, the problem of duplicate was an undoing of its source of strength. Nevertheless, Syafie stretched the importance of protecting D'yana's designs and measurements to mitigate the risk of being copied by the competitors during the management meeting.

e. Key Personnel

Even though the label is expanding rapidly, the management team remains as originally when it was established in 2013. Syafie and his wife oversee the operations across departments. There is no key personnel to focus on each core department. The management team agreed that the current structure might not be able to sustain when the label keeps growing. In view of that, Syafie noticed the importance of appointing heads to lead each core department and delegate the tasks to them, while he concentrates steering the company to success by developing and implementing necessary short-term and long-term plans of action.

Conclusion

Since 2013, the company has registered a multi-millions sales with the consistent cost reduction program due to its micro-managed policy. The entire system has progressed well resulting to company decision to open up opportunities for other entrepreneurs to start up business under their brand name. One of the key point that been addressed in this paper is the absence of expenditure on marketing for retail boutiques and online market especially during the normal season.

Nevertheless, D'yana is facing some difficulties to standardise the operation between wholly-owned boutiques and licensees' boutiques. It makes pretty obvious when customers complaining about the operation hours and promotions are varied across the boutiques. In addition, the company is also affected by internal and external factors such as staff incompetency, lacking in product differentiation and identity, and the reduction in spending power due to market instability. Therefore, taken into consideration on all the positive and negative factors, the management has sufficient information to come out with plans in order to achieve its sales target in 2016. What are the strategies that can be implemented? The recommendations should be based on the questions raised up to the management and conceptual framework.

The Humble Chef

Introduction

The Humble Chef was founded by Mr Rosman Hussin Rizal in 2010. At that time, the first location to highlight the idea that is in front of the Federal Territory Mosque in Jalan Duta. "With only two main menu of spaghetti bolognese and chicken, I decided to run my own business with little financial support from my mother. At that time, the business started in the afternoon where I was taking orders and I will cook every meal. Friday was the day's most well-received. Most who came to my truck are the government servant who's working nearby and majority of them is on probation for diet," said the graduate of Diploma in Culinary Arts, College of Legend, Kuala Lumpur.

As a starting point, Mr Rosman did not put high expectations and just hope to get daily returns of RM100 including profit and capital. After a few months in business, Mr Rosman decided to change the location of his business to Jalan Damanlela because of the nice ambience and beautiful night panorama around the road. The new location will also allow the passer by to easily spot their food truck.

"When we started our business here, the customer's reception was a little bit low. However, after Humble Chef has been reviewed by a well-known blog that is Bangsar Babe, our sales are getting much better and we also started to have our loyal customers. From no tables and chairs for customers, we finally add the equipment bit by bit," said the lad from Seremban, Negeri Sembilan.

As the name suggests, Humble Chef has revolutionized the way of Malaysian perception towards western food where they provide cheap and simple western food without compromise on its food quality. With the unexpected success, Mr Rosman decided to operate his own restaurant which at the same time still maintaining the food truck concept.

The concept of Humble Chef
The concept of Humble Chef is based on the desire of creating a convenient and casual environment for its customers. The simplicity of the trucks closes

resemblances to Asian style where people can have dined under the stars and simply to chat with their friends. In contrast to the Malaysian culture where western food is usually served in a high end restaurant, they only served it in a plastic container and food wrapping paper.

"As a former student of culinary arts, I am aware about food market and its trends in Malaysia. Malaysians liked the food which was cheap and it is important for the food to be simple", said Rosman. Although it has opened a restaurant, Humble Chef still retains menu, quality and most importantly, the same price as those sold in the truck. Thanks to his fellow chefs, their customer never complained about the taste and quality of the food. Customers are willing to queue and enjoy western cuisine in the street, talking among themselves.

Exhibit 1: Humble Chef's spaghetti served in plastic containers

Source: Bangsar Babe Blogsite http://www.bangsarbabe.com

"I am very concerned about the authenticity of the food. Every restaurant should have its own signature dish to attract customers regardless selling traditional food or western cuisine," he said on the menu at his stall that has become the choice of many celebrities.

The Humble Chef has been widely recognized by the Kuala Lumpur residents and also featured in several TV shows i.e. Best in the World (Asian Food Channel) and Bisnes Alternatif (Astro Awani) as well as being covered in local newspapers and magazines. As the business growing steadily as well as warm reception by the customers, Mr Rosman was thinking to expand its business. However, with the unstructured business organization, it will definitely slow down efforts to expand his business.

Exhibit 2 Customers queuing to buy food at Humble Chef's food truck in Pusat Bandar Damansara

Source: Smooch The Bone Blogsite http://smooch-the-bone.blogspot.com

Current Operating Scenario
At the moment, Humble Chef operate from two locations, food truck business based in Jalan Damanlela and also operates a restaurant in Bukit Damansara. They operate both locations on every day except on Sunday starting from 10.00 am until 3.00 pm and 6.00 pm until 12 am.

In Humble Chef, they offer western cuisine that consists of various types of pasta such as spaghetti bolognese, spaghetti olio and others. In addition, they also offer other menus such as kebab and omelette. To serve the food, Humble Chef is using the "eat and get rid of" where food is prepared in a plastic container and wrapping paper. As for drinks, the Humble Chef only offers canned soft drinks and mineral water only. Although the menu is somewhat limited, it still attracts customers because of the high quality and good taste. This is also one of the reasons why Mr. Rosman does not offer too many choices of menu that is to ensure the quality of the food.

In Malaysia, it is common where the price of western cuisine will bear an expensive price. However, Humble Chef managed to change that perception by offering a fully-affordable price. It is no exaggeration to note that the price factor is one factor why Humble Chef managed to retain its customers. Generally, customers Humble Chef consists of young people and the middle class. Normally, they would go to the Humble Chef for dinner after work. The relaxed atmosphere is also one reason why Humble Chef of choice for young people to socialize with friends while enjoying a meal.

The Dilemma

Because of the positive consumer reception, Rosman is planing to expand the business by opening another two branches in Puchong and Shah Alam areas of Kuala Lumpur. However, considering the current market conditions, ambitious planning to expand the business is looking infeasible. After series of discussion with his friends, Rosman has outlined several problems that would be improved in making their plan a success.

The Way of Doing Business

After operating for a quite some time, Humble Chef just practicing small-scale business operations. Although they operate one restaurant, the mode of operation is not much different with the food truck operation. At the restaurant, Humble Chef adopt self-service where customers have to queue to order food. Humble Chef Staff will then be sending food to their customers. Due to the growing popularity of Humble Chef, the number of customers visiting their premises is also increasing. While this is great for business, the method of operation sometimes cannot cope with the number of customers. As a result, customers had to queue and wait longer to get their food.

Increasing Competitors
Given the food truck industry is growing, is undeniably the number of competitors in this industry more and more. This is the most important challenge to be faced by The Humble Chef to expand its business. This is because competitors will attract loyal customers for Humble Chef. In addition, the menu offered by other competitors also more diverse. This differs from Humble Chef who only focuses on a limited menu. In addition, the competitors in the food industry also use equipment and vehicles that are more sophisticated. This makes them be able to operate in a bigger scale than the Humble Chef.

Location
Although Humble Chef is doing business using a food truck, they never changed the location of its business from the very start operating in 2010. The reason why is it aims to help customers to find their locations. Furthermore, the present location makes it easier for customers to park their vehicles because there is a fairly large parking space. However, doing business in one location only had limited Humble Chef from attracting more customers. Most customers who come to dine in can be categorized as their regular customers. Despite having regular customer is something good for business, the inability to attract new customers and to introduce it to a different business segment will hinder their plans to expand the business.

Unstructured Human Resource Management
As a small scale business, Humble Chef does not have the structured human resource unit. The recruitment and training was conducted by Rosman himself, whereby employees are required to observe and learn how things are done at the restaurant. Issues related to checkroll and leave are conducted via administration department.

All chefs currently working with Humble Chef are not formally trained. They were recruited based on their previous skills and experience. However, as their skills improved, current chefs started to think to switch to other restaurant. The reason being, Humble Chef does not provide advance training and there is no clear career progression path to its chef. More prominent restaurants in Kuala Lumpur such as Dome Café, Chilis, TGI Fridays and Ben's offered more promising career in culinary profession thus influencing them to switch. Some chefs are low on loyalty by making Humble Chef as a stepping stone to gaining experience in the culinary field.

Moving Forwards
After series of discussion with his close friend, Rosman has come up with several strategies to address the problem, and definitely there are many things need to be done. When Mr. Rosman received a phone call from his close friend asking about his business and going with his usual jokes with his friend telling him that he is going to expand the business abroad. While making that phone call, his longtime staff handed him a resignation letter. This particular staff member has been working with him as a lead chef for two years and had proven to be independent and hardworking. Even with his recent success, Mr. Rosman still unable to retain his employees. Such events are very troubling for him. Mr. Rosman knew that if his organization continues to be managed in such fashion, the Humble Chef is likely to be driven out of the market.

However, deep down, Mr. Rosman always has an aspiration to expand the food truck business. While the business at this point have not succeeded like other large franchises, Mr Rosman has a feeling that if he does not expand his business in one way or another, his company would slowly lose customers and he will not be able to compete with other large and growing brands and restaurants. Furthermore, the food truck industry competitors are on the rise and operating on the bases of smaller margins. Additionally, food business in Malaysia has a low barrier of entry, regulations and code enforcement, whereby anybody could operate overnight and become a potential competitor. In this highly competitive industry, literally anyone may offer similar product to customers. Unique characteristic such as good food, service, great taste and high quality is the only things that can make the decisive difference and play a big role in retaining customers and brands.

Finding new and strategic location
In order for new food trucks to attract customer as in the case of *Jalan Damanlela* location, Humble Chef must strategically locate a spot for the second food truck. To achieve this, Rosman had planned a comprehensive market research that includes online surveys, getting direct feedback from customers, and directly communicating with locals to identify new trends. Rosman wants to find potential locations that would have a maximum impact utilizing the popularity Humble Chef to attract new customers.

Implementing Structured Human Resource Management

To improve efficiency of human capital, Rosman had proposed a formal training program for all his staff including skills in food safety, marketing and communication. Such training program is anticipated to boost employees' morale and promote better loyalty among employee. Mr. Rosman also has in view the importance of providing the skill and competency required for career advancement. By providing strong career plans, this will provide a larger sense of hope in the future for his business.

Use of Social Media

Website and blog was the primary method of advertising for Humble Chef when they began operations in 2010. However, with the emergence of Facebook, Instagram, Twitter and other social media, Mr. Rosman feels that Humble Chef should make full use of social media as an effective tools of promoting the business. In addition, the use of social media will reduce the overall cost of promotion. This in turn will enable him to use these provisions to other operating activities. By using social media, the Humble Chef will come closer to its customers. Promotional campaigns, specials and new menu offerings will be delivered more quickly, enjoyably and effectively.

Joining the Truck- Food Community

For the purposes of long-term business development, Mr. Rosman felt it was time for Humble Chef to cooperate with other competitors in the same industry to advance the truck-food segment of the industry collectively. The potential for cooperation was initiated by Humble chef when joined the monthly *Food Truck Festival* organized by the Kuala Lumpur City Hall. With this, Humble Chef along with its rivals can work together in organizing and promoting the truck-food market. Humble Chef will also be able to identify the strengths and weaknesses of its competitors and as such, adapt to meet rising challenges.

Conclusion

From humble beginnings, Humble Chef is at the crossing roads between operating as a small business with simple informal operations and unstructured organizational functions, or to fundamentally change the ways of doing business. Being a typical small Asian business with completely centralized decision making by Mr. Rosman, it is only a matter of time before the owner comes to the realization that the old ways of doing business are not working in his advantage anymore. Lack of regulations, low entry barriers and increasing competition forced a new realization, that is change, or risk being driven out of business. The new plans laid out for Humble Chef with Mr. Rosman finally realizing the importance of change to the evolution of business will help transform Humble Chef from its humble beginnings to much better business with improved position in the truck-food market.

Jeonsa Centre

Introduction

Jeonsa Centre is wholly owned and managed by Classyca Holdings Sdn Bhd. Jeonsa Centre, founded in January 2015, is a multisport complex that offer a variety of services. In collaboration between Malaysian government and Classycca Holdings Sdn Bhd, Jeonsa Centre is mandated to educate the public to adopt sport culture by operating asset management through *Majlis Sukan Negara* (National Sports Council Act). Jeonsa Centre offers the public, an excellent sports center equipped with natural grass football fields, 18 badminton courts, multipurpose event hall, and other amenities such as sports cafeteria, changing room, sauna, and pray rooms with an affordable prices. With convenient and accessible location, being at the center of Kuala Lumpur, Jeonsa Centre attract guest looking for healthy lifestyle and those who want to spend leisure time with family and friends. Jeonsa Centre niche market is budget hotel residents, those looking for budget amenities and want to stay in comfort in relation to value for money. Jeonsa hotel's recreational facilities includes fitness centre, which is decorated and designed with the purpose of escape and relaxation. Jeonsa hotels provide business lounge, daily housekeeping, 24-hour front desk, fitness centre and Wi-Fi in public areas with safety and ample parking space to guests. The management of Jeonsa Centre ensured that the centre is equipped with qualified and knowledgeable staff to serve customers with all their sport needs. Acknowledging that customer are more demanding than ever before, Jeonsa Centre constantly attempts to provide real-time personalized experiences through social media platforms to secure potential customers.

Products & Services

Budget Hotel

Jeonsa Budget Hotel is located at Jeonsa Centre itself and provides conducive rooms for its guests. Jeonsa Budget Hotel consist of 32 rooms comprises of 10 deluxe and twin room, 22 sports dormitory rooms, air conditioning, LCD TV, sofa and fridge provided to help guests recharge.

Single Deluxe   Dormitory Room (8 bedded)   Deluxe Twin

Cafeteria
Jeonsa sports cafeteria is an ideal location for the sports enthusiast. High definition big screen Television is provided to showcase sports events, sports news, advertisement and promotions or any related TV programs and to ensure that customers do not miss out on big games. Jeonsa Cafeteria provides a diverse delectable menu to choose from breakfast, lunch, dinner with great daily specials for superb range of western and local cuisine.

Jeonsa Gymnasium
Jeonsa Gym & Fitness Centre, is fully equipped with cardio equipment including treadmills, cycles, cardiovascular, weight resistance machines and free weights. Jeonsa gym operates 24/7 with 365 days a year access. Membership and walk-in options are available with a contract-free, group session and professional classes available with certified trainers.

Badminton court/Multifunction hall

There are 18 badminton courts that offer badminton players a national standard and rubberized courts at Jeonsa Centre. Jeonsa provide high quality hall with high ceiling and regularly polished floor boards. Court booking is usually full with daily customers. Some of the regular customers are registered as member and given preferential rate whenever a booking is made.

Seminar Rooms

There is 3 seminar rooms available to the public or corporate for rent. The setups can be customizable according to the customer requirements and type of events such as private events, seminars conference session, leisure or meeting. All seminar rooms have complete media and presentation facilities such as desktop, projector, screen, flip chart, whiteboard, and presentation materials.

  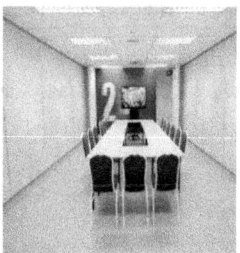

Classroom/workshop setup   Leisure setup   Meeting/Discussion setup

Football Fields

Jeonsa's Centre football field is a professional teams' stadium size with an area of 7140 square metres made of natural grass. The dimension and markings are defined of the field of play. The side-line field numbers are 6 foot high and by 4 foot designated with each 10 yard line marker. Along the restraining Line between the 30 yard markers with team benches.

JeonsaBiz Enterprise is the subsidiary of Classycca Holdings Sdn Bhd, a company that was incorporated in October of 2015. The management is currently in the planning and designing stage of the new business venture, which is designed to push the online sales of brands and products such as T-shirts, Jersey, caps, towels, calendar, diaries and others. JeonsaBiz also selling their local brand of football uniforms and jersey to local football Teams.

As of today, Jeonsa Centre has been operating for about one year in the market, with intensive promotional campaigns highlighting its facilities while maintain high quality services to remain as a market leader in their industry. While experiencing stable business growth and improved revenue within first year of operation, Jeonsa Centre has taken another step forward of diversification, by introducing new product line in their segments of the Malaysian industry, which is selling online sports merchandise and accessories.

The marketing manager at Classycca Holdings Sdn Bhd, Ms. Alysa is doing well by aggressively marketing Jeonsa Centre Sports facilities. During the first year of operation, she managed to increase revenues by 30-40% per month. Given the increasing demand for their products and services driven by sport enthusiasts, management decided to expand existing business by venturing into new line of products capitalizing on the online shopping segment. Ms. Alysa was appointed to become the director of *JeonsaBiz Enterprise* to lead the online operations and to ensure the continuous increase of existing sports facilities sales.

Industry Analysis

Sport industry growth have rapidly improved in Malaysia over the past decade. The Malaysia government concerned with rising diabetes amongst Malaysians largely because of life style and long work hours, is actively promoting the development of sport facilities and the adaptation of sport culture. Hence, government's involvement in the private sector encouraging entrepreneurs to establish sport centres helped the cause of Jeonsa Centre. This coincided with the rapid growth of urbanisation and movement to the main cities from rural areas.

Closest Competitors

Competitive analysis of the closest competitors revealed below:

Competitors	Descriptions
1) *Sports Planet*	Sports Planet is the ultimate futsal centre founded and began its services in November 2012. It offers facilities and services at affordable prices due to the increasing demand of futsal enthusiast especially youngsters in Malaysia. It is also a great futsal arenas and one of the best

	snookers in the Klang valley. Sports planet emphasize on continuous improvements of its facilities with excellent and efficient booking systems, membership privileges, quality pitch conditions, security, membership privileges, promotional and partnerships. Has 13 venues in Malaysia and 2 international venues that provide great facilities that cater massive audience through futsal promotional road shows and tournaments. Ultimately, Sports Planet guarantees outstanding and excellent facilities that created high spirit of sports development skills, inspiration, bonding communications as well as healthy lifestyle.
2) *Xtion Paintball Park*	Xtion Paintball Park is a recognized and established paintball park by members of International paintball industries founded in 2003 and officially launched by the Minister of Youth and Sports in 12th July 2005. The only paintball park operator in Malaysia that having latest facilities and well maintained park. It is also well known park in tournaments and events sanctioned by worldwide paintball governing bodies such as Paintball Sports Promotions USA and Millennium Series Europe. Besides, Xtion Paintball Park has become an official venue of Asia's biggest international tournaments such as Nation Cup (2004) and World Cup Asia (2012). As a recognized members and supported by the Sports Commissioner's Office and Ministry of Tourism Malaysia, Xtion Paintball Park promote paintball through road shows participation all over the country.
3) *National Aquatic*	National Aquatic Centre is one of the Premier venue for National and International Competitive Swimming,

Centre	Water Polo and Diving in Kuala Lumpur that established by the Government of Malaysia. Designed with the concept of floating Dome with 28000 square meters overall area and constructed with standards regulation by the International Swimming Federation (FINA).	
	Customers are usually fascinating with the surrounding circumstances here and the pond layout was built with the dramatic structure and well planned architecture. It became one of the great venue with the utilization of floats at the top of the pool such as product launches, fashion shows and mini concerts.	
4) Kompleks Rakan Muda	Kompleks Rakan Muda is one of the best sports centre around Kuala Lumpur and a good venue with sports facilities and multi-purpose hall to have multiple functions and sports event. It accommodates 450 people standing and 250 people seated and very good location for private and corporate sports events and oriented team building. It also have 120 sports dormitory rooms that can accommodate 900 pax in one time. Among facilities there offer to public is squash court, futsal court, aerobic room, gymnasium, snooker room, room for darts, carom and also table tennis.	
5) The Challenger Sports Centre	The Challenger Sports Centre is a best and quality badminton courts incorporated in May 2007 and the 1st centre located in Cheras, Taman Connaught. Due to high demand of badminton enthusiast while maintaining quality services, The Challenger Sports opened 2nd branch in Section 14, Petaling Jaya in April 2009. The Challenger Cheras is a well-maintain court flooring which only use rubberize mat. It is specifically designed lighting system particularly to ensure best playing environment with sufficient brightness.	

Target Market

Because of the diversity in the activities provided and available programs at Jeonsa Centre, the target marketing segment vary from dedicated die-hard workout enthusiasts, workers and office employees, football players, students, family, tourists and people who would like to spend few hours of leisure.

- ***Weekend Warriors*** – For special and periodic activities, Jeonsa target this group segment because they like the freedom to come and go without locked into any long-term commitments and expensive membership fees.
- ***Gym Rats*** – This target market consist of those who love to work out for a goal and healthy conscious. Gym rats tend to use the facilities quite frequently and mostly comprised of loyal customers. Members come to the gym to bulking up, increase power and flexibility and losing weight. Usually prefer special trainer to monitor and train every members to achieve their desired goals and fitness target.
- ***Families*** - This market segment is not very big as far as Jeonsa's activities are concerned, but it is an important market that tends to utilize some facilities such as private rooms and cafeteria. Jeonsa have "Something for everyone" that can attract the whole family to become a customers. The idea is not just to send kids to events, but to make them future customers through the adaptation of healthy life style and sport culture. Sport events are organized frequently and advertised on local TV stations. Activities are designed with the parents in min as well, parents who send their kids will have other activities to do themselves.
- ***Students*** –University and college students are Trgeted to enjoy facilities since there are few nearby university such as Unikl, UUM,UTM, Yayasan Selangor, Multimedia College with the fix discount rate of 20%.
- ***Footballers and fan clubs*** – Having a big screen helps attract events followers to watch games at the cafeteria while having dinner.

- ***Tourists*** – This is a small market segment for Jeonsa Centre, however oversea tourist may be attracted to the hotel accommodation located at the heart of Kuala Lumpur, which provides an easy access to the facilities and Kuala Lumpur attractions.
-

Other marketing activities

Determining the target market segments is key steps to successful marketing strategy. In order for Jeonsa Centre to succeed in the implementation of their marketing strategy, they need to effectively promote their services. Sport centers promotion is traditionally requiring aggressive salesmanship. In their case, an aggressive and constant healthy life-style promotion message means grabbing market share from their rivals. Jeonsa Centre must offer something extra to keep customers from turning away to other health clubs. The management team of Jeonsa Centre has identified few channels to help them reach potential customers as well as to maintain existing ones.

- Corporate Partnerships: To attract corporate client tell, Jeonsa Centre have built strategic alliances with universities and colleges. The chosen universities are UUMKL, UTMSPACE, KLMU, MMU College to promote Jeonsa accommodations and sports facilities. The agreement states that the university has to promote products while Jeonsa Centre give 20% discount for accommodations to all students. Staffs and students get additional special rates for other facilities such as seminar room, event hall also badminton courts. Thus students will get full package inclusive of meals, accommodations and other facilities to coordinate their events or programs.

- Social Engine (Agoda.com): Agoda.com is very popular in Malaysia and South-East Asia, and thus, it is an effective tool to promote sales. Agoda.com is a booking engine that tends to attract tourist from Indonesia, Vietnam, China, Philippine and the rest of the world to stay at Jeonsa hotel. As Jeonsa registered as an affiliate Agoda partner, the primary objective is to generate sales by getting more than 70% of commission from hotel rates driven by Agoda. Utilising agoda.com system with its established connections within more than 110 countries worldwide. Agoda.com help customers to choose their hotels within the desired budget and facilitate booking.

- Website: Jeonsa Centre utilizing their own website to convey information and communicate with the public on existing programs, specials, events and promotions. Tools are built in to facilitate customers feedback and enquiry.

- Social Media (Facebook page and Instagram): Facebook page is the number one social media tool and marketing medium prioritized by Jeonsa. Advertising through Facebook page help Jeonsa to reach out to wider customer base and build a network. Marketing teams will ensure the latest and interesting events are posted and communicated.

- Word of Mouth Marketing (WOMM): By telling others about their services, Jeonsa hopes to increase recommendations from members users friends and colloquies and gain new potential customers to use facilities. Management also do this in conjunction with close examination of complaints and reviews of existing feedback, to improve services.

Financial Projection

Financial projection is critical component and plays an important role in short and long-term planning. Practicing good financial control and cash flow planning, helped Jeonsa to evaluate current and future activities, opportunity, minimize risk, attract external funding and prevent planning mistakes or errors.

Actual and Projection Sales

	PRODUCTS/SERVICE	2015 YEAR 1 (ACTUAL)	2016 YEAR 2 (PROJECTION)
1	ACCOMMODATIONS		
	DELUXE	*11,278.00*	*13,675.00*
	QUEEN	*13,467.00*	*15,671.00*
	SPORTS DORM	*20,455.00*	*42,524.00*
		45,200.00	**71,870.00**
2	SEMINAR ROOM		
	SEMINAR ROOM 1	*15,678.00*	*19,876.00*

	SEMINAR ROOM 2	19,421.00	22,567.00
	SEMINAR ROOM 3	17,411.00	27,007.00
		52,510.00	69,450.00
3	**EVENT HALL**	48,276.00	82,500.00
4	**STUDIO**	47,600.00	85,250.00
5	**GYMNASIUM**	50,678.00	64,578.00
6	**FOOTBALL FIELDS**	78,900.00	104,226.00
7	**BADMINTON COURTS**	52,600.00	87,680.00
8	**CAFETERIA**	65,400.00	97,650.00
9	**PARKING**	89,500.00	132,546.00
10	**EVENTS**		
	KEMENTERIAN BELIA & SUKAN	16,789.00	55,670.00
	GENERAL HOSPITAL (HKL)	12,432.00	30,789.00
	CORPORATE COMPANY	10,000.00	32,908.00
	FOOTBALL CLUBS	5,689.00	33,456.00
	TAEKWONDO CLUBS	2,134.00	10,987.00
	OTHERS	8,956.00	34,640.00
		56,000.00	198,450.00
11	**SPORTS MERCHANDISE**	32,000.00	102,345.00
	TOTAL SALES ACTUAL & FORECASTED	618,664.00	1,096,545.00

Projection Income Statement

DETAILS	*2015* *ACTUAL*	*2016* *PROJECTION*
Income		
Capital Investment	500,000.00	
Accommodation	45,200.00	71,870.00
Badminton Court	52,600.00	87,680.00
Football Field	78,900.00	104,226.00
Gymnasium	50,678.00	64,578.00
Hall	48,276.00	82,500.00
Studio	47,600.00	85,250.00

Seminar Rooms	52,510.00	69,450.00
Parking	89,500.00	132,546.00
Cafeteria	65,400.00	97,650.00
Events	56,000.00	198,450.00
Sponsorships		250,000.00
Sports Merchandise	-	102,345.00
Total Income	**1,086,664.00**	**1,346,545.00**
Cost Of Sales		
COS - F & B	45,000.00	38,245.00
COS - Housekeeping	36,470.00	36,654.00
COS - Banquet	28,765.00	22,678.00
COS - Sports Equip	37,690.00	23,289.00
Total Cost Of Sales	**147,925.00**	**120,866.00**
Gross Profit	**938,739.00**	**1,225,679.00**
General Expenses		
Accounting Fees	5,000.00	5,000.00
Advertising	22,300.00	21,300.00
Astro Bills	5,862.00	5,862.00
Cleaning Services	3,450.00	3,100.00
Cleaning Maintenance	3,650.00	3,560.00
Consultation Fee	60,000.00	32,000.00
Football Team Dev	26,700.00	25,678.00
Directors Allowance	240,000.00	240,000.00
EPF-Employees Contri	24,000.00	24,000.00
EPF-Employers Contri	36,000.00	36,000.00
Electricity	6,421.00	6,515.00
Gas	3,958.00	4,045.00
Insurance	4,530.00	4,625.00
Laundry/Dry Cleaning	6,980.00	6,040.00
Lawyer fees	8,000.00	4,000.00
Marketing Expenses	36,000.00	15,600.00
MSN Rental	180,000.00	180,000.00
Office Rental	30,000.00	30,000.00
Photocopy Machine Rental	3,360.00	3,360.00
Printing	5,650.00	2,800.00
Repairs and Maintenance	34,500.00	15,000.00
Rental Machinery	34,250.00	12,300.00
Stationeries	5,420.00	4,876.00
Sports Accessories	37,654.00	20,100.00
Training & Development	5,800.00	4,000.00
Telephone & Fax	4,497.00	4,629.00
Uniforms	4,629.00	1,235.00
Unifi	7,900.00	7,950.00
SOCSO	4,580.00	4,612.00
Custom	2,550.00	2,760.00

Wages & Salaries	199,000.00	202,200.00
Water	1,850.00	1,990.00
License	3,900.00	1,500.00
Total General Expenses	**1,058,391.00**	**936,637.00**
Operating Profit	**(119,652.00)**	**289,042.00**
Income Tax		72,260.50
Cumulative Net Income	**(119,652.00)**	**216,781.50**

Actual and Projection Balance Sheets

BALANCE SHEETS	2015	2016
Assets		
Fixed Assets		
Hotel Equipments	129,465	116,518
Less Depreciation (10%)	(12,946)	11,652
	116,518	104,866
Café Equipments	95,000	85,500
Less Depreciation (10%)	9,500	8,550
	85,500	76,950
Sports Facilty Equipments	36,416	32,775
Less Depreciation (10%)	3,642	3,277
	32,775	29,497
Office Equipments	37,332	33,599
Less Depreciation (10%)	3,733	3,360
	33,599	30,239
Rennovation	83,381	75,043
Less Depreciation (10%)	8,338	7,504
	75,043	67,538
Computer & Software	54,062	43,250
Less Depreciation (20%)	10,812	8,650
	43,250	34,600
Furniture & Fittings	48,580	43,722
Less Depreciation (10%)	4,858	4,372
	43,722	39,350
Total Fixed Assets	430,406	383,041
Current Assets		
Bank	76,000	199,291
Cash	45,200	165,700
Trade Debtors	45,000	127,200
Prepaid Insurance	2,250	2,250

Total Current Assets	168,450	494,441
Inventories - F & B	13,000	25,700
Inventories - Housekeeping	16,700	27,900
Inventories - Banquet	7,800	24,700
Inventories - Sports Equipment	13,200	24,510
Total Inventories	50,700	102,810
Total Assets	**649,556**	**980,292**
Liabilities		
Long Term Liabilities		
Bank Loan	-	-
Current Liabilities		
Trade Creditors	166,700	157,700
Other liabilities	102,508	105,810
Total Liabilities	269,208	263,510
Equity		
Capital Investment	500,000	500,000
Retained Earnings	(119,652)	216,782
Total Liability & Equity	**649,556**	**980,292**

* All figures are in Malaysian Ringgit

Conclusion

Jeonsa Centre founded in 2015, is a multisport complex that offer a variety of services. In collaboration between Malaysian government and Classycca Holdings Sdn Bhd. With convenient and accessible location, being at the centre of Kuala Lumpur, Jeonsa Centre attract guest for looking for healthy lifestyle those who want to spend leisure time with family and friends. Jeonsa Centre niche market is Budget Hotel residents, those looking for budget amenities and want to stay in comfort in relation to value for money. Jeonsa hotel's recreational facilities includes fitness centre, which is decorated and designed with the purpose of escape and relaxation. Acknowledging that customer are more demanding than ever before, they constantly attempt to provide real-time personalized experiences through social media platforms to secure potential customers. To achieve their marketing plans with heavy capitalization on social media, they interact with customers to promote events through newsletter, website and Facebook pages. The business constantly examines customer's feedback through surveys, questionnaire, private message through

Facebook, WhatsApp and their website. Promotions and live events are also updated through broadcast groups and Facebook pages in addition to their own website.

Materialise

Introduction

Addictive manufacturing or known as 3D Printing is anticipated to lead the next industrial revolution through its impact on future processes and business models. 3D Printing revolutionizes the way we make things and has shown a good impact globally across industries. The healthcare industry is now a transformative business that has rising growth and potential enhancement. This case looks into the medical industry applications of 3D printing in Malaysia and Asia Pacific (APAC) through Materialise Sdn Bhd addictive manufacturing patient specific customization products and personalized surgeries in medical industry. It also analyses the potential of 3D printing in medical industry, challenges faced and the way forward to grow in Malaysia and Asia Pacific (APAC). It allows possible integration for surgeons, hospitals and patients to a high quality fabrication of highly customized implants and guides to provide solution for unique and complicated surgeries in a faster time and better recovery.

Background

Additive Manufacturing or 3D printing is a process of making three dimensional solid objects from digital file. It is refereed to nowadays and the future of technology innovation. 3D Printing will have vital impact on the processes and business models in many companies and through this technology, there are all many possible things made. It is a third industrial revolution.

Background of 3D Printing

3D Printing is a term used to describe a range of digital manufacturing technologies. It uses technology that produce component parts layer by layer through additional use of materials. The creation of a 3D printed object is by laying down successive layers of material until the whole object is created. These layers are seen as thinly sliced horizontal cross-section of the eventual project.

The beginning of 3D printing can be traced back in the year 1976 when the printer was invented. Late in year 1983, the co-founder of 3D Systems invented a printing process that enables a tangible 3D object to be created from digital data. The earliest development of 3D printing technologies happened in 1990s. Tradition manufacturing processes creates objects by taking away the material. On the other hand, addictive manufacturing recreates an object layer by layer from scratch by adding materials.

How does 3D printing work?

The 3D printing starts with designing a virtual object that we wanted. The virtual design is made in a Computer Aided Design (CAD) file using the 3D modeling process or by using the 3D scanner. A 3D scanner makes a digital copy on an object.

Using a 3D digital CAD as the blueprint, successive layers of material are precisely fused by a computer controlled into desired 3-dimensional shape object. This process does not require machining and thus no raw material is wasted.

Benefits of 3D printing

The 3D printing presents companies and people a wide and large range of technical, economic and social benefits. 3D printing has the potential to change the paradigm of manufacturing from mass communication to a world of mass personalization. It can lover the tooling and labor cost rates.

In addition, using 3D printing enable to reduce the need of fixed assets such as tooling, freeing up working capital within supply chain and reducing business risk in new product innovation. Fundamentally, 3D printing enhances manufactures to produce in lower cost in a very low unit volumes, down to batch sized of one part.

High complex shapes with very few geometric limitations could be produced using the nature of the 3D printing functionality. This is an added value as previously certain parts could not easily be made by the traditional methods.

Additionally, the manufacturing process of 3D printing itself can reduce the usage of raw material during production, placing a lower burden on the natural resources, commodity purchasing and environment.

The speed of 3D printing is faster compared to the traditional method. It can produce these products quickly, with minimal lead times which make additive manufacturing the ideal method in developing prototypes or low volume custom products. The higher the complexity part, the greater advantage the 3D printing has over the conventional method.

The Applications of 3D Printing

The worldwide 3D printing field is expected to grow steadily. Growth of this technology is predicted to transform almost all industries and change the way we live, work and play in future. And hence, it is anticipated to lead the next industrial revolution.

One industry that is evolving is the medical industry. Specialists and surgeons are beginning to utilize 3D printing in more advanced ways for advance surgeries in shorter time. All around the world, patients are experiencing an improved quality care through 3D printed implants and prosthetics that were never seen before.

Furthermore, the growth in the usage of 3D printing in aerospace and aviation field has been developed for larger parts in the metal addictive manufacturing sector. Currently, the use of 3D printing in automotive is showing better growth from relatively concepts models for functional parts that are used in test vehicles, platforms and engines.

Outside this main domains, addictive manufacturing is being used in production of toys, dolls, gifts, avatars and personalized keepsakes. The 3D applications have been utilized in the consumer electronics for the manufacturer of cases and covers for smart phones, mobiles, tablets and other portable devices.

Global market industry of 3d printing

The addictive manufacturing has evolved steadily in double digits during the past 15 years. Globally, 3D printing sales is projected to be calculated in billions by the 2018, propel by the development if newer technology, applications and approaches. The rising use of the technology bodes well for the market growth. The industry is expected to continue grow uniformly over the next several years.

3D printing will be leading the automotive, medical and aerospace applications more closely in year 2025. In the longer term, addictive manufacturing has the potential to rebrand the manufacturing community. It will give most impact to the industry for products that are made in small volumes that require high customization and more cost tolerant.

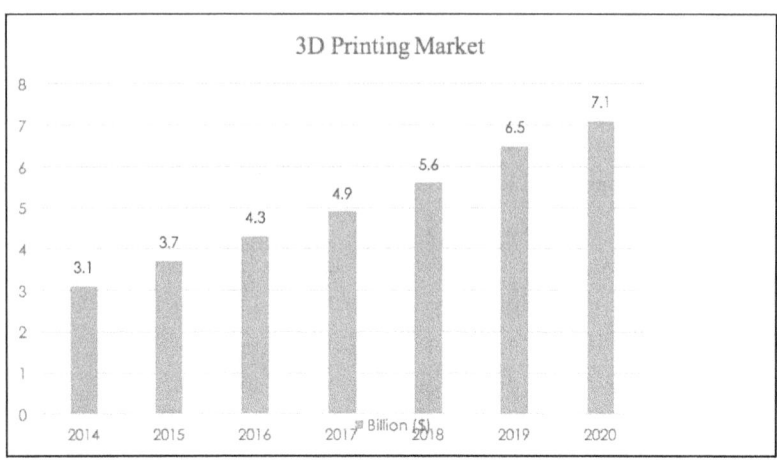

Chart 1: Global 3D Printing Market Value, 2014-2020
Source: Markets and Market Analysis

The technology is used for both making early model and manufacturing in jewelry, footwear, industrial design, construction buildings, civil engineering, engineering and construction (AEC), automotive, aerospace, dental and medical industries, geographic information systems, medical field, and others. Application of 3D printing technology in medical industry play a vital and major role and is the fastest growing segment. Furthermore, surgeons can produce and have an illustration of the patient's body that needed to be operated upon. They may be pre-planning earlier before the surgery and it help them to look over the complicated and complex surgeries. Furthermore, 3D printing technology interface in the aerospace industry as well. The manufacturing revolution in aviation area utilize the 3D printing technology to produce aircraft engine components and a variety of structural components. Addictive manufacturing solutions in the aerospace industry produces lighter and more durable components.

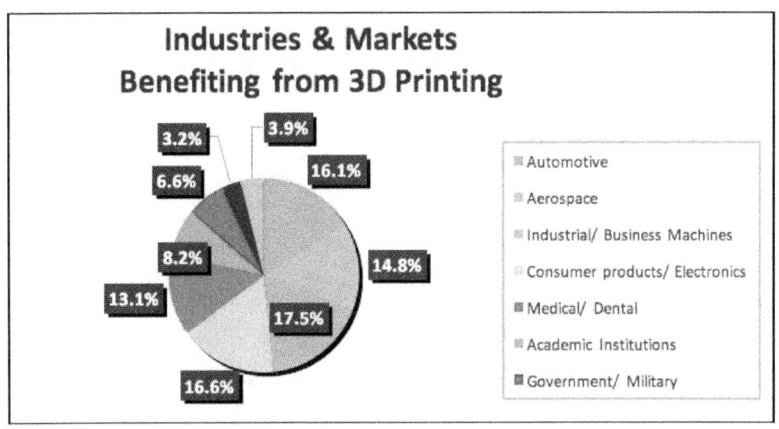

Chart 2: Industries and Markets Benefiting from 3D Printing
Source: Wohlers Associates, Inc 2015

The raw materials used in the 3D printing business are generally simplified into two main part that are plastics and metals. Plastic has been commonly used in addictive manufacturing and it play a vital impact to the major market share. On the other hand, metal is now rising and being used in high demand. Today's 3D Printing technologies make use a wide variety of raw materials such as ceramics and also biological materials besides plastics and metals. Even some companies are experimenting composite materials where they combine plastic and cellulose to form a wood-like material. Via using multiple print heads, different materials can be joined together or deposited at different stages, changing the characteristics and mechanism of the object and product.

The usual traditional manufacturing influences the economies with a wide numbers of items produced and manufactured. The 3D Printing has a mostly steady production cost. The 3D Printing allows for specificity and complexity to incline the independently of cost. The addictive manufacturing phases out the importance of inventory and leverages on the demand manufacturing and mass customization. The manufacturing cost for 3D printing will gradually drop but mostly it will remain steadily.

Figure 2: The Manufacturing Cost between Traditional Manufacturing and 3D Printing

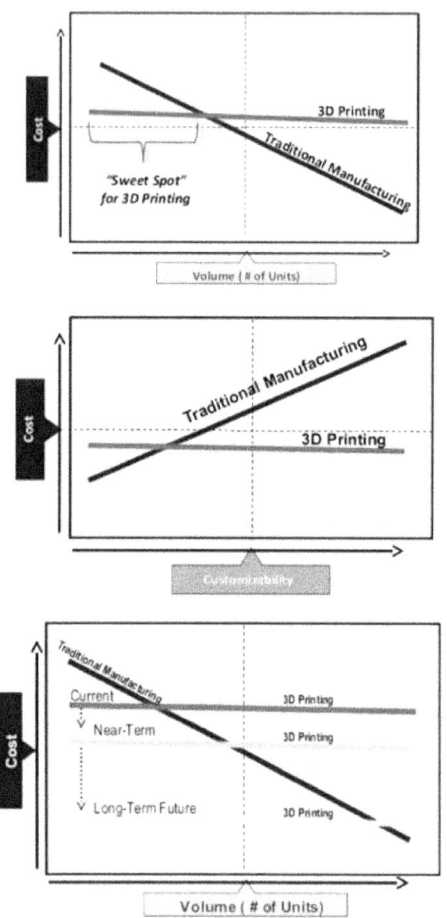

Source: www.slideshare.net, 2013

The vital tendency can be seen in 3D printing market globally are rising up the competition in the industry, increase of service of printing, mass customization, the demand and need for better and good materials and increasing of the usage of the 3D printing technology in more diverse and multifarious applications and industries.

Materialise global

Materialise was established in June 1990 by Wilfried Vancraen at Leuven, Belgium. Materialise was the first company to involve in Rapid Prototyping field in Benelux region. Rapid prototyping is known previously but now it is known as Addictive Manufacturing or in other word is 3D Printing. Since that, Materialise has grown steadily and today has established many offices in many countries on five continents. Their major offices are in Belgium, Malaysia, Ukraine and USA. They also owned offices at United Kingdom, Japan, France, China and Poland.

At this juncture, Materialise is one of the leader in 3D printing field and their aim is to create a better and healthier world. Their business structure is mainly divided into three main section that are 3D Printing, Engineering and Software Development.

Figure 3: Business structure of Materialise

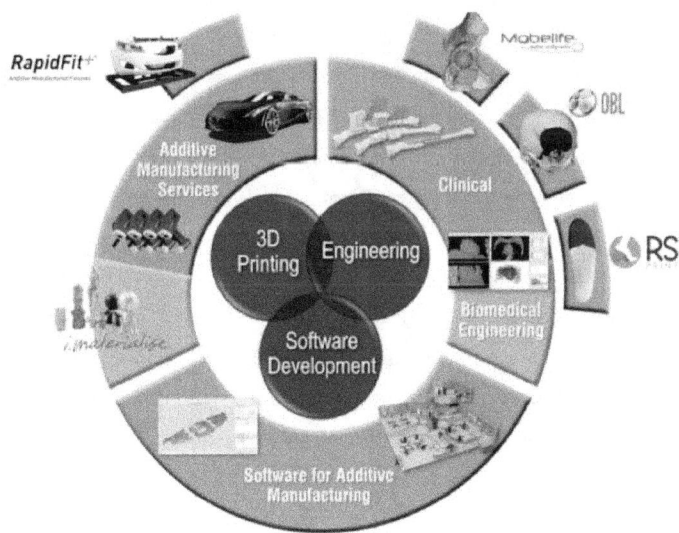

Source : Materialise Sdn Bhd Report

263

Materialise has the largest 3D printing service in Europe. It includes over 100 machines, manufacturing more than 300,000 products and parts per year. The manufacturing processes include are selective laser sintering, fused deposition modeling, multi jet modeling, streolithography and vacuum casting.

In addition, Materialise has focus on research and development in order to provide solutions for the transfer of data to the addictive manufacturing machines. The company released the Mimics software in 1991. The year after, Materialise released the Magics software. Mimics involves with image segmentation. Mimics calculated the surface of the 3D objects from stacked of images from computed tomography (CT), confocal microscope, magnetic resonance imaging (MRI) and micro CT. On the other hand, Magics imports data from computer aided design (CAD) format and then export it into the STL formal that can be printable.

Materialise enjoy a good image and reputation as the provider solution in innovative software. They have used their knowledge and experience in addictive manufacturing for industrial and medical applications and also by contributing biomedical and clinical solutions via medical image processing and surgical stimulations.

The added value of addictive manufacturing that have been used in Materialise are developing unique solutions for complexity situations that make a difference in world for its customers by their planning, prototyping, production and medical needs. Besides that, they have large group of customers from various range of industries such as engineering, automotive, consumer electronics and consumables sectors.

Materialise Sdn Bhd (Malaysia)

Materialise Sdn Bhd has been playing an active role in the field of Additive Manufacturing (also known as 3D Printing) since 1990. In addition to having the largest capacity of Additive Manufacturing equipment in Europe, they are also known for their innovative software solutions. BELGIUM-based innovator in 3D printing solutions Materialise, through its subsidiary Materialise Sdn Bhd, has made Malaysia its regional headquarters as the country has good infrastructure, skilled manpower and low cost of living. The company currently has more than 150 employees, with about half of them Malaysians, working in the engineering and software development side.

Materialise use this experience and expertise to create a better and healthier world through involvement in Additive Manufacturing for industrial and medical applications, and by providing bio-medical and clinical solutions such as medical image processing and surgical simulations.

Materialise mainly divided into four main departments. They are Human Resource (HR), Sales & Marketing, Online Services (ORTHO) and Research & Development (R&D).

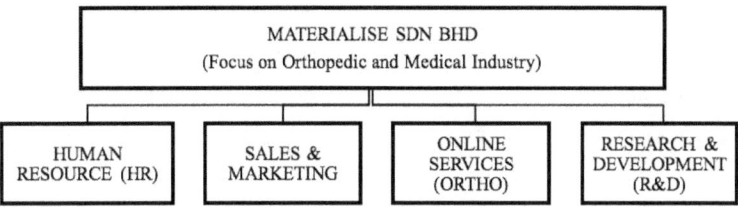

The HR department consists of three teams of Finance, Recruitment & Payroll Administrative. As for the Sales & Marketing department, it consists of teams such as Clinical, Software for Addictive Manufacturing (SAM) and Biomedical Engineering (BME). The online services are the team that involve in orthopedics and it consists of six teams. They are Biomet, Zimmer, Surgicase, Mobelife, Cranio-Maxillofacial and BME. Finally, the Research and Development department that includes the teams of 3-Matic, Mimics, BME and Clinical software.

The HR Department basically involve in the management of the Materialise Sdn Bhd. They are involved in organizing and managing the employees to align with company mission and vision. They are involved in a number of activities that include the training and development, employee wage and benefits, recruitment, performance reward and appraisal and finally company administrative work.

In addition, the Sales and Marketing department in Materialise focuses in developing and expanding the company hardware and software infrastructure through addictive manufacturing from diverse industries and fields such as automotive, medical, aerospace, fashion, research and development. But their main focus is the Medical Industry. Most of them are in contact with orthopedic surgeons in order to provide cutting edge implant technology for the medical cases. They are involved in promoting material and events and at the same time organizing events and product exhibitions.

The Online Services Department are the key of Orthopedic Industry in Materialise. They use Materialise software to add values to people lives by performing accurate 3D surgery planning and designing and customizing surgical guides for orthopedic surgery worldwide. They convert the 2D medical images (radiology, CT, MRI) into 3D bone models and following that, the preform pre-surgery planning on the 3D bone models using the software. Finally, customized surgical guides are designed and created to be used in the actual surgery.

Finally, the last department in Materialise Sdn Bhd is the Research & Development. This department work in developing and improvising the software used in 3D printing process such as software for the segmentation, planning and guide design. They involve in designing new modules of software and enhancement in align to the rise of addictive manufacturing field in Medical and Orthopedic Industry.

Materialise Sdn Bhd is mainly focus in medical and orthopedic field and industry. They involve in sales, marketing, designing and software development for providing solutions in medical and orthopedic field. The advantages of Additive Manufacturing have been used by Materialise Sdn Bhd to develop unique solutions that make a world of difference for many customers with their prototyping, production, and medical needs.

Market industry of 3d printing in Malaysia and Asia Pacific (APAC)
The 3D printing technology is in the early and development stage. 3D printing technology is seen as having high potential to have an impact in the growth of country's industrial sector. Malaysia is recognized as one of the Asian countries that has the potential to lead in technology advancement in the manufacturing industry. This is mainly because of the integration of micro technologies into products.

The 3d printing is largely adopted across fields and industries from the automotive field to the medical industries. This is because of the rising demand for an efficient, quick and low cost manufacturing solution for complexity designed products and objects in a largely usage raw materials. The technology is practically new and fresh in Malaysia as it is mainly involved in the advancement of prototypes in engineering, design and medical areas.

In addition, industry and medical experts are cognizant the impact of addictive manufacturing in education, healthcare, engineering, design, fashion and many more applications. The 3d printing is suspected to boost Malaysian industry robotic usage few years from now. Currently 3d printing is bringing closer industry experts, hobbyists and those with enthusiasm in educating and creating awareness of 3d printing technology and the impact on our everyday lives.

Asia is seen as one of the strategic region of development of 3d printing technology and in South-East Asia, Malaysia is one of the potential strategic hub. The Malaysia economy growth has now focus in manufacturing and services sectors. At this economy uncertainty, Malaysia is now venturing in emerging technologies such as 3d printing to find a niche that can provide the bases to compete with others. Malaysia now is targeting and focusing on technology that can add value in an innovative process and solution. This is to align with the mission target to enable Malaysia to become and 'Innovation Nation' by 2020.

In conjunction, there is an anticipated growth for Asia Pacific market, exhibiting a rise of 23.5% compared to the forecast demand. Asia Pacific region is targeted to have a convincing market demand in future as a factor due to the growing populations and the broadening demand on the applications of 3D printing in implants and surgeries. Below is the industry development in Asia region based on the Wohler's Report 2015.

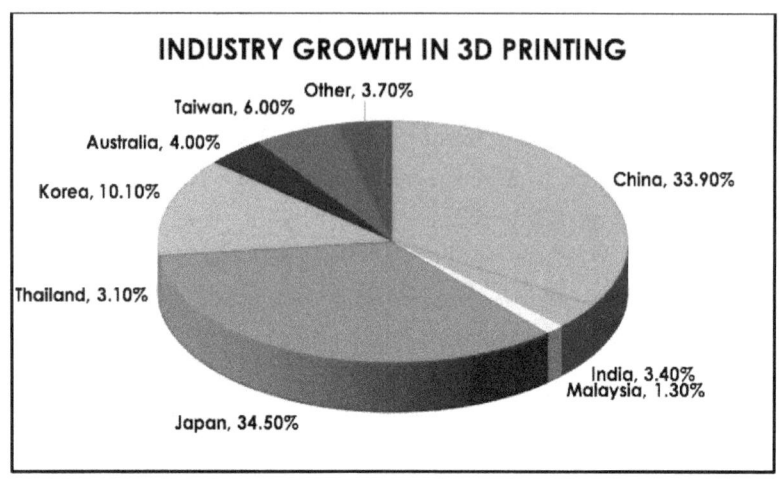

Source: Wohler Associates, Inc 2015

3D printing technology in healthcare industry

Previously, 3D printing has been the element in the mechanical engineering field where CAD software was traditionally used since 1980s. But now, it is developed more beyond the traditional market. 3D printing technology in medical industry is a transformative business that will have a rising growth and potential enhancement in the next five years.

The additive manufacturing in healthcare is remodeling the medical field and healthcare experts are focus and keen to inquire in improving quality of patient care solutions in lower cost and solution provider for complexity cases. 3D printing technology in medical industry has developed much elevation in recent years. This is due to the rising number of applications in medical, orthopedic and dental field with the evolution in tissue engineering.

The 3D printing includes technology such as implants, guides, surgeries and also prosthetic surgeries. The global healthcare market in additive manufacturing is rising speedily with a rise on 15% over the forecasted period. This is influence by the high demand for patient specific products in orthopedic and maxillofacial surgery. In addition, the 3D printing in medical field can be segmented as below;

Furthermore, in the healthcare industry, the 3D printing technology has been developing in a variety of applications. The technology is advancing in more complex medical modelling applications. With the scan image from computed tomography (CT), magnetic resonance imaging (MRI) and x-ray, patient specific product could be designed for every cases accordingly. This shows that 3D printing opens the potential of patient specific customization and personalized surgeries in medical industry.

Additionally, through 3D printing technology, custom made tools that will be used to perform surgical incision or wound opening surgery can be made uniquely suited for specific patients. The future of 3D printing would be the emerging technology on far more complex applications such as human organs. Currently researchers are recreating human cells in laboratories by hand such as skin tissues, blood vessels and other living body parts. But engineering a full model of organ is much more complicated with the complexity of cell structures and might cause controversial issues.

Key of business in Materialise (Malaysia)
Materialise business structure focuses on the 3D printing technology applications in Healthcare and Orthopedic Industry. There are three core competences that structure the business process. There is addictive manufacturing, digital CAD and medical image based engineering and manufacturing. These core competences are applied in medical and orthopedic field.

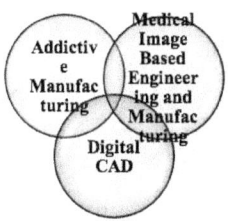

In Materialise, the medical applications in 3D printing are classified into three main group that are the cranio-maxillofacial, orthopedic and insoles. The cranio-maxillofacial basically include surgeries from head to trachea. On the other hand, orthopedic surgeries include from the anatomy of shoulder until foot. Insoles surgeries is done in the inner structure of foot.

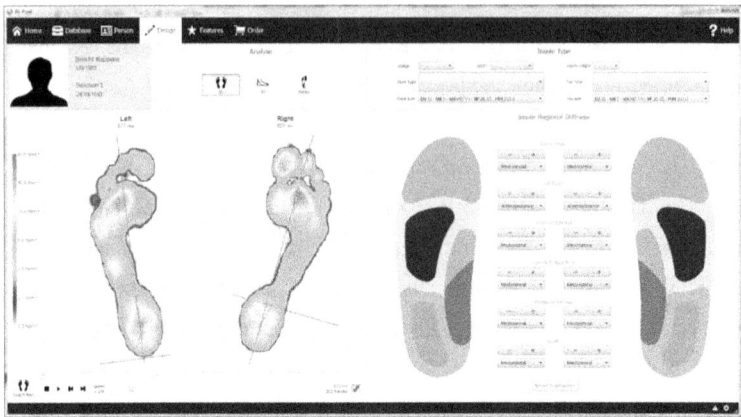

Clinical benefits

Addictive manufacturing has shown a positive impact on medical industry. 3D Printing guides and implants has proven a wide range of clinical benefits in the medical field. Below are the lists of clinical benefits that has been prioritize in using 3D printed guides and implants.

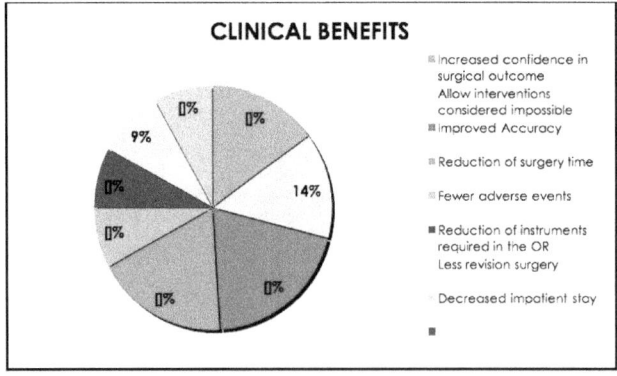

Chart 2: Clinical Benefits Percentage in Medical Field

Reduction of surgery time and improved accuracy are the most important clinical benefits that are inter-related. As this both clinical benefits could be achieved through this technology, it enhances the rise of confidence in the output and the recovery process of the surgery. The technology has become solution provider and allows interventions that was considered impossible to be a success.

Other benefits have almost the same importance where through the addictive manufacturing technology, lesser revision surgery is needed. Besides that, there are a reduction in using a wider range the instruments in operation theatre and a decreased on the stay of patient in the hospital after surgery. It has led to fever adverse events during surgery.

Challenges in Malaysia and Asia Pacific market

The main challenge for Materialise is to give technology to be more visible in Malaysia, as part of the marketing strategy in APAC. In order to market the services and product in Asia Pacific (APAC) and Malaysia, there are three main key factor that play important role. They are surgeon, patient and hospital.

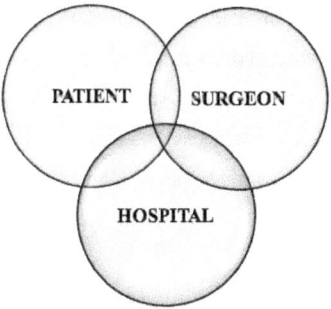

Surgeon

The targeted audience would be the Orthopedic Surgeons in Malaysia and APAC. The surgeons would be from the wide range of upper and lower surgeons from surgical and non-surgical field. Looking into the orthopedic surgeons' market in Malaysia and APAC, it can be explained that most of the surgeons are in the late majority cycle in the innovation adoption life cycle.

INNOVATION ADOPTION LIFECYCLE

The surgeons are basically in the range above 40 years old. They spend their time either in clinics, hospitals, surgeries or in lectures. At this range age of surgeons, they prefer direct sales approach. They tend to decline the calls to arrange meetings due to the incoming patients and patients that are already in consultation. It is difficult to determine their leisure period. About 70% of surgeon used to freebies such as lunch, dinner, drinks, sponsorship, gifts. Unfortunately, that is not the way of approach for Materialise. This group of surgeons also does not prefer email as their communication platform. They rely largely on telephone calls, SMS or WhatsApp.

The surgeons in the late majority cycle are normally older age, where they have more experienced in hands off, fairly conservative and less socially active. At this group of surgeons, they will tend to wait until an innovation has been accepted widely by majority. Once the price has dropped to adopt the new product, then only they will consider of using the services.

Patient

The market size for patient in orthopedic in the types of surgeries are big. But the reality is that the price has been a challenge for the patients. This surgery is not included in insurance coverage like the Europe and America continent. Currently, Australia is in the process on legalization to include the list of surgery in the insurance coverage. Apart from the cost of their solution, there are also additional costs involved such as consultation fees, hospital administration fees, medications. Price has been a concern for most of the patient. This is due to the fact that most of the patient are in the group of low or medium income. They would not afford to pay for the technology and would prefer to use the conventional way.

Hospital

Hospitals can be categorized into three; government hospital, private hospital and university hospital. In government hospital, the facilities are limited and the does not have much high technology equipment to aliased with the 3D printing technology for imaging. Both public hospital and private hospital can be done and implemented as basic technology needed. There is not any specific equipment needed. The difference could be the quality images of the scans but there are specific protocol in Images too.

The waiting list of patients are long and piled up for CT and MRI scan. The process and quality of medical checkup of patients varies due to the fact the surgeons are being changed time by time in government hospitals. As for the private hospitals, the cost and expenses are higher compared to government hospitals. They have much better and updated technology compared to government hospitals. The waiting lists are much lesser and patients can have faster scan of MRI and CT. It would much easier to get appointment from private hospitals and the surgeons compared to government.

SWOT Analysis

STRENGTH	WEAKNESS
Reliable, efficient, solution provider for hard cases, faster surgery, percise output, customization product	Costly, surgeons prefer conventional method, surgeons not familiar with new techology, surgeons mind set
OPPURTUNITIES	**THREATS**
Innovation technology has potential, Clinical Benefits for medical industry	Medical Industry growing fast, need to always follow up and keep close monitoring on the process to provide good quality

3D PRINTING INDUSTRY

Porter's Generic Strategies

Target Scope	Advantage	
	Low Cost	*Product Uniqueness*
Broad *(Industry Wide)*	Cost Leadership Strategy	Differentiation Strategy
Narrow *(Market Segment)*	Focus Strategy (low cost)	Focus Strategy (differentiation)

At Materialise, the focus of the strategy is on differentiation. The focus is on designing a product with unique qualities where the customers perceive as a better options and products in the industry.

This allows Materialise to desensitize prices and to focus on the specialized features that has added value. Materialise need to segment market accordingly thus generating higher price than the average.

First Mover Advantage

Materialise is rated as the first company in Malaysia and the third company in Asia Pacific in 3D Printing. In the medical and healthcare field, Materialise is rated the first. This gives an added value to as first mover in healthcare field in Malaysia. First mover advantage allows Materialise to achieve long-term competitive advantages goals by being the first to offer their customized guides and implants in the marketplace.

This build the company reputation as pioneer and market leader in 3D printing in the medical field. The market currently is free of competition. This in turn helps Materialise to establish brand loyalty where the company can protect its trade secrets or technology through series of patents.

Options and Alternatives

In order to have a growth in Malaysia and APAC, there are three pathways that need to be considered.

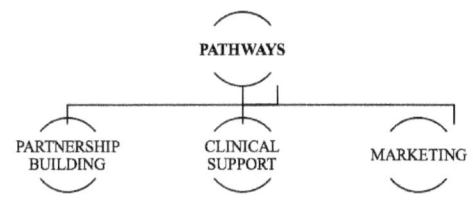

Partnership Building

Partnership building plays a big role in getting out products and services to reach surgeons and patients. This approach helps to get more products and services sold and enroll in APAC region. Partnership can be forged with Original Equipment Manufacturers (OEM). OEM partnering companies that are being consider currently are listed below.

Most surgeries need plates from the above OEM partnerships. In order for the surgeons to be aware of Materialise products, they need to be approached through OEM partners. Eventually, for most complicated cases, the solution provider tends to give an added value. OEM companies also constantly on the look out for potential partnerships, it gives them a greater chance to market their guides and implants. The partnership building process usually consist of three main stages as below:

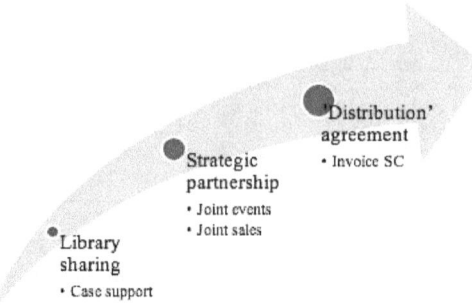

As we all know, the surgeons mostly are the late adopters. In order to approach them and new early adopters surgeons, Materialise need to build trust through Key Opinion Leader (KOL) surgeons that are fans of Materialise products and services. As most of Materialise KOL surgeons are influential and renowned experts in their field, this gives an added value in the effort of approaching other surgeons. Having a library agreements provides an oppurtunity for surgeons to access their products and services and all the cases review and process. This allows for the oppurtunity to work faster and more efficiently with a larger group number of surgeons. The simple and quick process on medical surgery can always be updated and discusseed amongst surgeons as they use Materialise platform for communication.

The next stage would be the strategic partnership. At this stage, they usually engage existing partners locally and add new local partners through rounds of partnership discussions. Annual joint workshops are held in order to give good visibility on hand approach of the technology and the solution approch for cases. It would be a case of business development via the KOLs and co-marketing, which allows a split of cost and resources. Additionally, the co-sales reduces the time on sales activities.

As Materialise started entering more markets, Materialise kept hitting a wall with payment since in most countries systems like that of Materialise' are not reimbursable if it is coupled with an implant. So the ideal situation would be to invoice via the implant as well.

Clinical Support

The second plan would be the clinical support. Materialise need to focus on clinical support and provice a good back up support to surgeons, patients and hospitals. This would enhance a platform for Materialise to find simple and complicated cases. Materialise need to have a effective accesibility. In order to achieve that, Materialise need to ensure that clinical engineers are knowledgable and experienced enough in guiding the surgeons and hospitals. This inculdes forming processes when the surgeons comes forward to use Materialise technology. From the image QC stage to surgery, Materialise must provide technical surgeon support. Materialise further need to have trainning material available for surgoens as reference guide. This mean that the current workflow need to be improved. There should be a clear and steady flow for the case processing as shown below. In order to be successful, Materialise need to provide full and as needed support for the entire process.

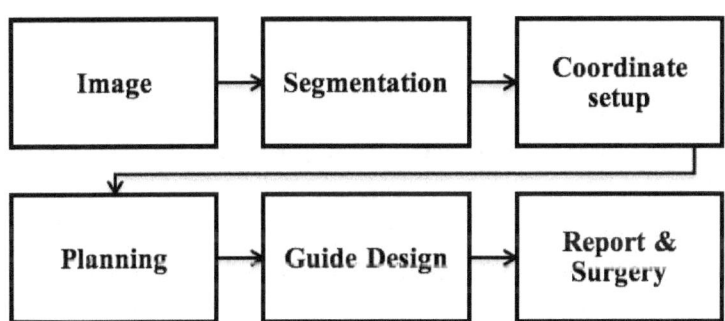

Marketing

Marketing is key for all a businness growth and development at Materialise. Marketing is needed as a tool for Materialise to approach surgeons, hospitals and directly patients. Event management is the method employed usually to achieve this marketing objective. Annual conferences, joint workshops, medical innovation banquets and sharing cases sessions by KOLs surgeons are examples of such events. Such events proved to be effective in Europe. Materialise Global organizes annual conference known as Materialise World Conference, whereby many surgeons and medical institutions join togather and exchange data, cases and knowledge. The same approach need to be implemented in Asia where an annual conference can be held somewhere in the APAC region. This will provide the needed platform to combine surgeons and interested candidates to participate and play a role.

Joint workshops also could be held in conjunction with conferences to provide clearer pictures mainly to surgeons to adapt and understand emerging applications of this technology. Medical innovations banquet venue to gather surgeons, government and non-governmental agencies. Such open platforms of discussion and exchange can be done on regular bases in Malaysia. The sharing case story is an effective method, once a special case is conducted, the success of the story should be shared with mass media, news, blog and television. Real and actual success is always the best marketing plan to attract users. This can also be done on annual bases whereby selected cases are talked about in social media by Materialise KOL surgeons or other interested surgeons. Writing a journal paper about Materialise clinical cases can support the collective effort to publicize Materialise technology.

Conclusion

In conclusion, 3D printing is the new era of technology development. The 21st century is promising a new industrial revolution lead possibly by 3D printing with its varying industrial applications. 3D printing is potentially lucrative market niche in the healthcare industry. The technology is providing solution to hard and complicated cases and has shown that the 3D printing healthcare technology applications is reliable, cost effective and efficient. Being the solution provider for complicated cases, 3D medical applications are much faster and proven to have a precise outcome. 3D provides every single patient to have their own customization products, which is an added value. 3D printing has also revolutionized scaffolding, medical instrumentations and human tissues area. The printing function of human tissue will be a game changer. Materialise Sdn Bhd is the leading company in Malaysia capitalizing on this technology and the 3rd largest in South East Asia.

Takaful

Introduction

Syarikat Takaful Malaysia Berhad (Takaful Malaysia) was incorporated on 29 November 1984 with authorized capital of RM500 million and RM162.817 million in paid-up capital. Operations begun on July, 1985. Takaful Malaysia was set up as a part of government effort to introduce an option for Islamic and Shariah (compliance with Islamic tradition) insurance in Malaysia. It was the first takaful operator in Malaysia and has been a catalyst and triggered the evolution of takaful sector and Islamic financial industry in Malaysia.

Company logo

Takaful Malaysia had a strong governmental support prior to establishment. A special task force committee was set up to study the market viability of Islam based insurance in Malaysia. The committee had concluded that a takaful company based on the principle of *al-Mudharabah* (form of partnership) will be well received given that the participants will be given an opportunity to save, invest and earn profits, while complying with Islamic business principles.

Going public was the next step for its expansion. Takaful Malaysia was listed on the Main board (known as "Main Market" on the Bursa Malaysia Securities Berhad). The move was essential for their growth, with an increment of RM 55 Million in capital and now stands at RM162.817 million to date.

Their primary business objective is for the Malaysian public to consider them as their preferred choice when it comes to insurance or Islamic takaful.

Meanwhile, Takaful Malaysia's mission is to exceed customer's expectation through:
i. Operational excellence
ii. Technology driven capabilities
iii. Product innovation
iv. Performance oriented culture

Such customers' expectation can be achieved while delivering shareholder value. Takaful has also established a tagline of "We Protect, We Care, and We Share" in order to inculcate the image of a takaful companies which will offers their customers protection, caring and most importantly sharing the weight of burden and difficulties at the time when most needed.

Takaful Malaysia's business model
Takaful Malaysia's business model was founded and based on the requirements and practices of Islamic Shariah and has taken the Islamic concept of *Wakalah* contract as main principle for contractual operations. Wakalah model enables them to employ the agency system efficiently and effectively in distributing Takaful products. Under Wakalah model, Takaful Malaysia will act as the agent, which manage the Takaful fund, on behalf of participants. Hence, Takaful will be entitled to a Wakalah (Service) fee for the services provided.

Through this business model, a concept of surplus distribution to the participants is provided. Contributing Tabarru' (donation), which is a certain amount of the takaful contribution that is agreed or undertakes to pay, as such, enabling the payee to fulfil his/her obligation of mutual help and joint guarantee in case any of the fellow participants suffers a loss. In the event of any surplus in the common takaful fund will be shared by both the participant and Takaful Malaysia. This is the common takaful fund, which is an essential make up of the business model.

Takaful Malaysia's corporate structure

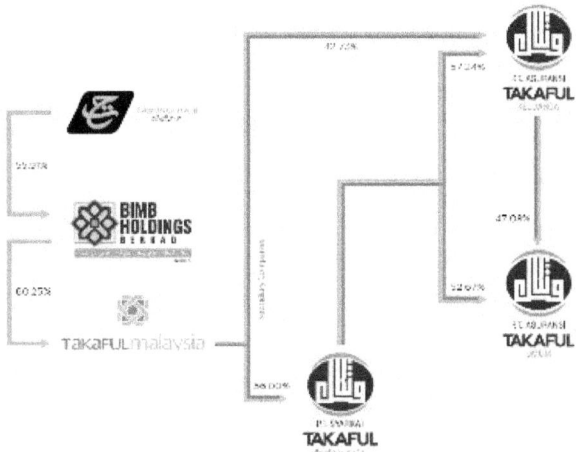

Source: Takaful Malaysia company profile

Takaful Malaysia's financial standings

i. *Financial report study*

Takaful Malaysia's profit has been increasing steadily from year to year. Although takaful companies are obliged to pay a sum of their total profit for zakat (Charity tax) payment, Takaful Malaysia is still making considerable profits for its stakeholders.

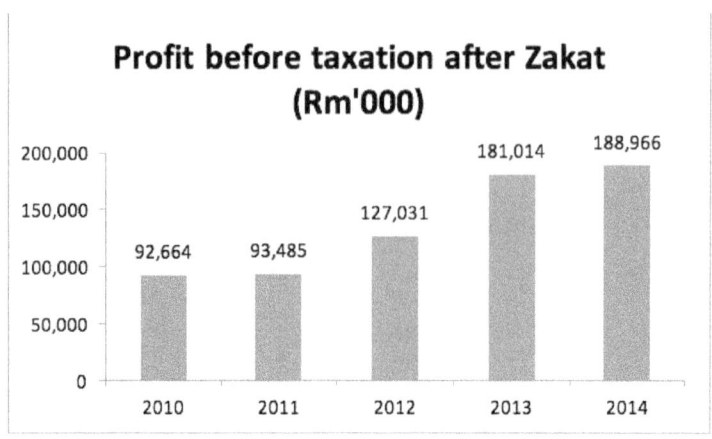

Source: Bursa Malaysia

Takaful Malaysia's profit has risen by more than double between 2010 and 2014. It is considered to be a very profitable business. This is partly because of the aggressive marketing and internal cost reduction strategies applied by management.

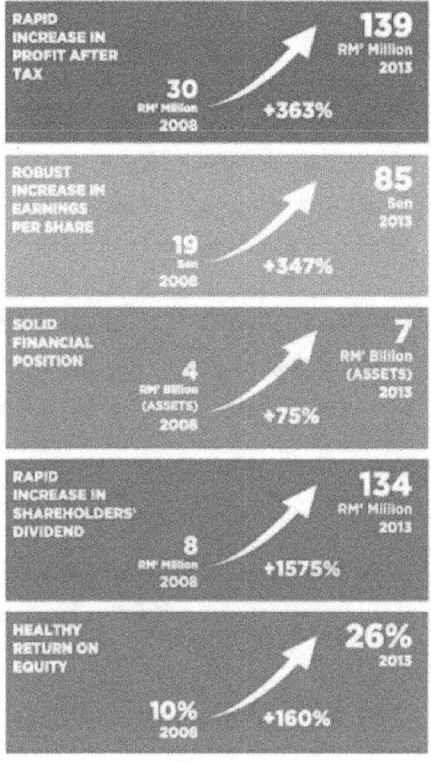

Source: Takaful-malaysia.com.my

Takaful Malaysia celebrated their 30th Anniversary in 2014. They have achieved a considerable growth and a healthy financial standing. As per the above figure, Takaful Malaysia has grown by 363% in 5 years since 2008. Total assets have also increased by 75% during the same period. From shareholders stand point, dividend received from Takaful Malaysia's share has been greatly appreciating by 1575% from 8RM million in 2008, to 134RM million in 2013. Profitability surely attracts investors. This is reflected by the share price listed in main board of Bursa Malaysia.

    ii.   Share price

Takaful's share price started off below RM 2.00 per share in 2009 and hiked up to more than 16.00RM per share in 2015. As the share price in 2015 became sky high for investors, Takaful Malaysia decided to do a stock split in second quarter of 2015. This kind of action is taken primarily as companies see their share price increase to levels that are either too high or beyond the price levels of similar companies in their sector. The main objective for the stock split is to make shares seem more affordable to small investors without changing the underlying value of the company.

After the split activity, Takaful Malaysia's share price has been more affordable, to its lowest point of 3.30 RM per share in May of 2015, since the split, while rising again to 3.90 RM per share in December of 2015. That is 18% increment in two quarters of the same year.

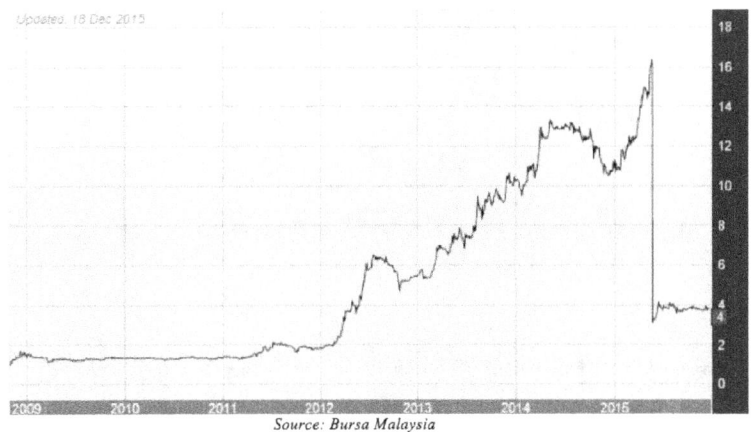

Source: Bursa Malaysia

Definition of takaful

Takaful is derived from an Arabic noun "Kafala", which means an act of protecting and safeguarding someone's needs and interests. Thus, takaful is an agreement between at least two parties to work together, protecting each other interest and equal profit sharing. The agreement also goes beyond sharing profits. Takaful companies and their customers also share the risk of loss should it happens. There are a few differences between takaful and the conventional insurance scheme. They can be separated based on the contractual content, responsibilities and liabilities of takaful provider and participants, and Islamic Shariah compliance of the fund investments.

Takaful is based on mutual cooperation between takaful operators and participants. All or part of the contribution paid to the operators by the participant is a donation to the takaful fund, which will then be used to help other participants by providing protection against potential risks. The accounts of collection derived from contributors' money, is also segregated from the company and shareholders' income. Should there be any surplus in the takaful fund, it will be shared among participants only, while the investment profits are distributed among Participants and shareholders. The investment to be made by the takaful operators companies should also be done in Shariah compliance investment funds.

As opposed to takaful, conventional insurance has a straight forward concept. It is based on an agreement of indemnity by the insurers to bear all expected and agreed risk in exchange of certain amount paid by the insured party to the insurers. However, this concept is rejected by Islamic scholars, in view that it lacks certain degree of fairness to both parties. Customers here transfer all risks to the insurance company by paying a certain premium amount. The collection of premium paid by the customers is then considered as an income to the company and their shareholders. There is also no obligation to which sector the insurance company should further invest their income, be it Shariah compliance or not which expose it to elements of gambling (*Maysir*), interest (*riba'*) and uncertainty (*Gharar*), which are forbidden in the Islamic system.

Overview of Malaysian Takaful Industry
The Malaysian takaful industry has seen a huge transformation and rapid growth since its establishment over 30 years ago. It has rapidly grown from an industry which consists of a single player with limited basic products, to a sustainable industry that has been swiftly integrated into the Malaysian mainstream financial system. This achievement was made possible through the efforts of Bank Negara Malaysia (Central Bank of Malaysia) and the takaful operators in developing a conducive, dynamic, resilient and efficient takaful industry.

Malaysia is a very conducive market for takaful to grow. According to Malaysian Department of Statistics, Malaysia's population in 2014 was at 30.1 million, and expected to rise to 30.5 million by the end of 2016. There poses a significant potential for the industry to grow, as the number of population increases. Malaysia's GDP has also growing smoothly from 2011 to 2014 indicating suitable and sustainable economic environment for takaful industry growth.

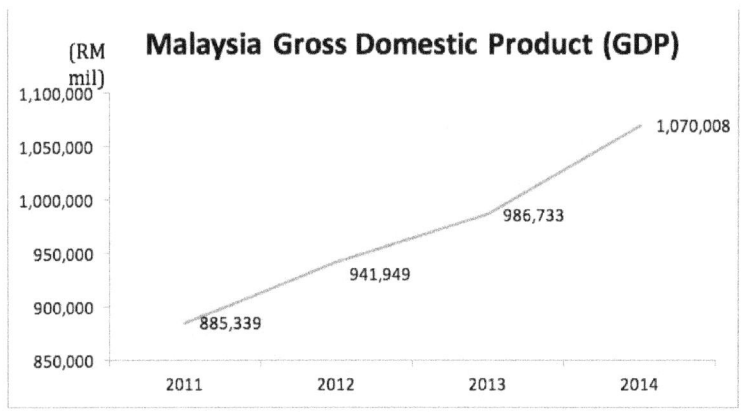

Source: Malaysian Department of Statistics

The growth prospects for the Malaysian insurance sector will remain favorable as the economy continues to expand. The growing middle-income population and awareness of varying risks among consumers will support higher private consumption, and will continue to drive demand for personalized products for transportation and real estate. Medical and health insurance are also likely to be the next segments that insurers and takaful operators are to concentrate on, as Malaysia's population ages with rising medical costs.

Takaful can be divided into two main groups of products namely, family takaful and general takaful. This division is accepted worldwide and used by Bank Negara to monitor the performance of takaful industry comprehensively. Basically, Family takaful is an Islamic form of insurance, which covers human life while insuring anything other than human life is called general insurance. Family takaful is normally a long term contract takaful with regular contribution. The schemes cover hospitalisation and surgical, education, mortgage, and investment-linked. General takaful schemes are usually based on annual or single contribution basis. Examples of general insurance are insuring vehicles against accidental damage or theft, or property against fire and vandalism.

Market for takaful in Malaysia has been steadily increasing on year-by-year basis. Net income from participant contribution has been in upward form from 2010 to 2014 in both takaful divisions recording RM 4.8 billion in Family takaful and RM 1.5 billion from general takaful. That is a total of RM 6.3 billion per year of industry income.

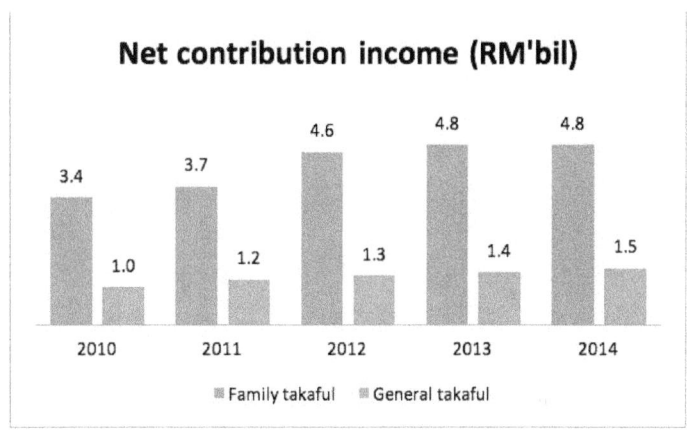

Source: Malaysian Takaful Association, 2014 Annual report.

The Malaysian government has been actively involved in promoting and assisting takaful industry's growth, mainly through Bank Negara and the associations of takaful industry. For example, in late 2013, Bank Negara proposed a paper called the "Life Insurance and Family Takaful for Everyone (LIFE) framework". The proposal included a wide range of areas covering operational flexibility, delivery channels, product disclosure, and market practices. Upon its completion, the initiatives was reflected in the relevant policy documentation to be issued under the Islamic Financial Services Act 2013 (IFSA) and Financial Services Act 2013 (FSA). Additionally, when BRIM 2 was announced during the Malaysia's Budget of 2014, which included takaful plan that provides protection of low income Malaysians, with monthly households' income of less than 3,000RM in the event of death or permanent disability due to an accident.

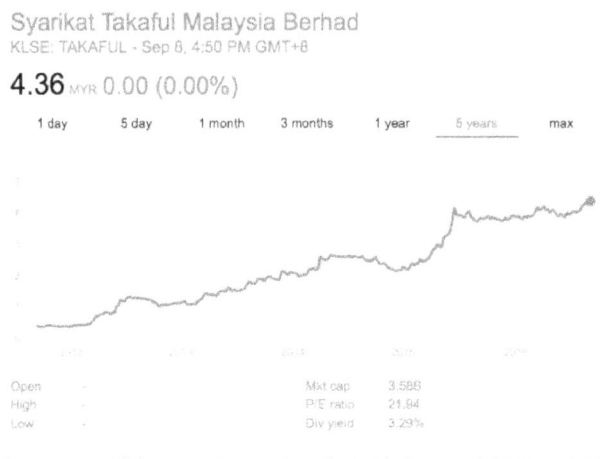

Takaful Malaysia products

Takaful Malaysia is one out of only three fully Sharia compliance company in finance sector listed in Bursa Malaysia according to Securities Commission (SC) latest updated of Nov 2015. In compliance to financial services act of 2013, Takaful Malaysia offers two types of takaful schemes which are Family and General takaful. Below is a list of products offered to participants based on the two products categories:

General takaful products	Family takaful products
- myPA Care Personal Accident	- Takaful myGenLife
- mySME Biz Partner	- Takaful myGen Medic
- Takaful myTravel Partner	- Takaful myHealth Protector
- Others risks (e.g Motor, Boilers and pressure vessels, fire, machinery breakdown, and products liability)	- Takaful myGroup Pro Save
	- Takaful myMortgage
	- Takaful my SME Partner
	- Group Term Family

| | - Group Medical Family |
| | - Group Credit Family |

Competitive environment and challenges
Losing market share in Malaysian takaful industry

Being a pioneer in takaful industry, Takaful Malaysia has done well in promoting and expanding takaful services to Malaysians. Profit growth has also been an increasing trend between 2010 and 2014. Profit before taxation in 2010 was 92.6RM million, and has been increasing by 0.9%, 36%, 42% and 4.4% between 2011 and 2014 respectively. In 2014, Takaful Malaysia was proud of their achievement, as profits before taxes reached 188.96 RM million, more than double when compared to 2010. This achievement has attracted the attention of both investors and competitors. Takaful Malaysia has received awards for their success, namely the Edge Corporate Award, second place for "Highest return for shareholders over 3 years" (2014), International Takaful Summit, Malaysia's best takaful company for (2014), and The Edge Corporate Award, third place for highest profit growth company with highest compound growth in profit before taxes over 3 years (2014).

However, despite the impressive growth performance, their penetration rate is still considerably low as compared to that of conventional insurance. Apart from competing with conventional insurance for a slice of Malaysian insurance market, Takaful Malaysia have to compete with its fellow takaful operators as well. There are currently eleven takaful operators in Malaysia registered with BNM and competing in the takaful industry. The companies are Etiqa Takaful Berhad, HSBC Amanah Takaful (Malaysia) Berhad, Hong Leong MSIG Takaful Berhad, MAA Takaful Berhad, Prudential BSN Takaful Berhad, Sun Life Malaysia Takaful Berhad, Takaful IkhlasBerhad, Great Eastern Takaful Berhad, AIA PublicTakaful Berhad, AmMetLife Takaful, and Syarikat Takaful Malaysia Berhad themselves.

Competing for the takaful market segment has become increasingly challenging over the years as more conventional bank see an opportunity in the takaful market, and therefore offering Islamic insurance product in additional to their product line. This can be seen with the entrance of conventional bank and insurance companies such as

HSBC bank, Hong Leong bank, Maybank (owner of Etiqa Takaful), Prudential and MAA into the takaful market.

Being a market pioneer does not guarantee Takaful Malaysia to be the market leader indefinatly. Any missed opportunity could lead up to their market share being lost to other takaful operators. The competition in the takaful industries today is so fierce, that even an experienced and a pioneer company such as Takaful Malaysia has to double their effort or become more creative to gain new market share. For example, in 2014, Takaful Malaysia ranked 5th in the Malaysian takaful market.

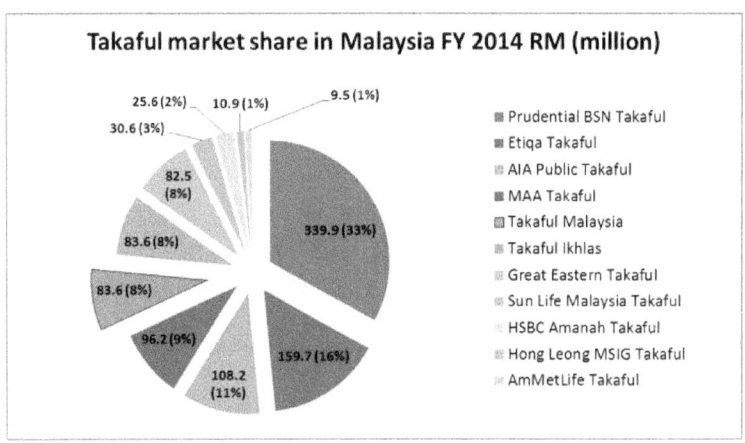

Source: *Malaysia Takaful Association, 2014 Annual report.*

However, Takaful Malaysia started the year of 2015 in strong position. According to *www.myinsurance.com* the takaful market share of Malaysia for the first quarter of 2015 was as below:

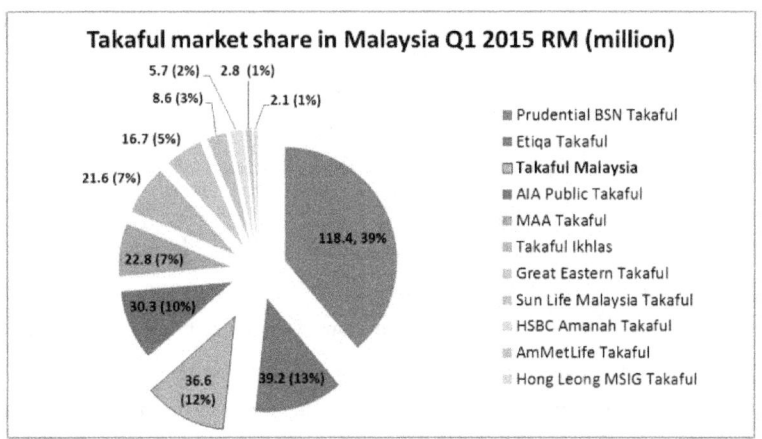

Source: *Malaysia Takaful Association, 2014 Annual report.*

However, the data above also shows that Takaful Malaysia is having fierce competition from other operators. Why does such a pioneer company in the takaful industry of Malaysia, with full support from the Malaysian government is finding it so hard to capture or corner the takaful market? With the experience and the managerial board which consists of Malaysian takaful regulatory setup board, why can't Takaful Malaysia maintain its leading position in the takaful industry? Why is that others players becoming more competitive than Takaful Malaysia?

In finding an answer to Takaful Malaysia's loss of dominance in the Malaysian market, one need to raise such questions as; does their current branding strategy work? was their marketing strategy effective in the past, and are there any new strategies? are they aggressively aiming at gaining new market share? Are they assessing their current market share for effectiveness and profitability? Are they concentrating on the wrong market segment? The 2014 financial year market share study based on Annual Premium Equivalent (APE) is a globally and widely accepted standard for measurement of insurance performance, which may provide some answers to the above questions when closely examined. It is important here to remember that premium in the takaful industry is called "contribution". Hence, takaful industry performance index is called Annual Contribution Equivalent (ACE).

The Annual premium equivalent (APE) is a measure primarily used to compare revenues generated from life insurance, through normalizing policy premiums into comparable annual payments. This practice is used by the insurance industry when sales has both regular premium and single premium. This practice allows for comparability between new business generated during a specific timeframe by life-insurance companies. An ACE is calculated by taking 100% of the amount of regular takaful contribution, and 10% of the total annual single takaful contribution, with the assumption that single payment of an average takaful policy lasts about 10 years. Hence, taking 10% of single takaful contribution annualizes the single lump sum payment over the duration of 10 years.

Takaful Operator	Regular takaful		Single takaful		Total ACE	
	RM (million)	Market share (%)	RM (million)	Market share (%)	RM (million)	Market share (%)
Prudential BSN Takaful	325.1	42.8	146.6	5.4	339.9	33.1
Etiqa Takaful	102.4	13.5	572.3	21.2	159.7	15.5
AIA Public Takaful	93.9	12.4	143.7	5.3	108.2	10.5
MAA Takaful	80.8	10.6	154.5	5.7	96.2	9.3
Takaful Malaysia	13.6	1.8	700.4	25.9	83.6	8.1
Takaful Ikhlas	70.5	9.3	130.7	4.8	83.6	8.1
Great Eastern Takaful	52.8	7	297.2	11	82.5	8
Sun Life Malaysia Takaful	1.7	0.2	288.5	10.7	30.6	3
HSBC Amanah Takaful	10.4	1.4	152.3	5.6	25.6	2.4
Hong Leong MSIG Takaful	4.8	0.6	61.3	2.3	10.9	1.1
AmMetLife Takaful	3.4	0.4	61.1	2.3	9.5	0.9

Source: www.myinsurance.com

Takaful Malaysia is performing well in the single takaful market, while losing market share in regular takaful to namely; Prudential BSN Takaful and Etiqa Takaful.

Competing with conventional insurance

Malaysia's takaful penetration is still considerably low at 5.2% of Malaysia's total gross domestic products (GDP) during 2014 (according to Malaysian Takaful Association Chairman Mr. Ahmad Rizlan Azman in the World Islamic Economic Foundation "WIFE" Forum 2015). As for terms of penetration rate, takaful is still low compared to its conventional counterpart. Malaysian Takaful Association indicates that the market share for takaful has been condensed between 2013 and 2014 by 0.8%. It coincides with Takaful Malaysia's loss of market share in takaful industry. This has lots to do with the number of players in the industry fighting for a limited market, and competition from the conventional insurance industry.

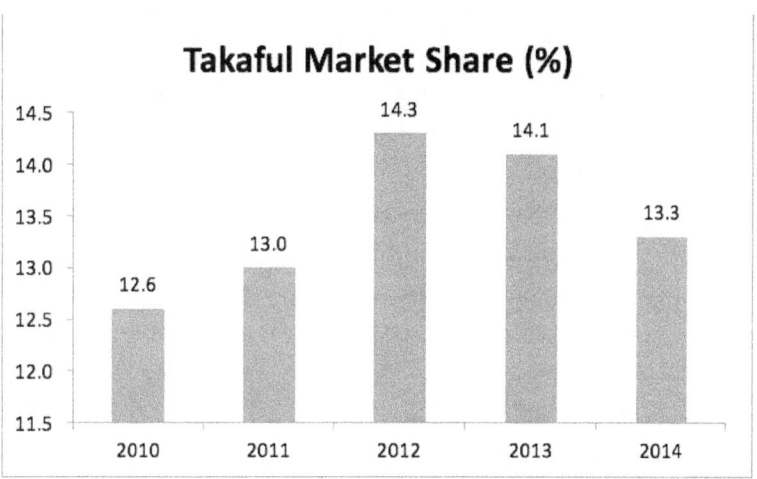

Source: *Malaysia Takaful Association, 2014 Annual report*

Even with 30 years of operations in the Malaysian market, takaful is still an unknown term to most people. This is attributed to number of reasons. Non-Muslims participation is very limited in a country segregated on religious and ethnic bases. Additionally, takaful is not strategically positioned to face the demanding financial ecosystem, and the marketability of takaful is not applied across the board to all ethnicities of the Malaysian public, the way it's marketed for the Malay.

Azrim Naim's research confirms the argument that numerous issues facing the takaful industry, including low level of Shariah compliance, lack of supporting laws and regulations, few takaful operators exist in the market, limited availability of Shariah compliance investment avenues, and available capital in the takaful industry is cconsiderably lower than that of conventional insurance companies.

Takaful Malaysia's marketing strategies

The biggest challenge facing Takaful Malaysia is how to maintain a competitive position in the takaful market. Government support and connection can only go so far. In this regards, Takaful Malaysia has taken several marketing and branding strategies with the aims of maintaining customers' loyalty, capitalizing on existing customers, and attracting new new segment of clients.

Takaful Malaysia has been very proactive and keen to regain their dominance in takaful industry by distinguishing their operations from those of conventional insurance operators. Their trategy largely applies an integrated marketing and branding initiatives to position themselves as the preferred choice of insurance. Other activities taken includes:

    i. Uplift operational efficiency and customer service through IT, to further develop 'customer-centric' approach to services provided throughout the company. Takaful Malaysia's website for example, offers innovative portal solution with added functions to make it easier for customers to enjoy service provided. The Motor Takaful calculator, Motor NCD enquiry and supplementary portals namely myTakaful Agent is an example of features added to their website for customers easy of experience.

    ii. Introduction of catchy tagline such as "We Protect, We Care and We Share" and "We Should Talk" has also been a central theme of the branding strategy to convey the image of friendly and caring company.

    iii. Promotions have also been a huge part of their growth plan. Takaful Malaysia claims that they are the only takaful operator to offer a 15% cash back for all general takaful products as a reward for no claims during coverage period. This promotion is widly advertised in newspapers and billboards strategically located along major highways across Malaysia.

Further action required by Takaful Malaysia

Takaful Malaysia has been a very successful company in the takaful industry and a major competitor in the insurance industry. Its past profitability should be used to expand operations further and capitalize on their success. Because they have potential to growth more by competing with existing rivals, they need to:

i. Expand market share by creating awareness of the advantages of takaful to every Malaysian regardless of their religious background. Advantages and the benefits of takaful should be made known to the public by targeting the Malaysia Chinese and Indian ethnicities through Chinese and Indian media. Taglines such as "Takaful for all" would create an image of universality and break the unnecessary religion barrier for their business to grow.

ii. Increasing the number of agents. Conventional insurance companies have a large network of agents offering their products. Takaful Malaysia should also increase the number of authorized agents especially in big cities such as Kuala Lumpur and in the rural areas, where internet access is limited and people prefer a personal relationship based on trust rather than through the Internet.

iii. Takaful Malaysia need to strengthen regular contribution products value and advertise these advantages. By focusing more on regular contributions, Takaful Malaysia could generate more constant income as opposed to single contribution, which is uncertain and considered as unfixed income. Customers' loyalty in single contribution is also low since customers are able to switch to other companies with no strings attached. For example, in Motor insurance customers can jump from one company to the other while maintaining their (No Claim Discount) NCD values should there is no claim made.

iv. To brand themselves as "The Takaful" company, Takaful Malaysia should capitalize on their existing strength in the market and remind customers that they are strong, stable and dominant takaful company. Aggressive advertising can help achieve the re-branding objectives. Takaful Malaysia should spend more on promotional. Newspaper, radio, billboards, and even social medias targeting all segments and ethnicities of the Malaysian society to create awareness of their inclusiveness. Future objectives should be that when people think of takaful products, the first company that comes to mind is Takaful Malaysia.

v. Go global with strategic alliances. There are 57 members' states in the Organisation of Islamic Cooperation. This means there is a huge untapped market that can be attained through strategic alliances. Going global, Takaful Malaysia will be able to have larger market share than the already saturated local Malaysian market.

Questions

1. Why does such a pioneer company in the takaful industry of Malaysia, with full support from the Malaysian government is finding it so hard to capture or corner the takaful market?
2. Given the experience of the managerial board, which consists of Malaysian takaful regulatory setup board, why can't Takaful Malaysia maintain its leading position in the takaful industry?
3. Why is that others players becoming more competitive than Takaful Malaysia?
4. What can Takaful Malaysia do to lead in their industry?

References used throughout the book

About Materialise. (2015).
Retrieved from http://www.materialise.com/about-materialise/

Abdou, H., Ali, K. & Lister, R. (2014) 'A comparative study of Takaful and conventional insurance: empirical evidence from the Malaysian market', *Insurance Markets and Companies: Analyses and Actuarial Computations*

ACSM'S Health & Fitness Journal: November/December 2015 - Volume 19 - Issue 6 – p. 24-31

All statements are supported by Figure 1 and an experience of becoming members at http://www.airasia.com/site/my/en/home.jsp.

AirAsia. (2015). AirAsia.com. Retrieved 27 Disember, 2015, from http://www.airasia.com/la/en/about-us/corporate-profile.page

AirAsia faces challenges throughout Southeast Asia as competition continues to intensify. (2013, August 1). Retrieved December 27, 2015, from http://centreforaviation.com/analysis/airasia-faces-challenges-throughout-southeast-asia-as-competition-continues-to-intensify-125261

AirAsia faces challenges throughout Southeast Asia as competition continues to intensify. (2013, August 1). Retrieved December 27, 2015, from http://centreforaviation.com/analysis/airasia-1h2015-results-the-regions-leading-lcc-regroups-for-the-long-run-reining-in-expansion-241169

Asohan, A. (2013, June 26). Stratasys' emerging markets. Retrieved from https://www.digitalnewsasia.com/

Avialite Sdn Bhd: Quality Manual, Brand Planning

Avialite Sdn Bhd: Quality Manual, Market Planning

Bamford, D. and Xystouri, T. (2005), "A case study of service failure and recovery within an international airline", Managing Service Quality, pp. 306-22.

Bank Negara Malaysia. (2014) Financial Stability and Payment Systems report 2014

BAE Systems Bofors AB Official Website Retrieved from http://www.baesystems.com

BAE Systems Inc. Official Website Retrieved from http://www.baesystems.com

BAE Systems Plc Official Website Retrieved from http://www.baesystems.com

Bank Negara Malaysia Annual Report 2014.

Bearak, M. (2015, June 22). AirAsia Faces Red Tape and Tough Competition in India. Retrieved December 27, 2015, from http://www.nytimes.com/2015/06/23/business/international/airasia-faces-red-tape-and-tough-competition-in-india.html?_r=0

Bala et al, (2005) Asian Academy Of Malaysian Journal, AAMJAF, Vol. 1, 81–104, 2005

BHIC Bofors Asia Sdn Bhd Official Website (2014). Retrieved from http://www.bhic-bofors.com.my

Bloomberg http://www.bloomberg.com/research/stocks/people/person.asp?personId=8399953&privcapId=2482172

Boustead Heavy Industries Corporation Bhd Official Website (2014). Retrieved from http://www.bhic.com.my/index.php

Boustead Holdings Bhd Official Website (2015). Retrieved from http://www.boustead.com.my/

Boustead Heavy Industries Corporation Berhad Annual Report 2014, Boustead Heavy Industries Corporation Berhad.

Boustead Heavy Industries Corporation Berhad (BHIC): www.bhic.com.my

Blackett, T. (2004). What is a brand. *The Economist Series: Brands and Branding*. New Jersey: Bloomberg Press.

Bloomberg Business. (2015, April 9). Islamic Fashion's Expanding Market Attracts Shariah Financiers, Retrieved from http://www.bloomberg.com/news/articles/2015-04-08/islamic-fashion-s-expanding-market-attracts-shariah-financiers

Business News Daily Retrieved from http://www.businessnewsdaily.com/5446-porters-five-forces.html

Bursa Malaysia – www.bursamalaysia.com

Carlos Garriga, Yang Tang, and Ping Wang (2014) *Rural-Urban Migration, Structural Transformation, and Housing Markets in China*

Castillo-Manzano, J. I., & Marchena-Gómez, M. (2010). Analysis of determinants of airline choice: profiling the LCC passenger. *Applied Economics Letters*, *18*(1),

49-53.

CIMB Itrade - http://itradecimb.com.my/

C.H. Williams Talhar & Wong. *Property Market 2014*, 2014. Kuala Lumpur. Online HSR International Realtors Pte Ltd. *Malaysia: Property Market Report 2013*. www.hsr.com.sg, 2014. Online

CK TAN (June 20, 2015) Malaysian developers shy away from competing with Chinese. *Nikkei Asian Review*.

Chamberlin, B. (2014, April 18). 3D Printing - A 2014 Horizonwatching Trend Summary Report. Retrieved from http://www.slideshare.net/

Chen (2015). Principle of Marketing Part 1: Strategic Marketing and Its Environment Retrieved from http://slideplayer.com/

Chiara, C. (2013). *LED Lamps Market to Grow at Light Speed.* Retrieved November 19, 2015 from http://www.frost.com/prod/servlet/press-release

Crude Palm Oil Futures (FCPO) on Bursa Malaysia, retrieved http://www.opf.com.my/blog/#sthash.fwm5noRA.dpuf

Davis, S. M. (2002a). Brand Asset Management: Driving Profitable Growths through Your Brands San Francisco: Jossey-Bass Inc

David, F. (2013). *Strategic management: Concepts and cases: A competitive advantage approach* (14th ed., global ed.). Harlow, England: Pearson.

Department of statistics, Malaysia - https://www.statistics.gov.my/

D'yana official website. (2015). Retrieved from http://www.dyana.com.my/

Economic Transformation Program (ETP) Handbook (2010), Performance Management & Delivery Unit (PEMANDU)

Economic Transformation Program (ETP) Annual Report 2014, Performance Management & Delivery Unit (PEMANDU)

Economic Transformation Program: www.etp.pemandu.gov.my

Economics Transformation Programme . EPP 2: Building Globally Competitive Shared Services and Outsourcers. Retrived December 19, 2015. From http://etp.pemandu.gov.my/Business_Services-@-Business_Services_-_EPP_2;_Building_Globally_Competitive_Shared_Services_and_Outsourcers.aspx

Ecoworld Official Website - http://ecoworld.my/

Eco World Development Group Berhad. *Eco World Annual Report 2012*. Malaysia.

Eco World Development Group Berhad. *Eco World Annual Report 2013*. Malaysia.

Eco World Development Group Berhad. *Eco World Annual Report 2014*. Malaysia

El Fegoun, M. A. B. C. Upstream Supply Chain Analysis for Oil Palm. 2015

Experience ACSM's Health & Fitness Summit & Expo 2015 RECAP. Spezzano, Michael J.

Fadzim Othman, Agricultural Land Use : Problems and Prospects, Jurnal Ekonomi Malaysia 25, 1992.

FGV Annual Report, 2014 Malaysia Palm Oil Council Websites
http://www.mpoc.org.my/Industry_Overview.aspx

Gambero. Dr. D. *Malaysian Property Market 2014 Outlook: The New Property Drivers and The*

Gilbert, H. (2008). *Introduction to Light Emitting Diode Technology and Applications* (2nd Edition), New York: Taylor and Francis Group

Global Naval MRO Trend Retrieved from http://www.asdreports.com

Growing Areas for High Return Investment. www.reigroup.com.my, 2014. Online

Groopman, J, (2014, November 24). How 3-D printing is revolutionizing medicine. Retrieved from http://www.newyorker.com/

Gunduz, F., & Pathan, A. K. (2012, November). Usability Improvements for Touch-Screen Mobile Flight Booking Application: A Case Study. In *Advanced Computer Science Applications and Technologies (ACSAT), 2012 International Conference on* (pp. 49-54). IEEE.

Hunstman, H. (2014). *Top LED Players Facing Tough Competition In LED Lighting Market*. Retrieved November 25, 2015 from http://bizled.co.in/top-led-players-facing-tough-competition-in-led-lighting-market/

Intellectual Property Corporation of Malaysia (MyIPO) website. (2015). Retrieved from http://www.myipo.gov.my/

Insurance Service Malaysia Berhad (2014) Statistical Yearbook: General Insurance and Takaful; Financial year 2014

iFAST Research Team, 2014, Is the Malaysian Sector Overviewd? Retrieved http://www.fundsupermart.com.my/main/research/viewHTML.tpl?articleNo=5019

iFAST Research Team, 2014 The Evalution of Malaysia Plantation Players , 2015 Fundsupermart

Is the Malaysian Sector Overviewed? Retrieved http://www.fundsupermart.com.my/main/research/viewHTML.tpl?articleNo=5019

Joshua, J. (2011). *History of LEDs.* Retrieved December 1,2015 from http://www.led-lamps.net.au/led-basics/history-of-leds

Khoo Khee Ming and D Chandramohan , 2002, Malaysian Palm Oil Indusrty at Crossroads and its Future Direction, Malaysian Palm Oil Board.

King, B. E. (2013). Transactional and transformational leadership: A comparative study of the difference between Tony Fernandes (Airasia) and Idris Jala (Malaysia Airlines) leadership styles from 2005-2009. *International Journal of Business and Management*, 8(24), p107.

Labuan Shipyard & Engineering Sdn Bhd: www.labuanship.com/corporate-about.asp

Lita Person & Swapnil Phalke. (2015). World 3D Printing Market - Opportunities and Forecasts, 2013 – 2020 Retrieved from https://www.alliedmarketresearch.com/

Marvin B. Lieverman and David B. Montgomery (2002). First Mover Advantages. Strategic Management Journal, Volume 9.

Malaysian Shipbuilding/Ship Repair Industry Report 2015/2016, Malaysian Industry Government Group for High Technology (MIGHT).

MalaysianDigest.com. *Encorp Banking On FIC's Strength.* http://malaysiandigest.com/business/509954, 2015. Online

Malaysian Takaful Association (2014) 2014 Annual Report

Malaysia Palm Council
http://www.mpc.gov.my/mpc/images/file/RR2014/RURB%20Palm%20Oil%20Report/OVERVIEW.pdf

Mellisa, N., Azizah, S., Zarina, Nur Hidayati and Diana Rose. (2011). Project: Information System In Company.

Naomi Ng, The Humble Chef, 29 June 2013, http://smooch-the-bone.blogspot.com/2013/06/the-humble-chef.html

Nancy Bota, Ethan Coppenrath, Danying Li and Michael Manning (2010). 3D Printing & the Medical Industry: An in depth analysis of 3DP'S potential impact on healthcare

Norman, C. and Seaman, P. (2013, March 12). 3D Printing Edge Manufacturing.

Retrieved from http://www.slideshare.net/

Outsourcing Malaysia. http://outsourcingmalaysia.org.my/ . Retrived December 18th, 2015. From http://outsourcingmalaysia.org.my/?page_id=18

Osterwalder, A., Pigneur, Y. *Business Model Generation*. New Jersey: Wiley, 2010. Print

Pew Research Centre. (2015, April 2). The Future of World Religions: Population Growth Projections, 2010-2050, Retrieved from http://www.pewforum.org/2015/04/02/religious-projections-2010-2050/

Quartz Business Media Ltd, 2015, Oils & Fats International retrieved at http://www.ofimagazine.com/news/indonesia-asks-eu-to-ease-indonesia-palm-oil-import-regulation.

Raine & Horne. *Living Within The Valley*, 2014. Kuala Lumpur. Online starproperty.my. *Felda Investment says Encorp buy will speed up property development.* www.starproperty.my/index.php/articles/investment/felda-in, 2014. Online

Raine & Horne. *Living Beyond The Valley*, 2014. Kuala Lumpur. Online theedgeproperty.com. *Highlight: Felda to take Encorp private.* http://www.theedgeproperty.com.my/content/highlight-felda-to-take-encorp-private, 2014. Online

RHB-FGV Market Analysis, 2014- Consumer Non–cyclical-Agriculture

Roderick B. Diaz et al. Impacts of Rail Transit on Property Values

Sarah Lim (15 April 2015) Eco World Berhad, A Rising Star. *Kenanga Investment Bank Berhad, Initiating Coverage*

Salman, S.A. (2014) Contemporary issues in Takaful (Islamic Insurance), *Canadian Center of Sceince and Education*, Vol 10. No. 2

Shavinina, L. V. (2006). Micro-social factors in the development of entrepreneurial giftedness: the case of Richard Branson. *High Ability Studies*, *17*(2), 225-235.

Ship building & ship repair (SBSR) industry: www.might.org.my

Shuk-Ching Poon, T., & Waring, P. (2010). The lowest of low-cost carriers: the case of AirAsia. *The International Journal of Human Resource Management*, *21*(2), 197-213.

Snack Attack – What Consumer Are Reaching For Around The World, September 2014, The Nielsen Company

Snack Nuts and Seeds – Sub-Category Report H2 2013, April 2014, Innova Market Insights

Spence, M. (1974). Competitive and optimal responses to signals: An analysis of efficiency and distribution. *Journal of Economic theory*, *7*(3), 296-332.

Spiros, K. (2010). *Light Sources: Technologies and Applications* (Vol 10. No.2), UK:CRC Press

Sustainable Sourcing Guide for Palm Oil Users, 2015 , Sustainable Food & Agriculture Markets.

Sudhir, K. (2001). Competitive pricing behavior in the auto market: A structural analysis. *Marketing Science*, *20*(1), 42-60.

Sue Lynn, The Humble Chef at Pusat Bandar Damansara, 5 April 2010
http://www.bangsarbabe.com/2010/04/the-humble-chef-pusat-bandar-damansara.html

Sweet and Savoury Snacks in Malaysia, February 2014, Euromonitor International

Takaful Malaysia. (2012) Annual report

Takaful Malaysia. (2013) Annual report

Takaful Malaysia. (2014) Annual report

Temporal, P. (2000). Branding in Asia: The Creation, Development and Management of Asian Brands for the Global Market. Singapore: John Wiley & Sons.

Teoh Cheng Hai, From Seed to Frying Pan, 2002, WWF Malaysia

Tim Whitaker, "LEDs Magazine"*,* Jul/Aug 2012 issue, PennWell Corporation, pp.109-111

Top 10 of Malaysia - http://top10malaysia.com/home/index.php/bursa-stories/bursa-malaysia-companies1

The Challenger (2012) Retrieved from http://www.thechallenger.com.my/

Themalaysianreserve.com. *FIC's Encorp set for first property venture.* http://themalaysianreserves.com/new/story/fic, 2014. Online

Therakyatpost.com. *Felda to delist Encorp?.* http://therakyatpost.com/business/2104/05, 2014. Online

Thestar.com.my. *Poser over Encorp's sale of loss-making construction unit for RM1.* http://www.thestar.com.my/business/business-news/2015/09/06/poser-over-encorp-sale-of-loss-making-construction-unit-for-RM1/?, 2015. Online

Thestar.com.my. *Encorp plans to leverage on Felda.* http://www.thestar.com.my/business/business-news/2015/06/25/encorp-plans-to-leverage-on-felda?, 2015. Online

Thestar.com.my. *Yeoh Soo Ann is lifting Encorp to greater heights in the post-Effendi era.* http://www.thestar.com.my/business/business-news/2014/03/15/taking-encorp-to-greater-heights-in-the-poste/?, 2014. Online

Thesundaily.com.my. *Effendi and daughter exit Encorp after stake disposal.* http://www.thesundaily.my/node/215534, 2013. Online

Thomson Reuters and Dinar Standard. (2015). State of the Global Islamic Economy 2014-2015 report, Retrieved from http://www.assaif.org/index.php/content/download/78258/380258/version/1/file/GIER+2014-2015.pdf

VADS BERHAD. Retrived December 18th, 2015 fromhttp://www.vads.com/integrated-ictservices/

VADS BERHAD. Retrived December 18th, 2015 from http://www.vads.com/integrated-business-process-outsourcing/Economics Transformation Programme. *EPP 3: Positioning Malaysia as a World-class Data.* Retrived December 19, 2015. From http://etp.pemandu.gov.

Valuation & Property Services Department. *Press release Malaysia Property Market 2014.* Putrajaya: Ministry of Finance Malaysia, 2015. Print

Valuation & Property Services Department. *Property Stock Report 2014.* Putrajaya: Ministry of Finance Malaysia, 2014. Print

Valuation & Property Services Department. *Property Market Report – First Half 2014.* Putrajaya: Ministry of Finance Malaysia, 2014. Print

Valuation & Property Services Department. *Property Market Report – First Half 2015.* Putrajaya: Ministry of Finance Malaysia, 2015. Print

Valuation & Property Services Department. *Wilayah Persekutuan Kuala Lumpur.* Putrajaya: Ministry of Finance Malaysia, 2015. Print

Valuation & Property Services Department. *Property Stock Report – H12015.* Putrajaya: Ministry of Finance Malaysia, 2015. Print

VPC Asia Pacific. *Property Country Report: Malaysia*, 2014. Johor. Online

Wohlers Associates. (2015). Wohlers Report 2015: 3D Printing and Additive Manufacturing State of the Industry Annual Worldwide Progress Report

Xtion Paintball (2015) Retrieved from https://xtionpaintball.wordpress.com

3D Printing in Malaysia Highlighted by Materialise Conference. (2013, June 19). Retrieved from http://3dprintingindustry.com/

3D Printing & Additive Manufacturing in the Aerospace & Defence Market 2015-2025: Top Companies in Prototyping, Manufacturing & Processes, Finished Parts. (2015). Retrieved from https://www.reportbuyer.com/

http://www.sipri.org

http://etp.pemandu.gov.my

http://www.avialite.com/

http://www.veeco.com/

http://www.matrade.gov.my

http://www.ledinside.com/

http://energy.sourceguides.com

http://www.bloomberg.com/news/articles/2015-12-01/unitedhealth-says-it-should-have-stayed-out-of-obamacare-longer

http://www.gcs.europassistance.com/sites/default/files/gcsebizplugandselleuropassistancecom/download-doc/pdf/gcsnewsletteroctober2015lr.pdf

http://www.liveplan.com/blog/2015/10/does-corporate-wellness-work-the-surprising-truth-about-employee-wellness-programs/

http://www.stadium.gov.my/index.php/en/arena/kompleks-sukan-negara-bukit-jalil/pusat-akuatik-nasional

http://www.takaful.coop/images/stories/Takaful%20Newsletter%20Issue%2020.pdf
https://en.wikipedia.org/wiki/Annual_premium_equivalent

http://www.bursamalaysia.com
http://www.takaful-malaysia.com.my

About the Author

Firend Rasch is an associate professor of business studies, holds a Ph.D in applied management and decision science (USA). Worked as investments banker with major banks in California, United States. Worked as management consultant with McKinsey & Company, KPMG, and Anderson Consulting advising U.S. Fortune 500 companies. Co-founded start-ups, and lectured in numerous countries including USA, Korea, Malaysia, Qatar, UAE, and now the UK, in the field international marketing, Entrepreneurship, Innovation & Technology. Currently serving on the board of directors of two Asian companies, and activly consulting with global firms. Served as editor in chief of international business journal as well as active researcher in the fields of global management and international business activities.

www.ingramcontent.com/pod-product-compliance
Lightning Source LLC
Chambersburg PA
CBHW070223190526
45169CB00001B/60